D0848911

The Phantom Respondents

Michigan Studies in Political Analysis

Michigan Studies in Political Analysis promotes the development and dissemination of innovative scholarship in the field of methodology in political science and the social sciences in general. Methodology is defined to include statistical methods, mathematical modeling, measurement, research design, and other topics related to the conduct and development of analytical work. The series includes works that develop a new model or method applicable to social sciences, as well as those that, through innovative combination and presentation of current analytical tools, substantially extend the use of these tools by other researchers.

GENERAL EDITORS: John E. Jackson and Christopher H. Achen

The Phantom Respondents

Opinion Surveys and Political Representation

John Brehm

Ann Arbor
THE UNIVERSITY OF MICHIGAN PRESS

Copyright © by the University of Michigan 1993
All rights reserved
Published in the United States of America by
The University of Michigan Press
Manufactured in the United States of America

2000 1999 1998   4 3 2

A CIP catalogue record for this book is available from the British Library.

Library of Congress Cataloging-in-Publication Data

Brehm, John, 1960–
    The phantom respondents: opinion surveys and political
    representation / John Brehm.
        p.   cm. — (Michigan studies in political analysis)
    Includes bibliographical references and index.
    ISBN 0-472-09523-4 (alk. paper)
    1. Public opinion polls. 2. Representative government and
    representation. I. Title. II. Series.
HM261.B694   1993
303.3'8—dc20   92-40475
                                                      CIP

For Kate, Robin, Laurel, and Joseph

Acknowledgments

I thank Steve Rosenstone, Don Kinder, Mary Corcoran, and Bob Groves for their patience, their comments on early drafts of this work, and their advice on my research.

I am grateful to Santa Traugott, the Board of Overseers of the National Election Studies, Tom Smith, the Detroit Area Studies, the Office of Management and Budget, and the Roper Center for providing me with the data used in this book.

In the course of presenting this work to various audiences, many individuals provided insights that could only be to my benefit. I would like to thank Chris Achen, John Aldrich, Mike Alvarez, Doug Arnold, Bob Bates, Bill Bianco, Henry Brady, Dennis Chong, George Downs, Bob Fay, Fred Greenstein, Paul Gronke, Don Herzog, Jane Mansbridge, Rick Matland, Ben Page, David Paletz, Gerry Pomper, Stanley Presser, and Lynn Sanders.

Contents

CHAPTER 1

Surveys and Representation

What are the duties of a political representative? Several tasks come to mind. We authorize representatives to act on our behalf, to design legislation, to enforce the law, to choose between alternative policies. We also expect political representatives to express our opinions and preferences, to say what we would have said if we were asked directly. This sense of "representation" is *authorization,* individuals entitled to choose, act, enforce, and speak for us. When we think of a political representative, we think of a political actor. But another sense of representation is *descriptive,* that of acting as a mirror of the people. When we think of representative government, we think of a body of people who stand for their constituents (Pitkin 1967).

Both concepts of representation are essential to a complete sense of what political representation means. The idea of representative government is virtually defined by actors authorized to choose on behalf of greater numbers of people. And representative government as a form of democracy is meaningless unless somehow the representatives stand for the people.

These aren't just word games. The descriptive sense of representation matters. One need only look as far as the rulings by the U.S. Supreme Court on apportionment to see the importance of descriptive representation. In *Baker v. Carr* (1962), the Court established the principle of one person, one vote. The Court explicitly tied apportionment and representation in a subsequent case, *Reynolds v. Sims* (1964):

> The idea that every voter is equal to every other voter in his State, when he casts his ballot in favor of one of several competing candidates, underlies many of our decisions (558).

Subsequent Court decisions made it plain that fair apportionment may require not just numerical equality across districts but equality in representation of political parties (*Gaffney v. Cummings* 1973) or redress for excluded ethnic and racial minorities (*United Jewish Organizations of Williamsburg, Inc. v. Carey* 1977). One person, one vote refers to the way in which seats are allocated to represent political interests, and not just a mere one-to-one correspondence of citizens and legislators.

Descriptive representation matters, too, when we examine the composition of a legislature. If the proportion of women and blacks in a legislature bears little resemblance to their proportion in the population, we speak of women and blacks as being underrepresented.

Further, descriptive representation matters in a conception of democratic government as a *deliberative* process (Mansbridge 1980). Mansbridge argues that democratic government is not merely a clash of opposing preferences but a debate among ideas leading to the development of policy. Kingdon (1984) develops a model of public policy formation based upon "streams" of ideas about policies and problems. The content of those streams limits what policies may emerge. One task of representatives is to relay the preferences and ideas of their constituents into political debate, to stand for their constituents in the streams of policies and problems.

If descriptive representation is acting as a mirror of the nation, polls and surveys are exquisite examples. Surveys strive to reproduce a portrait of the nation's goals and concerns, attitudes and characteristics.[1] Surveys and polls act as a conduit of political preferences and information, a way for citizens to express themselves and a means for leaders to learn about citizens. The usefulness of surveys as political representation is inextricably woven with how well surveys convey the attributes and characteristics of the public. This book examines how the representativeness of surveys affects our understanding of politics, indeed, the very fabric of politics itself.

Surveys and polls are ubiquitous in American politics.[2] From the

---

1. The idea that surveys with random samples are a form of representation inverts an argument made over a half-century ago by Swabey (1937). Swabey holds that elected representatives—indeed, representative governments in general—are a kind of sample of the public. Swabey was influenced by the ascent of the modern public opinion polling industry and saw analogies between surveys and democratic theory that presage some of the ideas I discuss here. People in the survey industry also saw polling as part of the modern democratic process. Gallup and Rae (1940) extol the virtues of polling as a means for leaders to assess a "mandate of the people," a way to prevent representative democracy from degenerating into elite rule.

2. I use surveys and polls interchangeably. Some survey practitioners might take umbrage at being lumped with pollsters, and vice versa. I mean no offense to either. When I discuss the roles of surveys and polls in politics, the reader should remember the context. The media generally conduct polls, while the federal government and academics generally conduct surveys. As for the particular threat to representation that I examine in this book, polls and surveys are equally victims.

polls in the legislators' frankings; to the media polls conducted by Gallup, Harris, and the like; to market research; to academic surveys conducted by organizations like the National Opinion Research Center and the Center for Political Studies; to surveys conducted by increasing numbers of candidates—we are an oft-interviewed people. There is hardly an aspect of American political life untouched by polling and survey research.

Most U.S. citizens will be interviewed sometime during the course of their lives. In an intriguing survey of survey exposure by the Roper organization in 1984 (employing a quota sample of 2,000), 59 percent of the respondents reported being interviewed at least once prior to the Roper poll (Roper 1986). In the "Industry Evaluation Survey," 23 percent of these respondents reported being interviewed by some survey in the last 12 months (Schleifer 1986). Considering that 20 million interviews are conducted in the United States each year (Sharp 1984), average citizens stand a more than fair chance of being interviewed several times during their lifetime.

Two-thirds of a century ago, Walter Lippmann warned of the inadequacies of the American public to meet the demands of the ideal democracy. *The Phantom Public* argues that very few citizens attend to the events of politics, that few are informed about the issues great and small that confront our society, that the vast majority of our public is preoccupied with the demanding occupation of mundane life. These observations mean that the mass public could never fulfill the requirements of idealistic democracy. As Lippmann puts it, "I set no great store on what can be done by public opinion and the action of masses" (1927, 199). The promise of surveys as a vehicle for political representation is that American government will become more responsive and that leaders will attend to the concerns of even the most preoccupied citizens.

By many accounts, we believe that surveys make a difference to the performance of government: 59 percent of the respondents to Roper's poll felt that polls make "some difference" in politics and an additional 21 percent felt that polls make "quite a lot" of difference (Roper 1986). These respondents were not misguided. In the pages to follow, I discuss just how pervasive and consequential surveys are in politics.

Surveys Pervade Political Life

Surveys influence the content of the media, structure political discussion, provide information that influences political choices, calibrate formulas for the allocation of funds, target campaign strategies, and possibly even influence election outcomes. I take up in turn these effects of surveys.

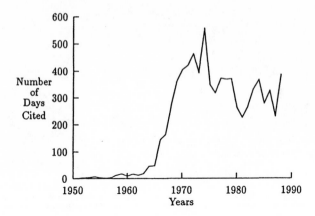

FIGURE 1.1. Number of Days Cited Under "Public Opinion" in the *New York Times*

Polls and the Media

No surveys are more conspicuous in modern politics than those reported in the American media. Polls are daily fodder for news reporting, probing attitudes toward politics and public figures. But this was not always true; it is a recent phenomenon. There is a clear explosion in the reporting of public opinion data in newspapers and on television.

A simple indicator of the recurrence of polling in the press appears in figure 1.1. This graph depicts a count of the number of days cited under the heading "Public Opinion" in the *New York Times Index* for every year from 1950 to the present.[3]

Only a handful of polls appeared among "All the News That's Fit to Print" in the early 1950s, but by the mid-1960s, the number jumped to over 100 stories per year. By the 1970s, the number of citations reached the current plateau of around 300 citations per year, or nearly 1 story a day. There is an interesting peak to the distribution in 1974 during the implosion of the Nixon administration. Between accounts of polls querying whether or not the public believed the president was personally involved with Watergate, whether or not Nixon should resign, and Nixon's approval ratings, the *Times* cited more than a poll a day.

Political subjects predominate in these polls, especially during elec-

---

3. The heading "Public Opinion" in the *New York Times Index* reflects all reports pertinent to public opinion in general. Of course, public opinion is a broader concept than just a gathering of poll results. However, these citations by and large report poll results, and only rarely reflections on public opinion in the broader sense.

tion years, and especially during the last weeks of the campaign. Over the course of an entire election year in the 1940s, Patterson (1980) reports that a typical newspaper's quota of poll-related stories would be 10 per year. In 1976, Patterson identifies 10 in the *Los Angeles Times* in the last week of the election alone. More recently, Ratzan (1989) tabulated the number of political front-page stories in the *Washington Post* and the *New York Times* during the last month of the 1988 election. He found that 42 percent of the *Post*'s and 48 percent of the *Times*'s political front-page stories were related to polls. Moreover, poll results featured in 19 percent of the *Post*'s and 9 percent of the *Times*'s headlines, suggesting that the poll's results *are* the story.

The flood of poll results reported in the newspapers hardly abates in nonelection years. Paletz et al. (1980) calculated that the *New York Times* in 1973, 1975, and 1977 featured a poll result at least once every three days. Considering that one-third of the nation's daily newspapers conduct their own polls (Atkin and Gaudino 1984), polls feature prominently in newspapers across the country.

Television news also reports poll results with regularity, although not nearly as frequently as newspapers. Over the same period (1973, 1975, and 1977), Paletz, et al., (1980) identify 83 stories on the NBC evening news and 40 stories on the CBS news about polls, nearly half of which appeared in the first 10 minutes of the newscast. As Wheeler (1976) argues, it makes sense that poll results would appear less frequently on television than in the press, but when poll results do appear on television, they are treated with more drama than are those in the newspapers.

> [T]elevision is a very bad medium for the reporting of polls because it demands emphasis on the dramatic and the visually interesting at the expense of things which are subtle and ambiguous. For a poll to get on the air, it must be timely and newsworthy. (Wheeler 1976, 202)

The content of the newspaper and television polls matters. Certainly, many of the media polls focus on the horse race of the presidential campaign: for example, that Clinton is seventeen points ahead of or behind Bush. And it is easy to understand the attraction of horse-race results: forecasts of the election make for snappy, exciting news with a kind of artificial precision. Paul Taylor of ABC News explains the attractions of polling results:

> I tell you there is institutional pressure. You spend a lot of money

on polls. You get a set of numbers back. The numbers have a reality of their own—a reality that in this ambiguous world we live in can be a very comforting thing. (Runkel 1989, 165)

Some journalists bemoan that the horse-race polls encourage journalists and other political observers to stray from reporting issues, and campaigners from debating issues (e.g., Germond 1980; Greenberg 1980). But the horse race is the dominant feature of the polls only every four years, times at which figure 1.1 plainly shows considerable activity throughout the last few decades.

Politicians attend to the non–horse-race polls, too. One staple of the political poll is the president's approval rating. This approval rating might be seen as a kind of Dow Jones Index for politics, the leading measure of public support for the president. This measure of public support affects support for the president among political elites. Rivers and Rose (1985) show that the effect of Gallup approval ratings on support for the president's legislative program in Congress is substantial, about half as important as the support from the president's party in Congress. Ostrom and Simon (1985) show the presence of a (potentially vicious) cycle where approval affects the president's success in Congress, in turn affecting the president's approval ratings. A 30-point drop in presidential approval means, on average, 31 additional roll-call defeats. The peak of figure 1.1 in 1974 is instructive, too: Nixon's miserable approval ratings undercut action on any policy during the waning years of his administration.

Approval ratings are akin to the horse-race election forecasts in that they are virtually contentless with respect to issues, policies, or problems. Approval ratings and election forecasts are a small facet of the business of surveys. Polls also regularly ask respondents how they feel about proposed policies and political problems. If polling is able to exert an influence on policy-making, one might think that the issue-related polls are paramount in the relation of polls to politics. Next, I consider how these polls influence political discussion.

Polls and Political Discourse

Our political folklore may depict politicians whipsawing to whatever trend emerges from poll results, but political reality is decidedly more ambiguous. There are times when poll results plainly influence political discussion; there are other issues—arcane, specialized, complicated, or just dull—where it is inconceivable that polls could affect outcomes.

Presidents from Roosevelt to Bush have kept a close eye on poll results. Johnson was famous for keeping a copy of the latest poll results in his pocket, which he would flourish if the results helped his argument. Carter also relied heavily on poll results gathered by his staff pollster, Pat Caddell, in order to bolster his case in Congress, although to little avail (Sudman 1982). Reagan's pollster, Richard Wirthlin, met with the president over 25 times and sent memos on over 40 polls in just the first two years of Reagan's tenure (Beal and Hinckley 1984). In fact, one of the tasks of the White House Office of Planning and Evaluation is to collect and analyze all major opinion polls. Surely, some of this attention to polls is just for rhetorical ammunition, but the magnitude of attention begs the question whether or not these presidents monitored polls in order to identify the public's needs.

Debates in the Congress occasionally invoke polls to support arguments. In the *Congressional Record,* a transcript of floor discussion and additional material submitted by the legislators, members of Congress cite poll results 15 or so times a year. What is both amusing and surprising is that the legislators hardly discriminate on sources and issues. The polls and surveys may have been conducted by the Survey Research Center of the University of Michigan, or a constituency survey attached to the frankings, or a poll conducted by the eighth grade class of Blair Junior High School for all the reputability of the survey organization matters to the debate.[4] The members of Congress invoke these varied polls to support the control of illegal drugs, aid to Chile, and sugar quotas or to prove there is too much taxation, too little taxation, or too much sex on TV.[5]

While a part of the political rhetoric, do poll results affect policy outcomes? There are specific recent policy debates where some observers claim poll results affected legislators' decisions. Scammon believes that polls helped stop a proposed congressional pay raise in 1989 (Elving 1989). And polls on abortion taken just after the Supreme Court's *Webster v. Reproduction Health Services* decision may have been the impetus for the first pro-choice victory (Aug. 2, 1989) on public funding for abortion since 1980 (Elving 1989). But is there a more systematic pattern?

---

4. These polls, respectively, were cited by the following members of Congress: Rep. G. V. Sonny Montgomery (Miss.), July 11, 1988, E2331–2332; half a dozen different representatives a year; Rep. Steve Gunderson (Wis.), May 24, 1988, E1661.

5. Polls were cited by the following representatives: Rep. Lawrence Couglin (Pa.), Aug. 3, 1988, E2607; Rep. Robert J. Lagomarsino (Calif.), Aug. 8, 1988, E2671; Sen. Daniel K. Inouye (Hawaii), Apr. 19, 1989, S8435–8438; Sen. Steve Symms (Idaho), Apr. 19, 1989, S4232–4233; Sen. William Proxmire (Wis.), Oct. 11, 1988, S15377.

Farkas, Shapiro, and Page (1990) claim that public opinion leads policy on some domestic issues. They compare changes in public opinion in national surveys from 1973 through 1978 with changes in spending. Although there are some problems with making causal inferences from their data (as they note), the patterns suggest that public opinion affects spending on the environment, space, education, and drugs. Stimson (1989) argues that politicians respond more to a general public mood (toward liberal or conservative policy), but that this mood is discernible from poll results in general.

In contrast, Crigler (1990) argues that public opinion, the media, and Congress rarely attend to the same agenda. And other research on the agenda of Congress concurs, noting that public opinion surveys are rarely specific enough to provide much guidance on the usually complicated policy matters before Congress. Nor are surveys often concentrated enough—in terms of geography—to provide much pressure on the congressperson (Kingdon 1984).

If public opinion polls appear in political discourse with regularity, it is virtually impossible to ascertain whether the polls affect the legislators' decisions or merely serve as verbal gunshot. But as Kingdon (1984) notes, it is equally difficult to identify *any* source of a particular public policy decision. One is left wondering whether the following remarks by Representative John Porter (Ill.) are rhetoric or self-observation:

> Politicians didn't get into office without being pretty good at marketing themselves. They know how to keep people happy, too. So we seem to be making public policy in America the same way: Take a poll and give them what they want. (*Congressional Record,* May 24, 1989, E1861)

What one might forget in all of this is that the media polls are only a tiny subset of the thousands of polls conducted in the United States each year. The federal government is both a major consumer and producer of survey research, the vast majority of which asks no questions about how respondents feel about policy matters. Surveys and polls are a form of political information, and these clearly affect policies.

Polls as Political Information

Surveys are source of political intelligence for all levels of government, used for program design and evaluation, assessment of needs, allocation of funds, and the enforcement of laws. The federal government is the single largest consumer of survey research, accounting for over 5 of the 20 million interviews conducted in the United States every year, not including the decennial Census (Sharp 1984). Although the vast majority of the surveys conducted by the federal government are not attitude surveys, these surveys are a potent source of political information. Some municipal levels of government conduct survey research to assess policy needs (Rosentraub and Thompson 1981). Industry uses the federally compiled data or may conduct its own surveys.

As an illustration of just how frequently departments in the federal government conduct survey research, consider the surveys requested by just one department (Health and Human Services [HHS]) in just one year (fiscal year 1991). We can track the use of survey research by the federal government by way of "respondent burden" reports that must be filed with and cleared by the Office of Management and Budget before any agency conducts any survey. Pursuant to the National Paperwork Reduction Act, every agency conducting survey research is required to detail the paperwork burden imposed on the United States. The paperwork burden is defined as the estimated length of the survey times the estimated number of respondents. Consequently, a survey with 250 respondents lasting an hour is equivalent in paperwork burden to a survey lasting only 15 minutes with 1,000 respondents. Table 1.1 displays the paperwork burden imposed by the agencies of the HHS in 1991.

In that year, HHS anticipated over 1 million respondent-hours in

TABLE 1.1. Respondents and Respondent-Hours for Department of Health and Human Services Surveys, FY1991

	Respondents	Respondent-Hours
Public Health Service		
Food and Drug Administration	26,281	9,704
Health Services Administration	33,393	11,259
Indian Health Service	1,311	8,466
Centers for Disease Control	453,781	498,087
National Institutes of Health	137,045	75,458
Alcohol, Drug Abuse, and Mental Health	208,727	156,867
Health Care Financing Administration	430,549	355,072
Social Security Administration	48,098	17,250
Administration for Children	1,714	1,045
Office of Human Development	80,186	155,125
Departmental Management	12,904	10,073
Total	1,437,102	1,205,387

"Respondent-hours" are the number of respondents times the approximate length of the interview.

interviews, and nearly 1.5 million interviews. (The difference between the burden and the number of respondents arises because many, if not most, of these interviews last well under an hour.) Consider the respondent burden for just one agency: the National Institutes of Health (NIH) accumulated over 75,000 respondent-hours—more than 35 National Election Studies (NES) conducted by one agency in just one year. A significant component of the NIH surveys, the National Health Interview Surveys, tracks the incidence of health problems in the national population.

Congress has its own agency for survey research, the General Accounting Office (GAO). Most of the surveys that the GAO conducts are not general population studies, but studies of very specialized groups such as veterans, native Americans, or West Coast growers. The GAO studies tend to be focused to particular policy concerns, supplying information to the committee that requests the work. The studies permit the committee members to congratulate themselves for effective oversight (if the survey finds no problems), to propose policy (if the survey shows the desired results), or to ignore the problem (if the survey shows unanticipated results) (Eckert and Vinkenes 1990).

The Census is a special case of the use of survey-type data for political information. According to the Census's report *Federal Legislative Uses of Decennial Census Data,* data from the Census enter into over 600 aspects of the U.S. Code (USC). Consider one of the more seemingly innocuous batteries of questions in the Census that concerns the respondent's journey to work. The data from this question are directly responsible for "defining local wage areas for setting Federal blue-collar wages under the Federal Prevailing Rate Act" (5 USC 5343a); for federal funds allocation to aid rural areas, encourage carpools, improve off-system (nonfederal) roads (23 USC 143, 146, 219); to formulate plans for "population protection and evacuation and protection of industrial capacity in event of nuclear attack, disasters, and other emergencies" (41 USC 5131; 42 USC 7701 et seq.; 50 USC 98; 50 USC app. 2061, 2251 et seq.); and to monitor federal auto emission standards under the Clean Air Act (42 USC 7401 et seq.). Likewise, the question about the number of rooms in the respondent's dwelling affects home mortgage insurance and housing assistance for the elderly (12 USC 1701q, 1709 et seq.), direct housing loans to veterans (38 USC 1811), and to determine selection criteria for Urban Development Assistance Grants (UDAGs) (42 USC Con 5318).

While the Census may be a special case for the breadth of the uses of its data, it is hardly a unique case. Our monthly unemployment statistics come from the Current Population Studies (CPS) conducted by the Bureau of the Census on behalf of the Bureau of Labor Statistics. Our monthly inflation statistics come, in part, from the Consumer Expenditure Surveys also conducted by the Bureau of the Census. Minute changes in either of these numbers drive stock markets up or down, trigger millions of dollars of wage changes, and affect consumer confidence in the status of the economy.

Probably the most significant aspect of the role of survey results in federal policy concerns the allocation of funds. Allocations for large federal programs are now keyed to survey results.[6] There are now about 100 different programs where the allocation of grants depends on counts of population, poverty, or unemployment. Some of the most conspicuous policies tied to these counts include Medicaid, Food Stamps, UDAGs, Head Start, Community Development Block Grants (CDBGs)—even hazardous waste management, coastal zone management, and public library construction.

The decennial Census is a component of most of these programs. The Census supplies population, income, age, and race data. About two-thirds of these programs, or about $28 billion of the federal budget in 1990, depend in whole or in part on these figures. And while the Census is not a survey per se, it resembles surveys in that it is an effort by the federal government to collect information about its citizens.

Surprisingly, the vast majority of the *funds* for formula grants depend not on the Census, but on assorted survey results. The Bureau of Economic Analysis supplies per capita income counts, and they account for $37 billion in allocations across such programs as the National School Lunch Program, Medicaid, and General Revenue Sharing. The Bureau of Labor Statistics publishes estimates of the labor force and unemployment, and accounts for $13.5 billion in allocations, of which $12 billion is taken up with the Food Stamps program. The CPS accounts for about $3 billion and affects programs like CDBGs and Social Services Block Grants.

One should certainly believe that the results of these surveys affect

---

6. The data in the paragraphs to follow from the 1990 budget come from the *1989 Catalog of Federal Domestic Assistance,* published by the Office of Management and Budget. This catalog lists every federal grant, including the assistance criteria. If there are formula criteria for a grant, the types of data for the grant as well as the source of the data appear in the listing. The numbers to follow reflect my tabulation across the entries. If there are mistakes in the total dollars reported, they reflect my omissions and are probably underestimates.

political decisions, and that legislators attend to these numbers. Nathan (1987) terms the effect of survey results "Printout Politics":

> No Member of Congress today would vote on an important grant-in-aid formula without a printout to see who wins and who loses. Of course, negotiating about who wins and who loses is not new. But it was speeded up [in a sense made more productive] by the new information-processing technology—a technology ideally suited to formula writing under conditions where the stakes involved warrant the costs of high-speed data (p. 341).

As the 1990 appropriations prove, there is little wonder why legislators attend to these survey results.

Survey results filter into policy design and evaluation and explicitly enter into the implementation of policy as part of formula-based allocations. Survey results affect who gets what from government.

Polling and Political Campaigns

Survey results also affect who gets into government. Polling comprises a significant part of campaign strategy—helping to target voters and potential issues. And this strategy determines the messages of the campaign and affects who wins and loses.

Polling the constituency is de rigueur campaign strategy. Amusingly, the first known use of polls was for George Gallup's mother-in-law, who was running for secretary of state in Iowa in 1932. Perhaps the first major use of polls came with Kennedy's campaign for president in 1960, when Lou Harris acted as a consultant (Salmore and Salmore 1985). As early as 1970, Nimmo claims that surveys themselves are the "most widely employed technique of campaign research." Candidates conduct polls during, broadly, three phases of the campaign. "Benchmark" or "baseline" surveys precede most campaign activity. These are moderate to large surveys (Sabato 1981). These benchmark polls provide detailed initial readings of the electorate—latent issues, recognition of candidates, and vote preferences (Salmore and Salmore 1985). During the main part of the campaign, there may be "trend polls" (Salmore and Salmore 1985) or even panel surveys to track drift in preferences and recognition over the course of the campaign. Finally, during the closing stages of the campaign, some campaigns will conduct "tracking polls." Tracking polls typically involve small samples (50-100 respondents), with moving averages used to compensate for the small sample size. The tracking polls permit quick response to the events of the campaign. Jacobson (1987) identifies some 1984 Senate campaigns that followed commercials of the opposing campaigns within 24 hours. Even if a campaign is bereft of the funds to conduct its own polls, some candidates will piggyback on polls conducted by larger campaigns (e.g., a House candidate who attaches questions to a Senate candidate's surveys) (Herrnson 1988).

The kinds of information provided by campaign polls permit campaigns to target voters who might be pulled away from the opposition. Once Eisenhower demonstrated that large blocks of peripheral Democratic voters might be convinced to vote for the Republicans, a primary purpose of campaign polls has been to identify soft votes (Salmore and Salmore 1985). Of the 15 Republican and Democrat contenders for the presidency in 1988, 11 admitted use of polls to develop their primary campaign strategies, most of which were simply tracking preferences of voters in key states. Only 1 of the 15 candidates (Jesse Jackson) explicitly rejected use of polls in the initial development of his strategy (Runkel 1989).

Surveys also allow political strategists to identify the issues of the campaign. By 1980, Caddell (Carter's pollster) attended every major meeting of the campaign staff as *primer inter pares* declaring which states the campaign would attack, where the money would go, and which issues the campaign would emphasize (Levy 1984). Wirthlin picked the signature themes of Reagan's 1980 campaign and later became a daily fixture in the White House (Beal and Hinckley 1984). Roger Ailes and Lee Atwater both admitted to a conference of campaign consultants held after the election that the Bush campaign employed focus groups and campaign polls to identify issues that could be used to Bush's advantage in the campaign.[7] Above all, the focus group results convinced them that the campaign would be largely issueless. The signature ad of the Bush campaign—attacking the prison furlough policy of Massachusetts as a revolving door—emerged directly from the focus group research and follow-up polls (Runkel 1989).

Evidence abounds indicating that polls have replaced more ad hoc determinations by precinct workers as the dominant method of assessing the attitudes of the electorate (Geer 1988; Ginsberg 1986; Salmore and Salmore 1985; Herrnson 1988; Wheeler 1976). The content of the election has been very much influenced by polling. Have polls also determined the results of elections?

---

7. In fact, the Dukakis campaign also found from its own polls that the Massachusetts furlough policy would be the single most damaging target for Bush (Runkel 1989).

Polls and Election Outcomes

One very worrisome effect of polls is their impact on election outcomes. If, as some believe, publicized poll results discourage people from voting for candidates well behind in the horse race, polls literally become self-fulfilling prophecies.

I wrote above about the extent of polling during elections and especially during the last month of the campaigns. One reason for the flurry of polling in the final weeks is that many voters change their preferences up until election day. (Rosenstone [1983] estimates that 10 percent of the voters in 1980 were undecided until election day.) Another reason for the proliferation of polls throughout the campaign is that our interest is, naturally, piqued to know who the next president will be, regardless of how well the election polls perform at forecasting the election.

Polls *are* how we, as citizens, find out who wins many elections, producing estimates of the results long before the official figures are released. The exit polls adopted by the major television networks figure prominently in the reporting of election day results. A concern is whether or not exit polls induce bandwagon effects in western states.

Jackson (1983) demonstrates that the early reporting of election returns and Carter's early concession speech discouraged marginally inclined voters from voting. (Those who intended, firmly, to vote or not to vote well in advance of election day were unaffected.) Jackson suggests that *Republicans* would have been less likely to vote after hearing the early results than Democrats. The implication is that exit polls did not induce a bandwagon effect (i.e., increased voting for the apparent victor), but the opposite. Moreover, the reverse bandwagon effect could only work if the election appeared to be close, up until election day.

But an alternate effect of polls on election outcomes occurs if polls' results discourage candidates from making serious efforts or by hampering their fund-raising. The evidence is largely circumstantial. Nelson Rockefeller withdrew from the GOP nomination contests before a vote had been cast on his candidacy; Wheeler (1976) claims Rockefeller withdrew because of some early poll results circulated by the Nixon campaign. Fred Harris (in 1976) and Bruce Babbitt (in 1988) withdrew from the Democratic primary campaign after early polls showed their candidacies garnering few voters. Furthermore, low name recognition or a poor standing in the polls may discourage contributions and hamper fund-raising (Wheeler 1976; Jacobson and Kernell 1981). After the 1988 campaign, Michael Dukakis' campaign managers complained bitterly about how swings in the polls severely dampened contributions to Dukakis's campaign (Runkel 1989).

Surveys percolate throughout politics. Campaigners conduct polls in order devise strategies; the media conduct polls in order to assess who's leading the campaigns and why. Practically every agency in the federal government involved with domestic affairs conducts surveys to calibrate implementation of policy. Polls influence the political discussion, affect legislators' decisions, and adjust outcomes of policy.

Surveys Dominate Scientific Research

Scientists in a wide range of disciplines depend on survey data for research. Those who rely on survey research include not only researchers in sociology, psychology, political science, economics, and anthropology but also epidemiologists, biostatisticians, educators, social workers, and scholars of business administration, public administration, market research, and labor relations.

One gauge of how greatly scientists depend on survey research is simply a count of the number of articles in the flagship journals for sociology and political science (probably the two social science disciplines that rely most on survey research) that depend on survey research as the primary source of evidence. Presser (1984) notes the stunning growth of articles in the major journals of sociology, political science, economics, and social psychology that employ survey data. (In sociology, the percentage of articles employing survey data grew from 24.1 percent in the late 1940s to 55.8 percent in the late 1970s. In political science, the same percentage jumped from 2.6 percent in the late 1940s to 35 percent in the late 1970s.) Furthermore, by the late 1970s, the vast majority of articles in sociology, political science, and economics employing survey data were secondary analyses of data collected by other survey researchers. These patterns continue through the present. For example, in 1986 alone, 21 of the 40 articles in the *American Sociological Review*, 16 of the 35 in the *American Journal of Sociology*, and 11 of the 43 in the *American Political Science Review* all employed surveys. Furthermore, there are academic survey organizations in at least 33 of the 50 states (Bradburn and Sudman 1988).

The best illustration of the importance of survey research to academics is the many cherished observations based on survey research. We know about the importance of party identification (Campbell, Gurin, and Miller 1960), education (Wolfinger and Rosenstone 1980), and economics to voting (Kinder and Kiewiet 1981) from survey research. More so, some of our most controversial debates arise out of how to best ascertain the public's thinking with surveys: pocketbook or sociotropic voting, ideological consistency or inconsistency among the mass public, or whether or not spending by incumbents affects election results.

As political scientists, too many of us trust survey research as *the* indicator of how the public thinks about politics. We are in a rather vulnerable position if something threatens survey research.

The Problem of Nonresponse

For the media, the government, and academics, regardless of the organization conducting the poll, or the sample design, or the quality of the questionnaire, there lurks a common threat to the representativeness of surveys: nonresponse. Survey nonresponse refers to respondents selected to the survey sample but, for various reasons, not interviewed. Some are those who refuse to be questioned, others are never contacted, and still others are unable to provide an interview. Nonresponse rates for even reputable surveys are quite high.

Nonresponse rates for surveys conducted by government organizations are usually comparatively low. The typical nonresponse rate for the CPS, the source for monthly unemployment statistics for the country, is about 5 percent, where the dominant component of the nonresponse rate has been refusals.[8]

Nonresponse rates for surveys by academic organizations typically range between 20 and 33 percent of the sample. The NES is probably the collection of survey data on elections used most widely by political scientists. The nonresponse rates for the NES in the 1980s have hovered around 30 percent. Surveys conducted by the National Opinion Research Center represent another major contribution to the regular public data collections for social scientists. Nonresponse rates for the General Social Survey (GSS) have been slightly lower, averaging around 25 percent. Surveys confined to relatively small geographic areas may encounter equivalent nonresponse rates. The nonresponse rate for the Detroit Area Studies (DAS) has typically been around 28 percent.

Nonresponse rates for surveys by commercial organizations are generally unavailable. A recent study by Crespi (1988) of survey organizations engaged in pre-election polling is informative. Typical *refusal*

---

8. The low nonresponse rates for the CPS surveys may be somewhat misleading in that the CPS interviews will accept reports from any eligible adult in the household, whereas the academic surveys reported above require a response from a specific member of the household. The proportion of responses to the CPS that were provided by proxies in 1984, to pick a typical year, was 40 percent.

rates for these organizations range from 30 to 50 percent, necessitating a *nonresponse* rate even higher than these numbers.

The current levels of nonresponse are worrisome enough. The pertinent question here is, are the 70 percent who participate in surveys identical to the 30 percent who don't? They are not. I show in chapters 2 through 8 that respondents and nonrespondents differ in a variety of consequential ways. This poses a large problem for drawing accurate inferences from surveys.

As if current levels weren't problem enough, there is strong evidence to suggest that nonresponse rates are getting worse. Accumulated folklore from the commercial survey industry has long suggested a decline in the cooperativeness of respondents (Reinhold 1975). Total nonresponse rates for the academic studies examined in this research have all risen from the quite low rates in the 1960s.[9] Total nonresponse rates for the DAS have risen from 12.5 percent in 1952 to 31.6 percent in 1988. Nonresponse rates for the GSS have also risen, but due to the shift of sampling frames from quota to area probability, the exact nature of the phenomenon is ambiguous.

Historical trends (Steeh 1981; Groves and Lyberg 1988) suggest that the refusal component of nonresponse is growing, while the other components decline. Steeh (1981) formally explored the composition of declining response rates. Figure 1.2 displays the change in refusal rates for the NES and the Surveys of Consumer Affairs from 1952 to 1989.[10] Refusal rates for the NES have climbed from well under 8 percent at inception (in the early 1950s) to current refusal rates near 25 percent. The refusal rates for the Surveys of Consumer Affairs climb at a virtually identical rate to the NES. Similar increases have been observed for other organizations.

Nonresponse rates are bad, and they are getting worse. Survey nonresponse explicitly threatens the representativeness of surveys. Nonresponse certainly undermines scientific representation, reducing the extent to which surveys provide an accurate portrait of the public. Nonresponse also threatens the *political* sense of representation.

Nonresponse and Political Representation

Somewhere, every day, someone is being interviewed. We need to worry

---

9. Probably the first systematic treatments of nonresponse as a problem emerged from the 1973 American Statistical Association conference.

10. I thank Charlotte Steeh for graciously providing me with the figures for refusal rates for the NES from 1952 through 1986.

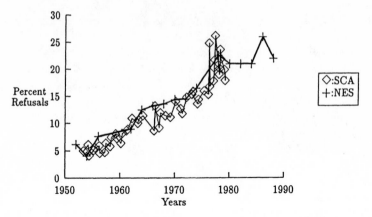

FIGURE 1.2. Refusal Rate for the 1952–1979 Survey of Consumer Affairs, 1952–1988 NES

about the representativeness of the surveys conducted daily by government, the media, market researchers, campaigners, and academics.

Surveys matter to politics, not just because they are used in politics. Surveys matter because of the unique opportunity of surveys to compensate for inequities elsewhere in politics.

It costs to participate in politics. Downs (1957) points out the implications of the costs of participating in as simple and as common an act as voting. It takes time and energy to trek to the voting booths; it may even require money to participate in other aspects of politics. People vote more frequently than they opt for any other form of political participation (Erikson 1981). Even with as widespread an act as voting, the better educated and wealthier one is, the more likely one is to vote. And this pattern holds with activities that extend beyond voting: Verba and Nie (1972) found that the most politically active people are more likely to be of a higher socioeconomic status than not. The costs of political participation pose an extra burden for lower classes.

Polls subsidize political participation. Polls bring the voting booth to the respondent's doorstep or telephone. You don't have to drive or walk to the polls—the interviewer comes to you. If you don't have the time now, the interviewer will come back (sometimes, even if you're not at home, the interviewer will return to give you a second chance). Poor or rich, the interviewer wants to talk with you and will accomodate your time and energy.

Polls equalize expression. Every voice in the survey counts as much as another, regardless of the intensity of expression. If you care deeply about abortion and oppose it, your voice counts as much as that of another who favors personal choice but really cares little about the issue. Of course, it is entirely possible for a researcher to opt to weigh individual cases differently, but ordinarily each case counts as much as another. Polls could be a builder's level for determining the tilt of citizen's preferences.

But surveys may have lost these opportunities to compensate for inequities of politics. There is strong evidence to suggest that polls disproportionately sample from the most interested, most informed, and most participative people in society. The problem of nonresponse means that surveys may be less representative than they seem or than one may hope them to be.[11]

If Lippmann told us that the people appeared in our democracy as but a "phantom public," this book meets a regeneration of that original claim. While surveys might vault the obstacles that many meet in expressing their preferences about politics, surveys themselves face the same problem in the "phantom respondents," who increasingly decline to respond to our surveys. Perhaps the missing respondents are immediately a problem for social scientists, but they are eventually a problem for wise and fair government.

Nonresponse and Science

Nonresponse is an epistemological concern for scientific research, a challenge to how well we know what we think we know. If survey participation is motivated by the same factors that influence participation in politics, we require that the respondents perform the very act we wish to study in order to even be seen in our study. We have a sturdier version of the "Heisenberg uncertainty principle"[12] to fear: instead of merely mea-

---

11. I borrow these concepts from Ginsberg (1986), who conceives the subsidizing and equalizing effects of surveys to be a problem. Ginsberg avers that surveys are a mechanism for the domestication of mass belief, a way for government to *avoid* responding to citizens' concerns. Equalized expression means that intensely held opinions are diluted in apathy. Ginsberg, too, should care whether surveys are more or less equalizing due to nonresponse than we thought. By his logic, one would prefer that surveys interview only the most interested and informed people.

12. Werner Karl Heisenberg's uncertainty principle is the German physicist's observation that if one measures light as a wave, light appears to be a wave, and if one measures light as a stream of particles (photons), light appears to be a stream of particles (Brehm and Mullin 1989). By extension, the concern for general science is that by measuring a phenomenon, one defines what the phenomenon looks like.

suring participation by looking for participation, we require participation in the first place.

Some social scientists are inclined to believe epistemology is a matter of taste, something to fear only if one's conscience directs one to do so. Is survey research akin to sausage making, where the squeamish don't want to know what goes into either?

Nonresponse is an epistemological problem with teeth. Nonresponse jeopardizes both the external and internal validity of our work. The external validity of survey research refers to the degree to which we can generalize from samples to some population. If nonresponse means that our samples no longer fairly represent a population, then our research on those samples is not generalizable either. The internal validity of survey research refers to the extent to which our findings hold for the sample at hand. If we shortchange the variabilility of our sample by eliciting interviews only among the most interested people in the population, then nonresponse lessens the apparent importance of interest *in our sample.*

Because survey nonresponse matters to politics and to science, we need a comprehensive sense of how the representativeness of surveys is at risk. There are two voids in our understanding of survey research:

•Why do people participate in surveys?

•What difference does nonresponse make to our understandings of political and social life?

The first question matters because if we know the reasons why people choose or refuse to participate in surveys, we may be able to reduce or correct nonresponse. By knowing why some refuse to be interviewed we might more effectively induce these people to change their minds. The survey industry has long known about the potential hazards of nonresponse (e.g., Hansen and Hurwitz 1946), but the response of the industry has been reactive: what can we do to reduce refusal rates or increase contact? These approaches would benefit from knowledge of the process that draws people in or out of our samples. Only if we know why people refuse can we adjust our analysis of the samples to fairly reflect the population as a whole. Over the last fifteen years, econometricians and statisticians have developed methods that are appropriate for repairing the damage caused by nonresponse. But every one of these methods requires a model of survey participation. Despite the value of a theory of survey participation, we have none. We have decades of research on the correlates of survey participation, but correlates don't make a theory. One aim of this book is to develop, and to test, a model of survey participation.

The second question matters because of the extent to which science and politics depend on survey research. It's not enough to say that nonresponse *might* undermine conclusions derived from survey research, even if one has the algebra to prove it. We need to know whether or not nonresponse causes us to draw substantially different inferences. The second aim of this book is to assess how nonresponse affects typical scientific research. The subsequent chapters tackle these two questions.

The Research Agenda

The problem of survey nonresponse demands exploration of the causes and consequences of nonresponse. This book proceeds by developing a theory of survey participation, and then using that theory to develop corrections for nonresponse. Armed with a battery of corrections for nonresponse, we can gauge what difference nonresponse makes to our understanding of social and political life.

In the chapters to follow, I examine the causes and consequences of nonresponse to surveys conducted by three academic organizations: the NES, the GSS, and the DAS. These organizations represent the state-of-the-art for survey research, especially with regard to how seriously they take the problem of nonresponse and their efforts to minimize nonresponse. If there are problems in these studies as a result of nonresponse, surveys that do not make efforts to reduce nonresponse must have greater problems.

Chapter 2, "Who Is Missing?" examines how the samples of typical academic surveys differ from benchmark estimates of the population. This first step in the study of nonresponse is simply to identify who is excluded from our studies.

In chapter 3, "Why Do People Participate in Surveys?" I model the process by which people are drawn into surveys as made up of three stages: contact, eligibility, and compliance. Drawing on multiple methods introduced in this chapter, I develop the components of a theory of survey participation as a set of relationships by potential respondents to the process of survey participation.

Chapter 4, "Structure of Survey Compliance," unites the ideas developed in chapter 3 and evaluates the model in three separate studies. This chapter then tests this model as a full structure of equations.

In chapter 5, "How Survey Nonresponse Damages Scientific Research," I review the statistical literature on how nonresponse undermines univariate and multivariate analyses of survey data. This chapter develops and presents corrections for nonresponse in multivariate analyses. Finally, I evaluate the sensitivity of these corrections to varying conditions of nonresponse.

The heart of this book is chapter 6, "Applications of Corrections for Nonresponse." In this chapter, I apply the model of survey participation developed in chapters 3 and 4 and the correction methods explicated in chapter 5 to a diverse set of standard results. This analysis reveals how nonresponse distorts our understanding of political behavior.

In chapter 7, "What If Nonresponse Worsens?" I examine what would happen to our analyses of politics if survey response rates were to sink even further, to levels approximating commercial polls.

Finally, in chapter 8, "Surveys and Misrepresentation," I return to a discussion of the role of public opinion surveys in the political process and how survey nonresponse jeopardizes political representation. In the end, I offer advice on how to handle nonresponse to researchers, survey practitioners, government decision makers, and citizens.

CHAPTER 2

Who Is Missing?

The first question to answer is simply, "Who is missing?" How do survey samples differ from the population? Do our surveys undercount or overcount particular groups of people? This information is valuable for two reasons.

If we know who's missing, we can assess the descriptive representativeness of surveys. Descriptive representation matters because the distribution of the ideas present in the debate on policy predisposes what kinds of policies are enacted and what interests are furthered. This must be true in a trivial sense: policy ideas and concerns must be part of political discourse to ever become law. But the mix of ideas and concerns may be more than simply the components of what becomes law; the mix itself may determine law. Kingdon (1984) suggests that policy emerges from a "primeval soup" of ideas, speeches, bills, and proposals, where the contents of the soup come from a variety of sources, including public opinion. According to Kingdon, the mating of a policy solution and a policy problem may be due to nothing besides the efforts of policy advocates who attach their policy to an opportune problem. If the set of policy problems and the set of policy proposals come from only a small segment of public opinion, then the other segments have fewer opportunities to redress their needs. To the extent that surveys affect policy, then any underrepresentation in surveys means an underrepresentation in the policy process as well.

Second, if we know who's missing, we may determine how nonresponse undermines the external and internal validity of survey data. External validity is affected to the extent that survey respondents differ from the population as a whole. If survey respondents are unrepresentative of the population, then one loses the ability to generalize from surveys to the population. Internal (and external) validity is at risk if the attitudes and characteristics of respondents differ from nonrespondents. We often use surveys to make raw descriptive statements such as "X percent of U.S. citizens approve of President Bush's performance as president," and also to make richer statements like "Y percent of

23

black U.S. citizens approve of Bush, while Z percent of white U.S. citizens approve of Bush." Internal validity is at risk in such a statement if black respondents differ more from black nonrespondents than white respondents differ from white nonrespondents.

Throughout this chapter I compare the demographics of respondents to academic surveys to benchmarks. The academic surveys I use are the National Election Studies (NES) and the General Social Survey (GSS), from 1978 through 1988. These studies represent the state of the art in academic survey research, particularly with respect to how they handle nonresponse. Both studies limit the scope of nonresponse by making multiple visits to households and attempting to convert refusals. Nonetheless, both surveys obtain significant levels of nonresponse, from 20 to 30 percent of the sample.

In addition, I include data from three NES telephone surveys, the 1982 Methods Comparison Project, 1984 Continuous Monitoring Study, and 1988 Senate Election Study. There are a number of difficulties with using the telephone data, which I discuss momentarily. Because telephone surveys represent the normal mode of operation for the vast majority of surveys (academic and otherwise) conducted in the United States every year, it is appropriate to include data from these three telephone surveys in order to assess the representativeness of telephone surveys generally.

The benchmark surveys I use are from the Current Population Studies (CPS) November supplements for the years 1978–1986, and the March survey for 1988.[1] The CPS is a reliable source for demographic characteristics of the population given that the nonresponse rate for the CPS typically falls well below 5 percent.[2]

---

1. As of this writing, the November 1988 CPS data are not yet published in electronic form. One feature of the November data sets is a measure denoting whether or not the respondent is a U.S. citizen. This variable is not present in the March collections. I restrict the CPS data to include only U.S. citizens, in order to make the CPS sample comparable to the NES and GSS samples. The reader should keep this distinction in mind when perusing the graphs and tables to follow.

2. I weight the NES (including the NES telephone studies) and GSS data by the inverse of the probability of selection (the number of eligible adults in the household). I do this because both studies are household samples, and the weight converts from households to adults. I weight the CPS data by their "standard person weight," which among other things is the CPS's correction for nonresponse. The reader should also be aware that the information for nearly half of the CPS cases are not supplied by the respondent, but by another member of the household. The informant's answers are less reliable than the respondent's answers. However, the informant's answers are probably not as unreliable for the demographic categories in this chapter (age, sex, race, income, education, residency) as for other questions in the CPS (e.g., whether

Of course, even if we assume that the CPS surveys yield reliable population estimates, simply finding that academic samples differ from benchmarks does not mean that the differences are solely due to nonresponse. Some differences between the sample and the population will be due to chance or sampling error. That is, it is just a matter of bad luck that the selected respondents are different from the population. But if one finds *consistent* differences (i.e., nonrandom differences that are consistently in the same direction) between the sample and the population across a range of surveys, as I do here, then sampling error as the source of difference becomes much less plausible.

Telephone surveys present their own difficulties for comparison to face-to-face surveys. For one, telephone surveys typically encounter response rates that are 10 percent higher than comparable face-to-face surveys. (The response rate for one of the three studies, the 1988 Senate Election Study, is considerably below the 1988 Pre-Postelection Study, with a response rate of about 45 percent). Thus, whatever effects nonresponse exerts on the differences between respondents and nonrespondents should be amplified. However, there are several confounding effects that may further amplify, or counter, any such differences. Obviously, telephone surveys can not reach individuals in households without telephones. Although the percentage of households in the United States without phones is quite low, that percentage is disproportionately likely to be poor, black, rural, and southern. Some questions seem to elicit higher *item* nonresponse, or refusals to particular questions, than do the equivalent questions in face-to-face studies. Questions about income, in particular, appear to elicit higher refusal rates. The absence of visual cues might induce some respondents to exaggerate their educational or social achievements. This much said, it is useful to compare the NES telephone surveys to the NES personal surveys in the field in the same year, as well as to the benchmarks.

The NES put the three telephone surveys into the field at different times, and in different ways. The 1982 Methods Comparison Project used a nearly identical questionnaire to the 1982 NES Postelection Study and was administered over the same time span as the 1982 study. The 1984 Continuous Monitoring Study (also known as the "Rolling Cross-section") ran for nearly an entire year as small weekly samples. For the results reported in this chapter, I pool frequencies across all weeks. The frequencies from the Continuous Monitoring Study are the most disparate of the lot. The sample frames for both the 1982 and 1984 tele-

---

or not the respondent voted in the general election or looked for work in the past week).

phone studies were Waksberg-Mitofsky cluster designs that are drawn from the same sampling frame as the NES and GSS areal probability samples. This is not the case for the 1988 Senate Election Study. This study draws cases with equal probability in every state, regardless of the population of the state. In order to make these numbers more comparable, I weight the frequencies from the Senate study by the state's population (see Gronke 1990).

One natural subject of interest is the demographic differences between respondents and nonrespondents. If one is able to claim that the sample is representative in the sense of mirroring aggregate population characteristics, one might be on firmer grounds to assert that the sample is reliable and fair. Conversely, if one can identify groups systematically missed by the survey sample, then one knows, at a minimum, to be wary of extending the analysis to the omitted subgroup. One might also be cautious about inferring population characteristics from a sample that is markedly unrepresentative. Furthermore, if we are able to identify the groups missing from our survey, we are in a better position to produce weights for the data we have, or to impute for the data we lack.

There are consistent and significant differences between the samples and the population for both the NES and the GSS. As a matter of fact, the nondifferences are as interesting as the differences, and I review those here as well. This chapter examines age, gender, education, race, and residency.

Age

There are good a priori reasons to be concerned about how surveys represent particular age groups. The age of the respondent may be related to how busy that respondent is, how available the respondent would be during particular hours, how amenable a respondent would be to participating in a survey, or how healthy a respondent might be. Both the GSS and NES face-to-face surveys underrepresent young adults and overrepresent the elderly. The answer is more mixed for the NES telephone surveys.

The proportion of adults less than 30 years old in the U.S. population as a whole has been rising (but dips in 1988, according to the CPS), while at the same time there has been a general downward trend in the proportion of survey respondents in this age group.[3] This difference holds for both the NES and GSS.[4] Figure 2.1 displays the percentage of

---

3. The raw percentages appear in tables in appendix A.
4. The reader might wonder whether or not these differences are statistically

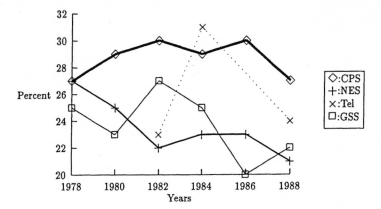

FIGURE 2.1. Percent of Respondents Less Than 30 Years Old, 1978–1988 CPS, NES, GSS, and NES Telephone

respondents under 30 years old for the NES and GSS, compared with that for the CPS (the external benchmark).[5] (The CPS estimates appear as the more boldfaced line throughout the figures in this chapter.) While the CPS estimate of the proportion of adults under the age of 30 is at 27-29 percent, the proportion is estimated as low as 21 percent in the NES and 20 percent in the GSS. The downward trend for GSS and NES estimates of this subgroup is plainly evident in this figure. In fact, the NES estimate for the proportion of adults under 30 is on target for 1978 (approximately 27 percent) but is quite off the mark by 1988.

Two of the three NES telephone surveys parallel the results of the NES and GSS face-to-face surveys (in 1982 and 1988). The 1984 Continuous Monitoring study achieves about a 31 percent fraction of respondents under 30 years old.

Figure 2.2 displays the fraction of respondents to the three studies who are 65 or older. The academic surveys (NES and GSS) *consistently*

significant and at what level. With sample sizes in excess of 1,000 cases for the NES and GSS, and in excess of 100,000 cases for the CPS, the largest possible pooled standard error is about .015, so that differences of 3 percentage points or more are statistically significant at $p < .05$.

5. The reader may notice that the plot of the CPS estimates is often smoother than the plots of the NES and GSS samples. There are at least two reasons for this pattern. One reason is that the substantially greater sample size of the CPS samples reduces sampling error. With samples in the hundreds of thousands instead of the thousands (typical for the NES and GSS), there is less variability due to chance. A second reason is that the CPS obtains a much higher response rate than the NES or GSS, reducing nonresponse error.

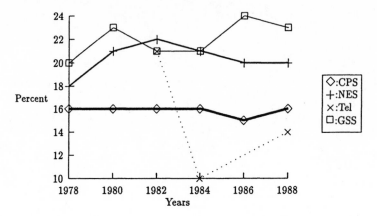

FIGURE 2.2. Percent of Respondents Over the Age of 65, 1978–1988 CPS, NES, GSS, and NES Telephone

overestimate the proportion of elderly respondents in comparison to the CPS. The NES and GSS are roughly equal in how far off the estimates are from the benchmark, overestimating by 2-9 percent the proportion of the population that are elderly. This might surprise some readers, but probably not an interviewer, whose folklore frequently features the elderly respondent who just loves the opportunity to talk with the interviewer.

Again, the telephone surveys yield a mixed message. The 1982 study overestimates the fraction of elderly respondents in the population (although only by the smallest amount in 1988). The 1984 Continuous Monitoring Study undercounts the elderly by about 6 percent, quite a sizable difference. In fact, in comparison to the two face-to-face academic studies in 1984, the difference is even more substantial. Both the 1984 NES and GSS yield estimates of the elderly around 21 percent, double that for the 1984 Continuous Monitoring Study. I do not think that we want to extrapolate too far from the representativeness of this particular study to the representativeness of telephone studies in general. The other telephone studies are closer to the norm of the face-to-face studies in terms of the count of the elderly.

These findings are consistent with the scholarship in survey research with regard to the lower response rates for younger ages (Dohrenwend and Dohrenwend 1968; Benus 1971; DeMaio 1980). However, considerable research has found higher *refusal* rates with increasing age (Cobb, King, and Chen 1957; Hawkins 1975; Goyder 1986; O'Neil 1979). Since

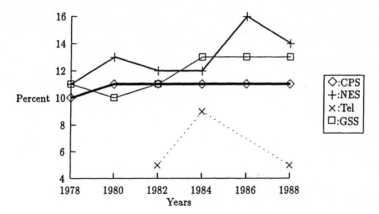

FIGURE 2.3. Percent of Black Respondents, 1978–1988 CPS, NES, GSS, and NES Telephone

refusal is only one component of nonresponse, these findings do not necessarily contradict the findings I report here. It turns out that older respondents are more easily contacted, but also more likely to refuse to be interviewed.

Race

Race plays a singularly conspicuous role in American politics and policy, from the Bush campaign's obsession with Willie Horton to the disproportionate numbers of the poor who are black. To the extent that polls influence campaign strategies or public policy, it is important to know whether or not blacks are underrepresented in public opinion surveys. At the level of a raw count of blacks and whites in these academic samples, this research suggests a surprise: blacks are often overrepresented in academic samples (see fig. 2.3).

Note that the CPS estimates that approximately 11 percent of those eligible to vote are black. The NES estimate always exceed the CPS estimate, by as much as 5 percent in 1986. The GSS estimate is closer and exceeds the CPS estimate for 1984–1986. In contrast, the NES telephone studies *underestimate* the proportion of blacks: the 1982 Methods Comparison Study found about 5 percent blacks, the 1984 Continuous Monitoring Study found 9 percent, and the 1988 Senate Election Study found about 7 percent. The consistent difference seen between telephone and face-to-face studies might well arise out of undercoverage of blacks

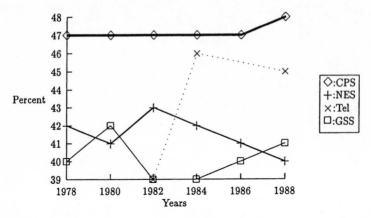

FIGURE 2.4. Percent of Male Respondents, 1978–1988 CPS, NES, GSS, and NES Telephone

by telephone sample: while the proportion of people who do not have access to telephones is small, that proportion falls heavier upon blacks.

The data from the NES, DAS, and GSS studies are consistent with previous studies, most of which find lower refusal rates for blacks (Weaver 1973; Hawkins 1975; O'Neil 1979; but see Goyder 1986).

Gender

There are good reasons to suspect that surveys might undercount men. Although the proportion of women in the workforce has been rising, there are still more working men than women. People working away from home may well be less available to be interviewed, or less amenable to being interviewed, than people at home. Both the NES and GSS samples, as well as the NES telephone studies, undercount men.

Figure 2.4 displays the proportion of CPS, NES, and GSS respondents by gender. The CPS estimate of the proportion of men in the population is a steady 47 percent from 1978 through 1986, jumping by a percentage point in 1988. The NES and GSS proportions of men in the sample always fall well below the CPS estimate with the surveys understating the proportion of men by between 4 and 8 percent. Notice that while the telephone samples undercount men in all cases, the telephone samples for 1984 and 1988 are much closer to the benchmark estimate than the 1982 Methods Comparison Project.

The finding here concurs with Smith (1979), who found declining proportions of men in the GSS samples (only after a switch of sampling method from quotas to full probability). What might account for the undercounting of men? Chapter 3 demonstrates that men are slightly less likely to be contacted than women, as well as more likely to refuse on certain grounds.

Education

We might expect a potential respondent's level of education to affect his or her likelihood of agreeing to be interviewed. Surveys might seem like tests to respondents, and perhaps those respondents with higher levels of education would more willingly subject 'themselves to these "tests" than those with lower levels of education. Some surprises lurk here: the NES and GSS samples overrepresent less educated respondents, while the NES also overrepresents respondents with college degrees.

Figure 2.5 shows that both the NES and GSS face-to-face studies *overrepresent* people with less than a high school education. For every study but one (the 1982 NES), the proportion of respondents without a high school diploma in the NES and GSS exceeds the CPS estimate. The GSS appears to overcount the proportion of those without a high school diploma by 5 to 7 percent.

The telephone studies are in striking contrast to the face-to-face studies. All three of the NES telephone studies underestimate the proportion of respondents without a high school diploma by at least 5 and as much as 12 percent. Two factors might account for the apparent underrepresentation of those without a high school diploma. It is possible that the telephone sample eludes undereducated respondents, who are likely to be disproportionately poor, black, and rural (all correlates of not having access to a telephone). A second reason is that the more impersonal nature of the telephone might encourage respondents to lie about their level of education.

The two academic survey organizations differ on estimates of respondents with a college degree for their face-to-face studies. As figure 2.6 displays, the NES tends to overestimate the proportion of respondents with a college degree (for 1980–1986), while the GSS tends to underestimate the same proportion (for 1978–1982 and 1986). The telephone studies appear to significantly undercount the fraction of respondents with a college degree by 10 to 15 percent.

The findings here run counter to a number of prior studies that found higher *refusal* rates among people without high school diplomas (Benson, Booman, and Clark 1951; Robins 1963; Dohrenwend and Dohrenwend

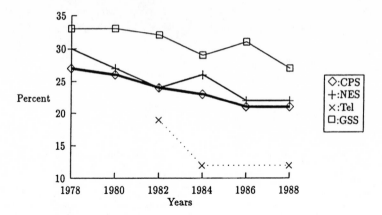

FIGURE 2.5. Percent of Respondents without HS Diploma, 1978–1988 CPS, NES, GSS, and NES Telephone

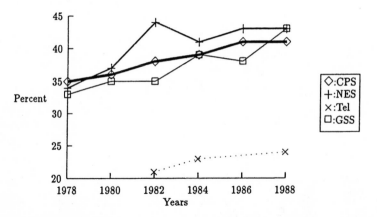

FIGURE 2.6. Percent of Respondents with a College Degree, 1978–1988 CPS, NES, GSS, and NES Telephone

1968; O'Neil 1979; Goudy 1976; Cannell et al. 1987). Again, refusals are only one component of nonresponse, and these earlier results are not strictly comparable.

Income

As with education, there are good reasons to be concerned about possible underrepresentation by income. For one, because surveys are an

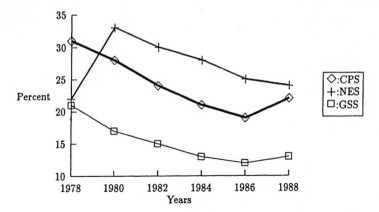

FIGURE 2.7. Percent of Respondents with Family Incomes less than $10,000, 1978–1988 CPS, NES, and GSS

important part of the formulas by which federal dollars are allocated to states and cities, one ought to be concerned whether the surveys underrepresent economic groups and thus lead to misallocations of federal aid. As with education, income may interact with political variables, themselves the concern of the study. As a result, we may misestimate the importance of income in politics if we underestimate income groups.

The NES overrepresents the poor; the GSS underrepresents them. Figure 2.7 displays the proportion of respondents to the 1978–1988 CPS, NES and GSS whose family income is less than $10,000.[6] The NES overrepresents respondents with family incomes less than $10,000, in comparison with the CPS. The GSS, on the other hand, always underestimates the proportion of poor families.[7]

Figure 2.8 displays the proportion of respondents whose family income exceeds $25,000.[8] The NES and GSS usually underestimate the

6. The three studies use different schemes to categorize income, and I have collapsed the categories to make them roughly comparable.

7. Unfortunately, we must leave off our comparison of the face-to-face and telephone studies, for two reasons. Most immediately, the coding of the income categories for the telephone studies makes it impossible to compare respondents and keep the same categories across studies. (As it stands, I have had to collapse income categories in order to make the NES, GSS, and CPS results comparable.) Secondly, there is significant item nonresponse to the income questions in telephone studies, and respondents in general appear to be reluctant to convey their incomes over the telephone.

8. Although one would probably prefer to have a higher threshold, the $25,000 cutoff is the highest level of income where both the coding of the income categories are

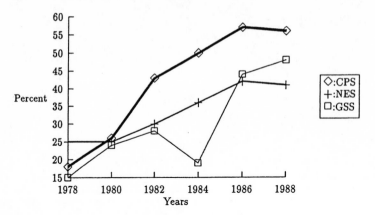

FIGURE 2.8. Percent of Respondents with Family Incomes more than $25,000, 1978–1988 CPS, NES, and GSS

proportion of families with incomes greater than $25,000 per year. Except for 1978, the NES estimate of families at this income level falls below the CPS estimates, by as much as 15 percent (in 1982). Except for 1988, the GSS also underestimates the proportion of families with incomes greater than $25,000. The NES and GSS estimates tend to be very close to one another (except for 1984 and 1988).

The estimates of the income of the respondents are necessarily more error prone than estimates of sex, race, and age. Some respondents will not tell the truth about their income to interviewers, but is it the CPS or the NES/GSS that is in error? Are respondents more likely to underreport income to the academic surveys, distrusting the interviewer? The CPS interview schedule includes a series of questions about the respondent's sources of income (from government subsidies, work, alimony, etc.), while the NES and GSS ask a much more limited battery. The extensive questions by the CPS may prompt respondents to recall sources of income that might slip the mind of the respondents to the NES and GSS. In short, misreporting of income may be only part of the problem. Such interesting speculations are unfortunately untestable with the current data.

As noted in subsequent chapters, the relationship of income and survey participation is more complex than one might have thought at

---

equivalent *and* present for all three studies for the full decade. The reader curious about the distribution of income at higher brackets should consult the tables in appendix A.

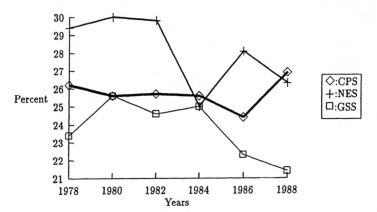

FIGURE 2.9. Percent of Respondents Living in Central Cities, 1978–1988 CPS, NES, and GSS

first blush. Income affects both accessibility and compliance, but in different ways. At this stage in the analysis the result is surprising: academic surveys underestimate the wealthy, not the poor (for results that run contrary to these, see Goyder 1986; Benus 1971; DeMaio 1980; Smith 1983).

Place of Residence

Where one lives might also influence how likely one is to be interviewed. Higher crime rates, busier lives, and more guarded entries might make a city dweller not only more reticent to be interviewed but also less accessible to the interviewer in the first place than someone who lives in rural areas. The GSS and NES contrast sharply in their estimates of the proportions of people living in cities and in rural areas.[9] Figure 2.9 displays the fraction of respondents to the three studies who live in the central city of a Standard Metropolitan Statistical Area (SMSA, the Census standard definition of an urban area). Except for 1980, the GSS underestimates the proportion of people living in central cities. In contrast, the NES overestimated the fraction of city dwellers for 1978, 1980, 1982, and 1986.[10]

---

9. Again, a comparison to the telephone surveys is not strictly possible. Since we do not know the address of the respondents when dialing to the cluster, that cluster might contain respondents who are both in and out of SMSAs.

10. The NES and GSS rely on highly clustered samples, especially in comparison to the CPS. As a result, the NES and GSS proportions of respondents by place of

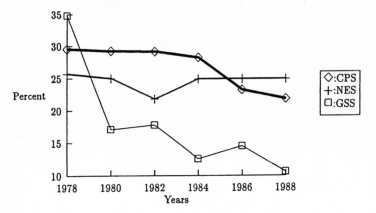

FIGURE 2.10. Percent of Respondents Not Living in SMSAs, 1978–1988 CPS, NES, and GSS

In Figure 2.10 we see the fraction of respondents to the three studies who live outside of SMSAs. The GSS consistently underestimates the fraction of respondents outside of SMSAs (except for 1978). On the other hand, the NES underestimated the fraction of respondents not living in SMSAs for all but 1986 and 1988.

The fact that the GSS and NES differ so sharply in the proportion of respondents by urban and rural categories reveals a larger point: where a potential respondent lives does not help very much in explaining his or her chances of responding. If location truly influenced response rate, one would expect that the response rate would be similar for two different studies conducted in the same geographical clusters. Figure 2.11 displays the response rate for the 1988 NES plotted against the response rate for the 1986 NES, *for the same cluster.* While there is a weak linear pattern, there is clearly more going on to influence response rates than geography. (The Spearman correlation is a modest .24.)

Some of the most striking research on correlates of response rates focuses on the respondents' place of residence. Steeh (1981) divides response rates for the NES and the Surveys of Consumer Attitudes by urban and rural areas noting an increase in refusal rates in urban areas over the last thirty years. House and Wolf (1978) observe similarly high refusal rates in urban areas and explicitly tie these refusal rates to increasing crime. An examination of response rates for urban areas in the particular studies of this analysis fails to confirm the earlier findings.

residence may be more variable than proportions for other demographic categories.

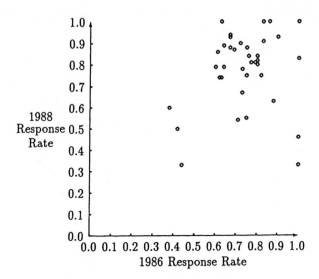

FIGURE 2.11. Response Rate for Identical Cluster, 1988 v. 1986 NES

Conclusions

There are some surprises among the findings in this chapter, and it is useful at this stage to recall the key differences and similarities by demographic categories among the three studies.

The NES and GSS both underestimate the number of young people and overestimate the proportion of the elderly.

The NES and GSS usually overestimate the proportion of black respondents. If one expected surveys to parallel divisions in society, one would be surprised at the greater participation of blacks.

The NES and GSS consistently underestimate the proportion of men. This is not a surprise intuitively.

The NES and GSS consistently overestimate the number of respondents without a high school diploma. The NES tends to overestimate the number of respondents with a college degree, while the GSS tends to underestimate the fraction of respondents in the same group. The NES tends to overestimate the number of poor families, while the GSS underestimates the fraction of the poor. However, both the NES and GSS tend to underestimate the number of wealthy families. These differences are startling, suggesting that the academic surveys tend to overrepresent people from poorer economic groups.

The two academic studies divide on how well they represent people by where they live. The NES overrepresents people in cities and underrepresents people in rural areas; the GSS underrepresents people in cities and in rural areas.

The differences between the NES telephone and the academic samples have been instructive on a number of counts. The telephone samples are occasionally less representative (further from the benchmark) than the face-to-face studies, and occasionally closer to the benchmark. What is perhaps most interesting is that for race and education, the telephone studies are on the opposite side of the benchmark from the face-to-face academic studies. The face-to-face studies overcount blacks and those without a high school diploma, while the telephone studies undercount those same groups.

At one level of analysis—the comparison of who is in the academic surveys—surveys appear to be a vehicle for representation of the economically and politically weak. Who is overrepresented in academic surveys? The elderly, blacks, women, the poor, the less-educated. Who is missing? Men, young people, whites, the wealthy. This is indeed a surprising finding. But it does not tell the whole story. We do not know *why* people respond to surveys, and at best the findings of this chapter are weak clues to the causes of nonresponse. We require more subtle approaches to understand survey participation. The next two chapters explore the process by which people participate in surveys.

CHAPTER 3

Why Do People Participate in Surveys?

Imagine that you have been selected to participate in a survey. What determines whether or not you agree to answer the questionnaire? The interviewer must first *contact* you; the interviewer must then determine if you are *eligible* to participate in the study and *capable* of answering the questions; and finally, you must decide to *comply* with the interviewer's request to be interviewed. Survey participation is a process, a sequence governed by differing factors.

This chapter develops a model of survey participation as a process with three stages: contact, eligibility, and compliance. Very different factors affect whether or not an individual moves from one step to the next. If the individual fails to cross any of these three thresholds, that individual becomes a nonrespondent. In order to become an interviewed respondent, one must cross all three steps. I display these stages as a flowchart in figure 3.1.

A clarification of terms is necessary. By *sample person,* I mean an individual that a survey organization selects as part of its sample and whom the organization intends to interview. A *respondent* is an individual actually interviewed for the study. A *no contact* is a sample person who is never reached by the interviewer. An *ineligible respondent* is a person the interviewer has contacted but who falls outside of the target population of the study. An *incapable respondent* is someone whom one can not expect to complete an interview, for reasons of health or otherwise.[1] A *refusal* is an individual who has been contacted by the interviewer, but declines to be interviewed. A *resister* or *reluctant respondent* is someone who refuses to participate on first contact but agrees on some subsequent contact. Refusals and no contacts are both *nonrespondents.*

The accessibility of the respondent heavily influences whether or not the interviewer *contacts* the sample person.[2] Security guards may

---

1. Many survey organizations refer to incapable respondents as "noninterview others" (Groves 1989).
2. The actions of the interviewer may also affect whether or not the interviewer

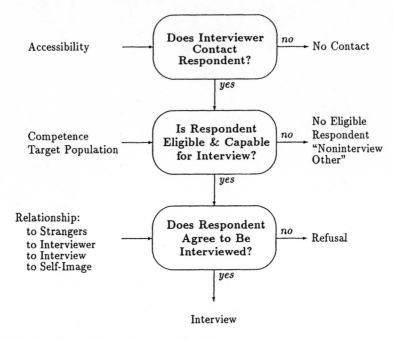

FIGURE 3.1. The Process of Survey Participation

routinely prevent interviewers or other strangers from reaching the front door. People without telephones can't be interviewed over the phone. Due to working schedule or life-style, some people may be rarely available to be interviewed.

Once contacted, the sample person must be eligible for the particular survey and capable of answering questions. Eligibility depends on the sample universe of the study. A study of voting may require that respondents all be of voting age and U.S. citizens, or even that respondents intend to vote in the election. Some studies may require that the respondent be over (or under) a certain age, be of a particular race or ethnic origin, or suffer from a particular disease. The interviewer also has to determine if the respondent can answer the questions. In many studies, if the respondent does not speak English, or if the respondent is not healthy enough to participate in the interview, a respondent may not be capable of being interviewed.

Once the interviewer contacts the sample person and determines

---

contacts a sample person.

that he or she is eligible for the interview, the respondent must choose whether to comply with the interviewer's request to be interviewed. This last step, the respondent's decision, is particularly important. Most nonrespondents are refusals, and the rate at which people refuse to be interviewed is increasing.

This chapter posits that four relationships determine the sample person's decision to participate or to refuse: a relationship to strangers, a relationship to the interviewer, a relationship to the interview, and a relationship to self-image. The targets of these four relationships (strangers, interviewer, interview, self-image) range from the respondent's connection with the external world to the respondent's sense of self. A potential respondent need not consider these four relationships in any particular order; any one of the four may be most important for any individual person. For convenience, consider the four relationships in order of specificity to the respondent.

Put yourself in the position of someone targeted to be interviewed. A stranger arrives at your doorstep, clipboard in hand. That stranger could be a salesperson, a political activist, a criminal, or, worse, an interviewer; some people would rather not talk with any of the four. How you feel about strangers will influence whether or not you will agree to listen to the interviewer, much less agree to the interview itself.

Once you establish contact with the interviewer, and discover that this stranger at your door is not a salesperson, political activist, or criminal, how you feel about this particular stranger—the interviewer—may determine whether or not you will proceed. The skill of the interviewer, his or (more often) her demeanor, even his or her voice or appearance may affect whether or not you will agree to be interviewed.

This interviewer explains why he or she is at your doorstep. A survey organization wants to know "your feelings on a variety of topics." How you feel about being interviewed at that moment, about the topics of the interview, and about the organization sponsoring the interview all weigh upon your decision to comply.

You now understand why this person is at your door, and what he or she wants you to do. Do you see yourself as the sort of person who complies with requests from strangers?

This chapter traces the steps by which someone becomes a respondent or nonrespondent to a survey. First, the chapter examines what influences whether or not an interviewer contacts a sample person. Then the chapter discusses what determines whether or not the contacted respondent is eligible and capable to participate. The third section discusses why a sample person would comply with the interviewer's request, exploring the respondent's attitudes toward strangers, the interviewer, the interview, and self.

Methodological Detour

One minor detour is necessary at this point: as the reader might ask, how on earth does one know anything about the nonrespondents? The interviewer hasn't even *seen* some of these people. How can one make statements about their demographic characteristics, much less about how they *feel* about strangers, surveys, or self? Unfortunately, the very best tool to examine the attributes of the nonrespondents is the survey the interviewer couldn't get. This chapter relies on a battery of complementary techniques that are substitutes for direct and intensive observation.

Interviewer-supplied information. One tactic is to use outside sources of information about the individual nonrespondents. If the interviewer has some contact with the nonrespondent, a neighbor, or another member of the household, the interviewer might be able to determine some demographic characteristics of the nonrespondent. Estimates of the nonrespondent's attributes are more error prone than those for the respondents. One might be able to guess the age of the nonrespondent, but that guess is likely to be less accurate than the age reported by the respondent him- or herself.

Three separate survey organizations accumulate data on individual nonrespondents as a matter of course. Interviewers for the GSS (from 1980 to 1985) completed a "Noninterview Report" (NIR) for each noninterview. These interviewers recorded the nonrespondent's age, income, race, marital status, and the number of adults in the household (estimating when necessary).[3] The NES (in 1986 and 1988) collected a similar set of information about nonrespondents in the "Interview Description Booklet" (IDB). These data included race, sex, age, approximate income of the nonrespondent, accessibility of the housing unit, reasons for refusal or a determination of "no eligible respondent," and the attitude of the respondent toward the survey.[4] The interviewers for the Detroit Area Study (DAS) (1989) collected parallel information about nonre-

---

3. Tom Smith, associate study director for the National Opinion Research Center, was gracious in providing me access to these files. Any mistakes in analyses contained here are strictly my own.

4. The Board of Directors for the NES provided me with these nonresponse data. These data are available to any researcher contacting the board, following specific guarantees of confidentiality of the respondent.

spondents: age, sex, race, approximate income, reasons for refusal, and accessibility of the housing unit.

Reluctant versus amenable respondents. A second strategy treats some portion of the respondents as proxies for the nonrespondents (O'Neil 1979; Ellis, Endo, and Armer 1970; Fillion 1976). The logic underlying the proxy nonrespondent approach is the belief that response to a survey is really a continuum, and not a dichotomy. The assumption is that most people probably agree or refuse to be interviewed depending on circumstances.[5]

For the GSS, NES, and DAS surveys, I treat any respondent who refused initially as a proxy for the nonrespondents. For the 1988 NES, the interviewers themselves determined whether or not a respondent refused initially. For the 1986 NES, DAS, and GSS surveys, I code initial refusals from the call records for the respondent.

Miniquestionnaire. I use a third approach only with the 1989 DAS: a ploy to obtain answers to a few key questions rather than the entire questionnaire. This approach is a "door-in-the-face" strategy. The foot-in-the-door strategy is used by salespeople to obtain sustained contact with an individual by first making some small request, followed with a larger request (Freedman and Fraser 1966). The door-in-the-face approach is in many senses the opposite: ask first for a large, impossible request; ask secondly for a smaller request (Cialdini 1984). The DAS staff instructed the interviewers to make the following statement to any respondent who refused on the second attempt (after a persuasion letter had been sent):

> I understand that you do not want to be interviewed, but I do have to provide a reason to my supervisor why I could not obtain the interview.
>
> A1. Why do you not want to be interviewed?

The interviewers then followed with questions on turnout ("Did you vote in the presidential election this November?") and vote choice ("Did you vote for Dukakis, Bush, or someone else?"). Surprisingly, 64 percent

---

5. Furthermore, treating the most reluctant respondents as proxies for nonrespondents mimics the field procedures of many, if not most, survey organizations. In a survey of survey organizations conducting pre-election polls, Crespi (1988) found that a full third of the organizations make only one attempt to reach a respondent at the household and that 82 percent of the organizations do not attempt to convert refusals into interviews.

of the refusals were willing to answer question A1, 43 percent were willing to answer the turnout question, and 15 percent were willing to answer the vote choice question.

The three methods I use in this chapter, combined, give a portrait of the demographic and attitudinal characteristics of respondents and nonrespondents. With the interviewer-supplied information, we have estimates of key demographic characteristics and a record of the refusals' reasons. With the short-form questionnaire, we have the refusals' self-expressed reasons for refusing and (for many of the refusals) measures of their turnout and vote choice. With the reluctant-amenable respondent comparisons, we have measures of the attitudes and demographics of the people most like the nonrespondents. I now use these methods to explore the sequence of steps required to interview a respondent.

Contact

The interviewer must first be able to contact the designated sample person in order to get an interview. A sample person's accessibility determines his or her "contactability." Physical barriers between the interviewer and the sample person decrease the chances of contacting the sample person. People who are not at home at the time that the interviewer calls the household may also never be contacted, even if nothing prevents the interviewer from reaching the door.

Physical inaccessibility is a common occurence in modern life, and particularly in urban areas. On several occasions in the course of administering the 1989 DAS, interviewers found it was impossible to speak directly with any member of the selected household. A locked front door with a security guard barred the interviewers from entering the building, even to use the intercom, unless the respondent made prior arrangements. Locked doors, security guards, or absence of intercom systems all make sample people inaccessible.

Sometimes, physical inaccessibility arises out of physical threats to the well-being of the interviewer. Mail carriers may have to go to the mailboxes of households with vicious dogs; interviewers often will not. A sad comment on modern life and inaccessible respondents follows from the prestudy planning of the DAS. There was a small debate among DAS study staff as to whether crack houses would be counted as "nonsample" or as "businesses." There was no debate about whether or not the interviewer would attempt to contact anyone in the crack house.

A sample person's household may be easily reachable by the interviewer, but that person may never be at home. People with long working hours will be less available to be interviewed than others. Individuals whose social life takes them out on the town every evening won't be accessible to interviewers.

We can exploit what information the interviewer could gather about no contacts from neighbors or by observation. Table 3.1 presents probit analyses of the likelihood of contact as a function of various demographic characteristics for the 1986 and 1988 NES and the 1980–1985 GSS. The dependent variable is contact with the sample person, coded 1 for contact, 0 otherwise.[6] The rows display the bivariate probit coefficients, where contact is regressed on each row variable, one row variable at a time. For example, the coefficient for *restricted access* in the top row of table 3.1 is the slope coefficient of the probit regression of *contact* on the dummy variable for *restricted access* alone.[7] A variable-by-variable approach may introduce spurious causality: if we find that an elderly person is 23 percent more likely to be contacted than a nonelderly person, is it because the elderly are also more likely to be poor and living alone, or is contactability associated with age? The variable-by-variable approach is useful as a descriptive tool only.

These measures illustrate what influences accessibility of respondents. Two of the more powerful explanations for acessibility pertain to the residence of the respondent. In this descriptive analysis, the most potent variable is whether or not access to the household is restricted in any way.[8] The probit coefficient is −.79 (1986 NES), which means the interviewer is 29 percent less likely to contact the respondent if access to the respondent's household is restricted.[9] The population of the

---

6. I assume that all cases are identically and independently distributed in order to compute the standard errors for this and all subsequent analyses in this chapter. The NES, GSS, and DAS employ clustered sample designs, thus the true standard errors will be larger than the standard errors used here. In this chapter, I pay closer attention to *patterns* of point estimates than to their confidence intervals.

7. Several of the measures are unavailable for some of the GSS. "Restricted access" and the log of the population size are not available in the GSS data sets for any year. The measure of the number of children in the household is unreliable for 1983–1985. Furthermore, coefficients from any probit model that did not converge are not reported in this table.

8. Restricted access includes any of the following situations: locked gate, no trespassing sign, loose dog, contact must be established by intercom, doorman or guard blocks access, secure apartment or condo with no means of contacting anyone for access.

9. I calculate the net change in probability from the probit coefficients using the method of first differences (King 1989): calculate the probability for the maximum of the range (here, that the household is restricted, or restricted access = 1), holding all the other variables constant at their means, and subtract the probability for the minimum of the range (here, that the household is not restricted, or restricted access

TABLE 3.1. Bivariate Probit Analyses of Contactability of Sample Persons, 1986 and 1988 NES, 1980–1985 GSS

	NES			GSS				
	1986	1988	Pooled	1980	1982	1983	1984	1985
Restricted Access?	−.79							
Log of Pop. of City	−.04	−.05						
Elderly Person	**.55**	**.65**	**.61**	**.69**	**.65**			
Children in Household	**.39**	**1.26**	**.23**	**.53**	**.56**			
Income	**.29**	.07	**.10**	.10	.07	.12	.15	.00
Number of Adults in Household	−.03	−.10	−.02	−.01	−.03	−.01	−.02	−.02
Male	−.03	−.10	**−.20**	−.14	−.14	−.39	−.24	
N	3,261	2,984	9,351	1,899	1,886	2,001	1,762	1,813

Boldfaced entries are statistically significant at $p < .01$. Dependent variable is contact, where contacted sample persons are coded 1 and "no contacts" are coded 0.

respondent's place of residence matters, too. The probit coefficient on the log of population size is −.04; interviewers would be 11 percent less likely to contact a respondent living in a city at the median population size for the NES sample than a respondent living in the most rural area of the NES sample.

Five demographic measures are related to whether or not the interviewer will contact the respondent. First, interviewers are more likely to reach the elderly (sample persons over age 65) than the nonelderly. The probit coefficient ranges from .55 (1986 NES) to .69 (1980 GSS). Interpolating the middle of that range to .62, an interviewer is 23 percent more likely to contact a respondent over the age of 65 than a respondent under the age of 65. This makes sense: respondents over age 65 are more likely to be retired, and hence at home.

Secondly, whether or not there are any children in the household increases the odds that an interviewer will be able to eventually talk with the sample person. Interviewers reached households with children more frequently than households without children: the probit coefficients range from .23 to 1.26, all positive. This observation is also quite sensible: families with children more often require someone at home to take

---

= 0), holding all the other variables constant at their means. One might choose to report only the probabilities, but this depends on some assumptions: that the other variables are held to their means, and that the range of change is relevant to the individual reader. I choose to report the probit coefficients in the tables, and to report selected probabilities in the text. That way, readers who are curious about the net probability of sample persons with other combinations of characteristics may do so.

care of the children and will be more accessible. The care-giver at home may well be the respondent or would be able to make appointments for other respondents in the household.

Thirdly, interviewers are more likely to reach people with higher incomes than lower incomes. The probit coefficients range from .07 (1982 GSS) to .29 (1986 NES), with the exception of the 1985 GSS (0). One might conjecture that many poorer sample persons live in inaccessible areas (more urban, greater number of stories to the buildings, etc.) or have life-styles that are less predictable (such as irregular work-hours). This remains a conjecture, as the data here do not permit much further examination. One should also note that the interviewers could only guess the income of the noncontacted sample persons, while the actual respondents reported their income. Income is probably the least reliable measurement of the seven used in this descriptive analysis.

Surprisingly, interviewers had more difficulty contacting houses with many, as opposed to few, adults. This is counterintuitive: one might think that additional adults in the household would increase the chances of finding someone in the household when the interviewer knocks at the door. However, an increase in the number of adults yields a small but statistically significant decrease in the probability of contact. Households with large numbers of adults may be unusual: households with adult children living at home, multiple young adults sharing an apartment, elderly adults without spouses but living together. Perhaps the unusual nature of these households is what accounts for lower chances of contact.

Fifth, interviewers are less likely to contact men than to contact women. The probit coefficients for probability of contact given that the sample person is male are all negative. One plausible explanation is that men may be more likely to work outside the home than women and thus be less likely to be contacted.

The descriptive analysis here does not allow tests of what *causes* some respondents to be accessible and others inaccessible. However, this approach describes who is generally reachable: the elderly, people with children, women, people with higher incomes. The features of accessible respondents make sense.[10]

---

10. The reader should note that there might be common causes of contact and compliance. If interviewers are less likely to contact busy people, busy people may also be less likely to consent to be interviewed. In the discussion about the third, compliance, stage of the survey process, there is some evidence to suggest that busy people are less likely to agree to the interview. "No contacts" may be more like refusals than researchers have previously thought. Interviewers will certainly share

Contacting the respondent is only the first step. The respondent must be part of the sample universe and able to answer questions. The respondent must also agree to be interviewed. The next sections follow these stages.

Eligibility and Capability

Once the interviewer contacts the respondent or another member of the household, the interviewer's next step is to determine whether or not the sample person is eligible and capable of being interviewed. Eligibility depends, in great part, on the purpose and target population of the survey. Is the survey a study of the voting age population? A study of the health of a particular subpopulation? A study of the income or spending habits of welfare participants? Eligibility for a survey depends on the goals of the study.

The proportion of ineligible respondents in the NES, for example, is tiny. Among *all* coversheets dispatched by the field staff for the 1986 and 1988 NES—nonsample cases plus interviews and nonrespondents— less than 5 percent of the coversheets targeted ineligible respondents (of which 3.1 percent were "No Eligible Respondents" and 1.4 percent were "Noninterview Others" for 1986, there is no further specification in the coversheet records). As a point of comparison, twice as many coversheets targeted vacant houses as ineligible respondents.

While the number of ineligible respondents to the NES is tiny, remember that this proportion is utterly dependent on the target population. The fraction of ineligible respondents in some studies may not be negligible.

At the same time that the interviewer must determine whether or not the sample person is eligible to be interviewed, the interviewer must

---

stories about respondents who hide behind closed doors, pretending not to see the interviewer at the doorstep. These are "hidden refusals": situations where respondents are actually refusing to be interviewed, but masquerading as uncontactable. Hidden refusals may be part of the interviewers' folklore, but one must suspect that their number must be small. A more likely scenario is a "latent refusal": a situation where a respondent is not only too busy to be contacted but also too busy to be interviewed should he or she actually be contacted.

Some surveys with unusual populations of interest may be especially prone to both latent and hidden refusals. For example, a survey of victims may have great difficulty locating respondents who have moved since the crime (even when starting from a listed sample). One might well suspect that the victims would refuse, even if the interviewer were able to contact the sample persons. Their moving may signify a desire to be left alone.

TABLE 3.2. **Multivariate Probit Analyses of Capability of Contacted Sample Persons, 1986 and 1988 NES**

	1986 NES		1988 NES	
	B	SE	*B*	SE
Age 30–50	**.91**	.09	.15	.16
Age 51–65	**.56**	.09	.09	.18
Age > 65	**−.24**	.09	**−.79**	.15
(Constant)	1.05	.05	2.13	.20
N Incapable	141		161	
N Capable	3,000		2,683	

Dependent variable is capability, where capable respondents are coded 1, 0 otherwise. **Boldfaced** coefficients are statistically significant at *p* < .01.

also determine whether or not the respondent is *capable* of being interviewed. The fraction of incapable respondents is also small—around 5 percent of all sample persons for both the 1986 and 1988 NES. As the sample person's age increases, the chances that he or she will be capable of being interviewed decrease.

An interviewer may have difficulty determining whether or not a sample person is capable of being interviewed. One reason is that the actual health of the respondent may be ambiguous. For the NES and the GSS, respondents who are not healthy enough to participate may be ruled incapable. But the determination that a respondent is not healthy enough to be interviewed often comes from an intermediary in the respondent's household—a nurse or other family member. Some respondents consent to an interview on their deathbed. Some respondents with only minor illness refuse to be interviewed, but with an intermediary warding off the persistent interviewer.

A second gray area is in the language skills of the respondent. The NES interviews in Spanish. The DAS does not interview in Spanish. And neither the NES, GSS, nor DAS conduct interviews in languages besides Spanish or English. Non-English speakers may still be part of the sample universe, those eligible to vote.

With the NES, the most potent factor explaining likelihood of being capable of being interviewed is age. Table 3.2 displays a multivariate probit analysis of likelihood of capability as a function of age.[11] The dependent variable is capability, coded 1 if the respondent is capable and 0 otherwise. I represent age as a set of dummy variables.

---

11. From this point forward, all of the probit analyses are multivariate. The reason is that we want to have a sense of how the demographic characteristics interact (e.g., whether it is income or race that accounts for a particular reason for refusing).

Capability declines with age. Sample persons over 65 years old are the least likely to be capable of being interviewed: 6 percent less likely in 1986 and 7 percent less likely in 1988 than a respondent 30 years or under. (There is also a monotonic, although nonlinear, pattern to the coefficients, suggesting that capability drops continuously.)

The first two stages of the survey process account for little nonresponse in the studies examined here. The interviewers for the NES, GSS, and DAS persistently attempt to contact respondents, and their persistence pays off in relatively low no contact rates. Additionally, few respondents are incapable of being interviewed or ineligible for the interview. These two steps in the survey process may be relatively unimportant in understanding nonresponse in the NES, GSS, and DAS, but may take on added significance in more specialized studies. The most interesting, most important stage of the survey process is the next step in the flowchart: does the respondent agree to be interviewed?

Compliance

The third stage of the survey process produces most of the nonresponse. In the typical case, the interviewer contacts the respondent and determines that the respondent is eligible to be interviewed. The interviewer then explains the purpose of the study, and that the respondent's answers will be held completely confidential, identifies the institution conducting the research, and finally asks to conduct the interview. Unlike the prior stages of the survey process, this time the respondent can make the decision. The prior stages are heavily organizational or administrative problems, the compliance stage of the survey process is a behavioral problem.[12]

Why would you *refuse* to be interviewed? For example, the interviewer does her best to persuade you that the study values your contribution. She explains that the study will help your community, let the politicians in city hall or in Washington know how *you* feel. The interviewer praises the virtues of random sampling for having selected you as a unique representative for thousands of other people like yourself. She tells you that you'll feel good to express yourself. The simple fact is

---

In this particular table, I conduct a multivariate probit analysis to get a sense of how capability *changes* with age.

12. Of course, there are also respondents who hide behind doors or feign illness (hidden refusals), or who would refuse even if contacted or eligible (latent refusals). The discussion to follow applies to the latent and hidden refusals in the same manner as the observed refusals.

that you may hate surveys, fear strangers, prefer to keep your opinions to yourself, or just can't spare the time while you try to take care of two children and a spouse with the chicken pox.

Why would you *agree* to be interviewed? Interviews are often long, tedious, and intrusive—how would you feel about 40 minutes of questions about brushing and flossing? You rarely receive a tangible reward for answering all those questions.[13] And who knows if politicians really pay attention to poll results? The simple fact is that you may like to talk about yourself and your opinions, enjoy the company of strangers, see yourself as someone who likes to help others, believe that surveys will lead to a cure for AIDS, or just desperately need someone to talk to after taking care of two children and a spouse with chicken pox for the last two weeks.

This section repeatedly uses the reasons that respondents and refusals offer for their decisions. Many readers might doubt that any reason provided by a respondent or a refusal, in truth, reflects the basis of his or her decision. Skeptical readers might wonder whether the refusals' reasons are just the first coherent thought that pops into mind, and not the cause behind the decision. By this thinking, the refusal might feel threatened by the interviewer but tell the interviewer, "I'm too busy." Other skeptics might believe a refusals' reason is just what that person thinks will convince the interviewer. More extreme skeptics might even doubt that the refusal is capable of knowing why he or she chose to refuse.[14] Such skepticism is probably well-founded. On the other hand, why not treat what people say as useful information? What I ask of the skeptical reader is a partial suspension of doubt. If we treat the offered reasons as true reasons, do they help us understand compliance? As the reader shall see, there are coherent and sensible patterns to the types of people who express various reasons for refusal.

A set of four relationships determines why people choose or refuse to participate in surveys. The respondent's *relationship to strangers* influences whether or not that respondent agrees to talk with the inter-

---

13. My household had the privilege of being an Arbitron family for one week. (Arbitron is a nationwide polling organization assessing television and radio use, much like the more famous Nielsen ratings.) Arbitron sends its respondents two crisp, brand-new dollar bills, one before and one after, but both with a sticker thanking the respondent for keeping a diary of radio use for the week.

14. Nisbett and Wilson (1977) report experiments that demonstrate that people readily provide spurious reasons for their behavior. Even if the patterns of people that express certain reasons make sense and are consistent, there will always be grounds to assert that the refusals' reasons aren't *why* they refused. Of course, this is anathema to survey research generally, so we needn't feel alone in our misery.

viewer. The respondent's *relationship to the interviewer* also influences the chances of complying with the request. If the respondent has no specific objections to strangers or the interviewer in particular, the respondent's *relationship to the survey* comes to bear on the respondent's decision. If the respondent has no specific objection to strangers, the interviewer, or the survey, the respondent's self-perception, or *relationship to self-image,* influences whether or not the respondent agrees to participate. In the pages that follow, I discuss how these four relationships individually influence compliance.

Relationship to Strangers

An interviewer arrives at your doorstep. You have no idea why this stranger is there. Should you listen to this stranger? Should you even open the door? Are you *suspicious* of strangers? Do you fear a breach of your *privacy and confidentiality?* The interviewer at the sample person's doorstep is a specific instance of a common situation: an encounter with a stranger. In this section, I examine suspicion and confidentiality as indicators of the respondent's relationship to strangers.

There is some evidence that people refuse to be interviewed because they are suspicious of the interviewer. Among 643 refusals to the 1988 NES, the interviewers classified 17 percent as suspicious, 22 percent as rude, 22 percent as hostile, 3 percent as threatening, and 69 percent as polite but firm.[15] Most of the refusals were polite, but many were more antagonistic.

Which sample persons tend to be marked as suspicious by the interviewers? Table 3.3 displays the results of a multivariate probit analysis examining the demographics of people that the interviewers labeled as "suspicious" (refusals and respondents). The dependent variable is 'suspicious,' coded 1 if the interviewer rated the sample person as suspicious, 0 otherwise. Only one coefficient is statistically significant: interviewers are 4 percent more likely to rate blacks as suspicious than nonblacks (again using the method of first differences). The patterns on the other coefficients, although not statistically significant, are instructive nonetheless. Interviewers are 2 percent more likely to rate Hispanics as suspicious than non-Hispanics, although the standard error on this

---

15. Interviewers for the 1988 NES completed an "Interview Description Booklet" for all refusals, "no contacts," and resisters. The interviewers marked whether or not the respondent exhibited any of the five attitudes (suspicious, rude, hostile, threatening, or polite but firm). Percentages do not add up to 100 percent because a refusal may exhibit more than one attitude.

TABLE 3.3. Multivariate Probit Analysis of Respondents and Refusals Labeled as Suspicious by Interviewers, 1988 NES

	B	SE
Age	.00	.00
Income	−.01	.05
Black	**.28**	**.10**
Hispanic	.16	.13
Male	−.13	.08
(Constant)	−1.53	.15

Dependent variable is whether or not the interviewer coded the sample person as "Suspicious," coded 1 if the interviewer rated the respondent suspicious, 0 otherwise. **Boldfaced** coefficients are statistically significant at $p < .05$. There were 643 refusals and 2,040 respondents in 1988.

TABLE 3.4. Reasons for Refusal, Refusals Only, 1986 and 1988 NES, 1989 DAS

	Percentage Mentioning		
	1986 NES	1988 NES	1989 DAS
Not Interested	68	19	47
Bad Experience	4	56	33
Very Ill	4	9	4
Too Busy	70	56	33
Family Stress	6	9	4
Confidentiality	19	10	8
# Refusals	824	643	219

coefficient is quite large. The interviewer is 2 percent less likely to label men as suspicious than women.

Refusals and resisters to the 1986 and 1988 NES and the 1989 DAS occasionally mentioned violations of privacy or confidentiality as reasons for refusal. A summary of reasons for refusal appears in table 3.4.[16] As one can see, privacy and confidentiality are *not* the most prevalent reasons for refusal, but not uncommon either. Fewer refusals mentioned reasons pertaining to confidentiality, compared with the substantial pro-

---

16. Interviewers for the three studies marked the respondent's reasons for refusal or resistance on an IDB. In 1986, the interviewers marked reasons as answers to an open-ended question. In 1988, the interviewers checked off a list of possible answers, in addition to the open-ended question. In 1989, the DAS interviewers checked reasons for refusal from an expanded list of alternatives. In addition, the DAS interviewers attempted to ask respondents themselves why they refused to be interviewed. Because the data for the three studies were collected in radically different ways, it is *not* appropriate to compare relative percentages *across* studies. Furthermore, the percentages will not add up to 100 percent as a refusal may have more than one reason for refusal.

portion of refusals who claimed they were "too busy" (70 percent in 1986 NES, 56 percent in 1988 NES) or "not interested" (68 percent in 1986, 19 percent in 1988).

We can identify the demographic attributes of those people who refused being interviewed on grounds of confidentiality. Table 3.5 displays a multivariate probit analysis of the demographic characteristics of sample persons who refuse on grounds of confidentiality. The dependent variable in this analysis is whether or not the sample person mentioned privacy or confidentiality as a reason for refusal. Hispanic refusers are far more likely than any other group to cite confidentiality as a reason for refusing: 19 percent more likely in the 1986 NES and 31 percent more likely in the 1988 NES.

Other researchers report that Hispanics resist or refuse to be interviewed at unusual rates. Lewis (1987) found that nearly all Hispanic respondents were reluctant to participate in a 1983 special *Los Angeles Times* survey. He suspects that the reason is fear of problems with immigration authorities: 21 percent of the foreign-born Hispanic respondents admitted to being undocumented aliens. Given that the NES surveys are national surveys, one might suspect that problems with immigration authorities are less conspicuous than in Lewis's Los Angeles surveys, but a potential problem nonetheless.

There are several reasons why respondents might be suspicious of the interviewer or fear an invasion of privacy. One explanation is fear of crime. A comparison of the amenable respondents to the reluctant respondents in the GSS suggests that trust and fear of crime might be two factors underlying responsiveness to the survey. Table 3.6 displays the percentage for amenable respondents (those who agree to be interviewed

TABLE 3.5. Multivariate Probit Analysis of Confidentiality as a Reason for Refusal, 1986 and 1988 NES, 1989 DAS, Refusals Only

| | 1986 NES | | 1988 NES | | 1989 DAS | |
	B	SE	B	SE	B	SE
Age	.00	.00	.01	.01	.01	.01
Income	.08	.09	.08	.12	.19	.22
Black	.00	.24	.31	.27	−.06	.37
Hispanic	**.77**	.32	**1.10**	.41		
Male	−.04	.14	.11	.20	.54	.32
(Constant)	−1.53	.31	−2.01	.37	−2.57	.68
N	824		643		219	

Dependent variable is "Confidentiality" as reason for refusal, coded 1 if mentioned by the refusal, 0 otherwise. **Boldfaced** coefficients are statistically significant at $p < .05$.

TABLE 3.6. Comparison of Levels of Fear of and Exposure to Crime of Amenable and Reluctant Respondents, 1980–1985 GSS

	1980	1982	1983	1984	1985
Afraid to Walk at Night?	−.09	−.06		−.07	−.07
Are People Fair?	−.01		.06	.04	
Can People Be Trusted?	−.06		.01	.05	
Safe at Home?		.00			
Ever Burglarized?	−.01	.00		.00	.02
Ever Robbed?	.01	.00		−.03	.01
N of Respondents	1,467	1,494	1,593	1,400	1,459

Cell values are the percentage of the category agreeing with the statement for amenable respondents, less the same percentage for reluctant respondents (initial refusals). **Boldfaced** coefficients are statistically significant at $p < .05$. Blank cells in the table are there because the questions were not asked in those years.

at the first contact) less the percentage for reluctant respondents (initial refusals). One can read this table as amenable respondents are more (if the value is positive) trusting, etc., than the reluctant respondents. Trust of people in general, or the belief that people are fair, might work against suspiciousness.

The reluctant respondents were more afraid to walk at night than amenable respondents for the 1980, 1982, 1984, and 1985 GSS, and to a statistically significant degree.[17] But the other differences are less clear. In 1983 and 1984, the amenable respondents were more likely to believe people are fair and can be trusted. (In 1980, the situation is reversed.) The differences are statistically significant only for whether or not people are fair, and only in 1983. There are no statistically significant differences between amenable and reluctant respondents for reports of burglarization or robbery.

Fear of crime isn't the only explanation for suspiciousness. Two studies show that concern about government intrusions affect responsiveness to surveys. A joint Survey Research Center/Census study found that most respondents doubt that Census records are truly confidential (National Research Council 1979). Goyder (1986) found that response rates to surveys declined at the same rate that complaints in newspapers about the intrusiveness of the Census rose.

How respondents feel about strangers is just the first of the four relationships that affect the respondent's likelihood of compliance. Several points are already apparent. The reasons people express for refusing or complying make sense. Hispanics are from 19 to 31 percent more likely

---

17. The question was not asked in 1983.

than non-Hispanics to refuse on grounds of privacy or fear of breach of confidentiality. People who are more reluctant to be interviewed are also more fearful of crime. Furthermore, interviewers are more likely to label blacks as suspicious than whites. Is this racism on the part of the interviewers, real suspicion on the part of blacks, or both? More of this acrimony between respondents and interviewers of different races appears in the relationship between respondents and interviewers.

Relationship to Interviewer

The first time you see the interviewer, you know the interviewer's age (roughly), sex, and race. This interviewer may be a cheerful, pleasant person. Or the interviewer may be just the sort of person you can't stand. The appearance, skills, and demeanor of the interviewer affect the respondent's chances of agreeing to be interviewed. In this section, I examine how one specific attribute of the interviewer—the interviewer's race—affects the respondent's likelihood of complying.

Why focus on the interviewer's race? One reason to focus so exclusively on race is that the competing explanations—the interviewer's skills, sex, age and experience—yield no consistent patterns of refusal or compliance in the 1986 NES, 1988 NES, or the 1989 DAS.[18] Unfortunately, one could argue that there was no fair test of the alternate explanations: except for the 1989 DAS student interviewers, the interviewers did not vary much in experience. For example, more than half of the interviewers for the 1988 NES were interviewing for the first time, and nearly three-quarters of the interviewers worked for the SRC for two years or less.

Second, there are good theoretical grounds to suspect that race affects both responsiveness *and* the character of response. Physical differences between a requester and a requestee accentuate social distance. Byrne (1971) demonstrates that people prefer requesters who are most similar in social status. Dohrenwend, Colombotos, and Dohrenwend (1968) found that social distance affected interviewers' success rates. Increased social distance also decreases the chances of the respondent empathizing with the interviewer (Batson and Coke 1981; Hornstein, Fisch, and Holmes 1968).

---

18. Specifically, none of the following attributes of the interviewers were statistically significant predictors of the respondent's likelihood of compliance using multivariate probits for the 1986 NES, the 1988 NES, and the 1989 DAS: age, years of experience, number of languages, and sex. Race of the interviewer was a statistically significant predictor for the 1986 NES and the 1989 DAS, but of opposite signs in the two studies.

TABLE 3.7. Multivariate Probit Analysis of Race of Interviewer—Race of Respondent Effects on Compliance, 1986 and 1988 NES, 1989 DAS (Refusals and Respondents)

	1986 NES		1988 NES		1989 DAS	
	B	SE	*B*	SE	*B*	SE
Black Respondent	**.35**	.14	**.47**	.23	**.48**	.10
White R–Black I	**−.40**	.08	−.13	.22	.18	.15
Black R–White I	−.07	.16	**−.52**	.25	−.43	.30
(Constant)	.58	.03	.95	.03	.75	.06
N of Refusals	824		643		219	
N of Respondents	2,176		2,040		916	

The dependent variable is compliance, where respondents are coded 1 and refusals are coded 0. The omitted group is White Respondent–White Interviewer. **Boldfaced** coefficients are statistically significant at $p < .05$.

The interviewer's race may even affect the respondent's answers. As early as 1942, Hyman demonstrated differences as high as 20 percent depending on the race of the interviewer on innocuous questions. More recent research replicates Hyman's early work, although with considerable variation in the magnitude of the effects of the race of the interviewer on response (Schuman and Converse 1971; Anderson, Silver and Abramson 1988).

Race of respondent and interviewer interact in a consistent pattern across the 1986 and 1988 NES and the 1989 DAS: respondents who see an interviewer of a different race are more likely to refuse than respondents who see an interviewer of the same race. Table 3.7 displays probit analyses of likelihood of compliance given different racial characteristics of interviewers and respondents. Controlling for race of interviewer, black respondents are more likely to grant an interview than white respondents: 10 percent more likely in the 1986 NES, 8 percent more likely in the 1988 NES, and 5 percent more likely in the 1989 DAS, all statistically significant at $p < .01$. Most importantly, respondents are more likely to refuse to be interviewed by interviewers of a different race than by interviewers of the same race. The interaction term on black respondents and white interviewers is negative, and statistically significant for the 1988 NES and 1989 DAS. The interaction term on white respondents and black interviewers is also negative for the 1986 and 1988 NES, but only statistically significant in 1986.

"Race of interviewer–race of respondent" effects are disheartening, but altogether expectable. Although the field managers of the Survey Research Center do their best to avoid situations where respondent and interviewer are of different races, the occasions where races interact point

TABLE 3.8. Interviewer's Assessment of the Attitude of Refusals and Respondents, by Race of Interviewer and Respondent, 1988 NES

	Rude	Hostile	Suspicious	Threatening	Polite
Whole Sample	8	8	12	1	20
Whites	7	7	11	1	20
White R, White I	7	7	11	1	20
White R, Black I	8	11	14	4	21
Blacks	10	10	18	3	16
Black R, Black I	0	0	21	0	19
Black R, White I	12	12	17	3	15

Cell entries are the percentage of respondents and refusals who were marked by the interviewer as displaying the attitude in the column heading. There were 643 refusals and 2,040 respondents in 1988.

to respondents' resistance to interviewers of a different race than their own.[19]

Situations where the respondent and interviewer are of a different race lead to more than a simple refusal: the interactions of respondents and interviewers of different races often lead to antagonism. Recall that interviewers classified many respondents as suspicious, hostile, rude, threatening, or merely polite. Further examination of the interviewer's assessment of the respondent's attitude underscores racial origins of antagonistic relationships. Table 3.8 displays the interviewers' report of the attitude of black and white respondents.

For every one of the antagonistic attitudes (rude, hostile, threatening and suspicious), interviewers reported black respondents as more antagonistic. There is a strong suggestion that this acrimony emerges most strongly when white interviewers contact black respondents. Black interviewers reported black respondents as rude, hostile, or threatening with negligible frequency (less than .5 percent). In comparison, white interviewers reported black respondents as rude or hostile in 12 percent of those situations (this difference is statistically significant at $p < .01$). At the same time, black interviewers found white respondents to be only slightly more antagonistic than white interviewers rated white respondents.

This finding raises disturbing questions. Do white interviewers find black respondents to be more antagonistic because of racial attitudes

---

19. In the 1988 NES, white sample persons (respondents and refusals) were interviewed by black interviewers in about 3 percent of the attempted interviews with white people; black sample persons were interviewed by white interviewers in about 85 percent of the attempted interviews with black people. Situations in which a black respondent is contacted by a white interviewer are clearly much more prevalent than situations in which a white respondent is contacted by a black interviewer.

toward blacks, or is this hostility real? We can't tell. The number of times white respondents were contacted by black interviewers is tiny (3 percent of the time), while the black respondents were contacted by white interviewers more often than not (86 percent of the time). There is also a problem of nonrandom assignment of the interviewers in general. And without being an omniscient fly-on-the-wall, we don't know whether or not interviewers recorded these attitudes fairly. Nonetheless, it is disturbing to see that white interviewers frequently found black respondents to be rude or hostile, while black interviewers did not find black respondents to be that way at all.

There are positive sides to the respondent's relationship to the interviewer. Respondents who *empathize* with the interviewer may be more likely to comply. Batson and Coke (1981) attribute some compliance to the requestee's belief that complying aids the interviewer. And one-fourth of the DAS respondents answered that they agreed to participate in the study out of a sense of empathy with the interviewer. What stands out in this analysis of the relationship between respondent and interviewer is how race adversely affects rapport.

Relationship to Interview

You now know why the interviewer is at your door: the interviewer wants to ask you some questions. How you feel about surveys influences whether or not you will agree to participate. Are surveys a waste of time, or are surveys sources of important information? Have you been interviewed before, and did you think the earlier experience was good or bad? What's in it for you? Do you have the time to participate? Do you feel as though you can answer his or her questions? In this section, I examine views of survey compliance that emphasize the rational consideration of costs and benefits and views that explore potential respondents' information and interest.

Costs and Benefits

The respondent may, quite reasonably, view the interview as a task. Some respondents choose or refuse to participate after weighing the costs and benefits of doing so. The most obvious cost of a survey is the time it takes to answer questions, but there is also the cost of being bored or feeling foolish. The most obvious benefit of the survey is whether or not the respondent expects to enjoy the experience (26 percent of the

DAS respondents talked in terms of what they expected to get out of the study when asked why they decided to participate).

The respondent's amount of free time constrains his or her decision. Interviews, after all, may take upwards of an hour to complete. There is evidence that respondents *do* think about their available time. The most common answer from nonrespondents about why they refuse is simply "I'm too busy." Is this response just cultural shorthand for "Go away?" Perhaps, but certain demographic groups use this reason more than others.

Table 3.9 presents a multivariate probit analysis of the people that claim to be "too busy." Wealthier *refusals* are the most likely people to resort to "I'm too busy" as a reason: the coefficient on *income* is positive and substantial for all three studies. It is *not* necessarily true that rich people are busier, merely that rich people are the most likely to refer to time as a reason for refusal. Comparing the wealthiest to the poorest refusals, the wealthiest refusals are 23 percent more likely in 1986, 31 percent more likely in 1988, and 55 percent more likely in 1989 to claim to be too busy to participate. The probit analysis strongly suggests that the wealthier respondents resort to time as the excuse, independent of how busy they may actually be.

Older *refusals* are unlikely to claim to be "too busy." The coefficient on *age* is negative, and substantively large. Since *age* is measured in years, an elderly refusal is very unlikely to claim to be "too busy." Comparing a 65-year-old refusal to a refusal at the mean age for the samples, the 65-year-old refusal is 10 percent less likely in 1986, 8 percent less likely in 1988, and 20 percent less likely in 1989 to claim to be "too busy." This is also sensible: retired people would have more time

TABLE 3.9. Multivariate Probit Analysis of "Too Busy" as Reason for Refusal, 1986 and 1988 NES, 1989 DAS, Refusals Only

	1986 NES		1988 NES		1989 DAS	
	B	SE	*B*	SE	*B*	SE
Age	**−.01**	.00	**−.01**	.00	**−.04**	.01
Income	**.24**	.08	**.24**	.10	**.50**	.18
Black	−.36	.19	−.19	.21	−.21	.27
Hispanic	−.10	.31	−.07	.39		
Male	.04	.11	.11	.15	−.24	.24
(Constant)	.44	.25	.11	.26	.80	.46
N of Refusals	824		643		219	

Dependent variable is "Too Busy" as reason for refusal, coded 1 if mentioned by respondent, 0 otherwise. **Boldfaced** coefficients are statistically significant at $p < .05$.

to be interviewed, and that is perhaps what the *age* coefficient is picking up.

In short, if "too busy" is just cultural shorthand for "go away," it is only a definable subset of the population that uses this excuse. Wealthier respondents are the most likely to use time as the excuse. Older respondents are the least likely. It is still possible that "I'm too busy" is just a *sub*cultural shorthand for "go away."

Time is the clearest example of costs entering into the sample person's decision to choose or refuse to be interviewed. But respondents also talk about what they expect to gain or lose from the experience of being interviewed. There is no systematic demographic pattern to the sorts of people who refuse on grounds of having a bad prior experience with surveys, but one probably would not expect to find such a pattern. Nonetheless, the value of the experience does enter into the decision of some potential respondents. There is support for the belief that respondents make a considered decision when deciding to participate.

Interest and Information

We need not constrain the potential respondent's relationship with the interview to material costs and benefits like time or expected pleasure. *Interest* and *information* also enter into the respondent's relationship to the interview. How interested respondents are in being interviewed affects their experience. Some 20 percent of the DAS respondents claimed that they responded because they were interested in the interview. Conversely, many refusals and resisters expressed lack of interest in the survey: 68 percent in 1986, 19 percent in 1988, and 47 percent in 1989. Furthermore, how informed, or capable of answering survey questions, respondents feel to be may also affect compliance. Interest and informedness might be seen as aspects of rational deliberation *or* as a step prior to rational consideration.

We can compare the reluctant and amenable respondents' interest in the topics of the survey. The NES surveys discuss politics, and thus interest in and attention to politics is an appropriate basis of comparison. Table 3.10 displays levels of interest for the amenable and reluctant respondents. In every case, amenable respondents are more interested in politics and consume more media about the campaign than reluctant respondents. Four of the measures yield statistically significant differences at $p < .05$ and beyond.

The respondent's informedness affects compliance as well. While in-

TABLE 3.10. Comparison of Interest in Politics, Amenable and Reluctant Respondents, 1988 NES

	Reluctant Respondents	Amenable Respondents	t Value
Interested in Political Campaigns	44	52	−3.41
Listen about Campaign on Radio	26	32	−1.88
Read about Campaign in Newspaper	42	50	−2.49
How Much Attention to Newspaper	24	29	−2.27
Watch Programs about Campaign on TV	47	53	−2.55
Much Attention to TV	53	60	−0.75
Number of Days Read Newspaper (Number)	3.74	3.97	−1.18

Table entries are percentages. There were 2,040 respondents in 1988.

terviewers try hard to persuade sample persons that the interview is *not* a test, surveys must appear to be tests to many respondents.

By comparing reluctant and amenable respondents, there is a strong suggestion that refusals are less informed about politics than respondents. Table 3.11 presents the differences between amenable and reluctant respondents in levels of political information for the 1988 NES. Amenable respondents are better informed than reluctant respondents on *every* measure. The difference in recall of the congressional candidates is striking. Only 7 percent of the initial refusals could recall the name of the house incumbent, while 28 percent of the amenable respondents could. Similar patterns emerge for recall of the challengers and Senate candidates.[20]

Another measure of political information is to require the respondents to identify the political jobs of a list of political figures. In 1988, interviewers asked respondents to identify Ted Kennedy, George

---

20. By the way, it is possible to produce an estimate of how much the 1988 NES overstated the population's level of recall. If one uses the reluctant respondents as proxies for the nonrespondents, then the estimate of the population value is:

$$
\begin{aligned}
\text{Recall of House Incumbent} \quad &= \quad (\text{reluctant's recall}) \times (\text{nonresponse rate}) \\
&\quad + (\text{amenable's recall}) \times (\text{response rate}) \\
&= \quad 7 \text{ percent} \times .30 + 28 \text{ percent} \times .70 \\
&= \quad 22 \text{ percent}
\end{aligned}
$$

Because the percentage of respondents to the NES who could recall the House incumbent was 28, this means that the 1988 NES overestimated recall by 6 percentage points, or over one-fourth.

TABLE 3.11. Comparison of Political Informedness, Amenable and Reluctant Respondents, 1988 NES

	Reluctant Respondents	Amenable Respondents	*t* Value
Recall House Incumbent	7	28	−7.43
Recall House Challenger	1	9	−4.81
Recall Senate Incumbent	9	29	−7.04
Recall Senate Challenger	5	18	−5.32
Identify Political Figures	13	40	−14.64
Interviewer's Assessment of R's Informedness	40	53	−6.93

Table entries are percentages. There were 2,040 respondents in 1988.

Schultz, William Rehnquist, Mikhail Gorbachev, Margaret Thatcher, Yasser Arafat, and Jim Wright. The amenable respondents identified, on average, 40 percent of the political figures' jobs compared with only 13 percent of the reluctant respondents.

A final measure of political information is the interviewer's assessment of the respondent's level of information.[21] The difference in the interviewers' assessments of the reluctant and amenable respondents is instructive: interviewers placed well under half of the initial refusals below average levels of information, while they placed amenable respondents just above average.

Interest and informedness affect the respondent's relationship to surveys, and the respondent's chances of complying. Furthermore, respondents who are amenable to being interviewed in the first place manifest greater interest in politics and more information about politics than respondents who resist being interviewed.

Interest and information may be viewed as part of the respondent's rational deliberation. If one views the response "I'm not interested" to mean "I don't expect to get anything out of this," lack of interest means that the refusal sees the benefits of participating as less than the costs. Similarly, a sample person who refuses because he or she feels uninformed might be seen as someone who expects to experience a high psychic cost in the form of feeling foolish.

---

21. At the thumbnail sketch after the interview, the interviewer completes a short questionnaire describing the situation of the interview. In one of the questions, the interviewer is asked to assess the respondent's level of information. This measure is surely endogenous to a great extent: the thumbnail sketch comes at the conclusion of the interview, after all other interactions between interviewer and respondent, and is influenced by everything the respondent has said thus far. Zaller (1985) demonstrates that the interviewer's assessment, while endogenous, coheres closely with a more robust information measure derived from an extended battery of questions.

Alternatively, interest might precede rational consideration. Taylor and Fiske (1978) argue that one must pay attention to a decison before evaluation and consideration become possible. A refusal might be a "top of the head" answer—one where the respondent has spent virtually no time deliberating, has gathered no information, yet answers nonetheless. If "I'm not interested" means "I don't pay any attention to surveys," then lack of interest may imply that refusals haven't yet made the decision to consider the costs or benefits of participating. For this refusal, lack of attention to surveys is a way of screening out noise. The more that one believes "I'm not interested" is a contentless response, a way to politely tell the interviewer to go away, the more the answer resembles a predeliberative response.

Relationship to Self-image

How a respondent sees himself or herself may also affect a respondent's chances of agreeing to be interviewed. Is the respondent the sort of person who helps others, a person who does this sort of thing?

People who see themselves as helpers may be likely to comply with the interviewer's request. Fourteen percent of the respondents in the 1989 DAS identified themselves as helpers. However, there is no consistent demographic pattern to these people. (Nor would one probably expect to find that how helpful people are varies by their age, sex, race, or income).

The respondent's relationship to self-image may be circularly related to the respondent's health and family situation. An ill respondent or a respondent under a stressful family situation may have a depressed self-image in addition to the extra burdens posed by the illness or stressful situation. After all, some respondents will grant interviews while quite ill, while other respondents will refuse because of a cold.

We have very few measures for how respondents' self-perception influences their likelihood of agreeing to participate. But information from other sources suggests that the people who are most likely to participate in polls are also more likely to participate in society generally. In a 1985 poll on polls, the Roper organization asked a quota sample of 2,000 respondents what they thought about polls, how often they participated in politics, and the number of times they had been interviewed previously. This is, naturally, a biased sample since nonrespondents to other surveys would not be likely to participate in Roper's poll either, but some patterns are fascinating.

Table 3.12 displays an OLS regression of the number of times the

TABLE 3.12. OLS Regression of Times Interviewed Before, as a Function of Participation in Politics, 1985 Roper Organization Poll on Polls

	B	SE
Political Participation	0.201	0.025
Hispanic	−0.522	0.239
Male	−0.297	0.095
Age	0.029	0.018
Black	−0.161	0.167
Income	0.087	0.022
Education	0.113	0.046
(Constant)	0.283	0.236

Dependent variable is the number of times interviewed prior to this interview. There were 2,000 respondents to this quota sample.

respondent has participated in polls on a scale of participation in politics and controlling demographic variables. The scale of participation in politics is a simple count of the number of political activities in which the respondent has participated, from a list of 12 activities.[22] The coefficient on political participation is strongly positive (.201) and statistically significant at $p < .01$. In other words, the more often the respondent participates in politics, the more times that person has participated in an interview. Note also that the demographic measures move in sensible ways. Wealthier, better educated people are more likely to participate in surveys than poorer, less educated people—echoing findings about general political participation (Wolfinger and Rosenstone 1980; Verba and Nie 1972).[23] Blacks and Hispanics are less likely to have participated in prior surveys. Older people are more likely to have been interviewed previously—which is quite sensible, given that the older one is, the more opportunities one would have to participate.

My evidence of the respondent's relationship to self-image is the weakest in this chapter. We have the information that many people who comply with surveys claim they did so because they see themselves as

22. The list of activities included writing a letter to Congress, attending a rally or speech, attending a public meeting, running for political office, serving on a local committee, serving as an officer of a club, writing a letter to a paper, signing a petition, working for a party, making a speech, writing an article, and being a member of a political group.
23. Wealthier refusals may be more likely to resort to claims of being "too busy" as a reason for refusal, but wealthier people are not less likely to agree to be interviewed. A simple probit model of compliance as a function of the demographic characteristics shows that as a person's income increases, so does that person's likelihood of agreeing. (This model appears in Table 6.3, if the reader wishes to jump ahead.)

the sort of person who helps others. But we don't have the contrary evidence that people who refuse do so because they see themselves as the sort of person who doesn't like to help. (And it would be difficult even to think of how one might collect this information.) We do have the information that the people who are most participative in surveys are also more participative in politics, implying that some people are more participative generally than others. But we don't have the information that this is related to general participation and not to, say, a common interest in participating in politics and in surveys about politics. Only limited exploration is possible with limited information. To explore this relationship further requires better tests of how respondents see themselves.

Summary

I ask the reader to digest a great deal of data about a great variety of surveys. It is time to pull together the principle findings, and to place these findings in a broader context. In this summary, I first review the major factors affecting the three stages of the survey process: contact, eligibility, and compliance. In this summary, I also reflect on two broader points: the usefulness of both rational and nonrational paradigms in understanding survey compliance and political participation as a metaphor for survey participation.

First, the interviewer must be able to contact the respondent. The likelihood of contacting a sample person depends on the accessibility of that person. The elderly, people with children in the household, and wealthier people are more likely to be contacted than younger, poorer people or people without children. Men are less contactable than women. Characteristics of the sample person's place of residence affect contactability also: people who live in households where access to the door is limited and people who live in cities are less contactable than others.

Once the interviewer contacts the sample person, the interviewer must determine whether he or she is eligible for the study and capable of answering the questions. Very few sample people are *ineligible* for the studies I examine in this chapter: only those who are not U.S. citizens of voting age. Whether or not a sample person is *capable* of being interviewed might vary by the respondent's health or the languages he or she speaks, but the only meaningful predictor of a respondent's eligibility is age: the older a respondent is, the less likely the respondent will be capable of answering questions.

The contacted, eligible, and capable sample person must decide whether or not to comply with the interviewer's request to be interviewed. In this chapter, I discuss four relationships between the sample person and differing targets that influence that person's decision.

How respondents feel about *strangers* affects their likelihood of compliance. Some of the aspects of this relationship include concerns over privacy and confidentiality, fears about crime, and suspiciousness, and some of these appear to affect nonwhite sample people most of all. Hispanic respondents are much more likely (from 19 to 31 percent more) than non-Hispanic respondents to refuse to participate in these studies because of a fear of breach of confidentiality. Interviewers are about 10 percent more likely to find black respondents suspicious than white respondents (but we do not know whether black respondents are more suspicious in fact or if this is the interviewer's perception). Those respondents who were most reluctant to be interviewed in the first place (but did grant an interview) are more fearful of crime than those who agreed at the outset.

The attitudes that respondents have toward the *interviewer* also affect whether they agree or refuse. Sometimes this relationship may be positive: a quarter of the DAS respondents said that they agreed to be interviewed out of a sense of empathy with the interviewer. But what stands out in this chapter are the situations where the rapport between respondents and interviewers is negative: respondents who confront an interviewer of a different race are less likely to agree to be interviewed. And interviewers are more likely to say that black, not white, respondents are rude, threatening or hostile.

How the respondents feel about the *interview* influences their chances of participating. Some aspects of how the respondent thinks about the interview are the time the interview will take, whether or not the respondent is interested in the interview, and whether or not the respondent feels informed enough to answer questions. More respondents refuse to be interviewed on the grounds of being "too busy" than any other reason. Perhaps this is merely the polite way to tell the interviewer to go away, but it is clear who uses this as the reason. The wealthiest refusals are from 23 to 55 percent more likely to refuse on grounds of being "too busy" than the poorest refusals. The respondents' level of interest and informedness also appear to affect their chances of agreeing to be interviewed. Respondents reluctant to be interviewed are less likely to be interested in politics or to be exposed to television or newspaper stories about politics than respondents who readily agree to be interviewed. The reluctant respondents are much less informed about politics than the amenable respondents: only a quarter as many reluctant respondents as amenable respondents can identify political figures or their representatives.

Finally, how the respondents see their *self-image* influences their likelihood of agreeing to be interviewed. About 14 percent of the DAS respondents said that they agreed to be interviewed because they think of themselves as the sort of person who helps others. And from the Roper poll on polls, we know that the people who participate most in polls are also more likely to participate in politics.

How do these four relationships deepen our understanding of political and social behavior in general? At one level, the four relationships tell us about whether or not people comply with requests from strangers after rational deliberation. And at another level, the participation of people in surveys tells us something about why people participate in other social and political activities. I take these two topics up in turn.

Rational and Nonrational Paradigms of Survey Participation

The respondent's choice to refuse or comply with the interviewer's request echoes a debate over the basis of other social behavior. Is the respondent's decision based on rational calculus, a weighing of expected costs and utilities? Or is the respondent's decision grounded elsewhere?

The answer, according to this model, is that rational calculus enters most clearly in one of the four relationship—the respondent's relationship to the survey—but the other three are more ambiguous. While it is possible to construct a rational story behind each of the four relationships, the relationship need not be rational in the least.

Respondents who fear strangers may have a simple rational basis. Some respondents may have had problems with immigration authorities. Some respondents may be afraid of crime. But it is also possible that these fears are not based on experience. In fact, the reluctant respondents to the 1980–1985 GSS were afraid to walk at night more often than the amenable respondents, but were not victimized any more frequently. Fear of crime without greater exposure to crime certainly might be seen in terms of rationality, a form of risk-aversion. But we could just as well view fear of strangers as the product of psychological disorder.

The respondent's relationship to the interviewer seems very much *uninfluenced* by rational calculation. The most potent explanation for the respondent's negative feelings toward the interviewer is simply that the interviewer is of a different race.

The respondent's relationship to surveys may be heavily influenced by consideration of the costs and benefits of participating. A very common reason for refusal is that the respondent doesn't have time to be interviewed or had a prior bad experience with a survey. These reasons clearly reflect the costs of agreeing to be interviewed. But just as many respondents simply convey no interest in the survey as they do any other reason. Lack of interest may as much represent lack of attention as lack of value (Taylor and Fiske 1978).

Finally, it seems somewhat ludicrous to consider a rational basis for one's attitude toward oneself. Is it possible locate a cost or benefit for how one perceives oneself?

The four relationships vary in the extent to which a rational model even makes sense. Phrased another way, the relationships also vary in the degree to which the target of the relationship is central to the respondent's decision. The model presented here is quite consistent with Petty and Cacioppo's (1986) central-peripheral model of persuasion. When one person persuades another to perform a task, they argue, the persuaded's logic may move through either central or peripheral routes. Central routes to persuasion concern the exact features of the task at hand. Peripheral routes to persuasion invoke characteristics of the source, the message, and the recipient, but not the content of the message. The respondent's relationship to surveys may be very much a central route to persuasion: this relationship may well involve explicit considerations of what the respondent expects to gain or lose by participating. The other three relationships suggest a more peripheral route: attributes of the interviewer and of the respondent become the basis of the respondent's decision.

The idea of alternate routes to persuasion makes for messier models, but it also provides for comprehension of complicated decisions. This chapter shows the plausibility of the four relationships and gives a sense of what motivates and influences these relationships. The next chapter welds the four relationships into a structural model of compliance.

Political Participation as a Metaphor for Survey Participation

The respondent's decision to participate in surveys may share common factors with a citizen's decision to participate in politics. Considering the importance of polls and surveys to contemporary politics, some respondents may view participation in the survey as a political act. One has to wonder if the same respondent who views participating in a survey about politics as political would also view a survey about dental hygiene in the same light. One need not go the extreme of considering survey participation an inherently political choice to see that there are some common features between survey participation and political participation.

The respondent's attitude toward surveys may be the most akin to a political relationship. After all, the interviewer is asking the respondent to perform a task. If the respondent sees value to the general community in performing that task, there is a similarity to other forms of participating in the community.

Interest and information affect not just participation in the survey, but also participation in politics. Political scientists have long been able to demonstrate that people who are interested in politics, who care about the resolution of political problems, and who pay attention to politics are people who are likely to participate in politics (Berelson, Lazarsfeld, and McPhee 1954; Campbell, Gurin, and Miller 1954). Well, people who pay attention to polls, care about survey results, and who are interested in polls are more likely to participate in polls. Similarly, people who are better informed about politics, who can discriminate between political alternatives, are also likely to participate in politics (Milbrath and Goel 1977).[24] As this chapter demonstrates, people who have greater political information are more likely to participate in surveys about politics.

The similarities between political participation and survey participation may arise from a spurious cause: both forms of participation may be seen as participation in society. People who like to participate in society, by this argument, are more likely to participate in both politics and polls.

In brief, one would have good reason to believe that political participation and survey participation share common underlying causes. Whether or not they are both a product of general social participation or whether or not information and interest affect both, there is good reason to consider political participation a metaphor for survey participation.

If political participation is a metaphor for survey participation, analysis of survey data on political participation is in jeopardy. Is a major source of information about who participates in politics merely a replication of their participation? As chapter 5 explains, scientists have

---

24. The causal order between information and participation is the subject of an interesting dispute, with serious normative implications. Some hold that information is a prerequisite for participation (Schumpeter 1942; Berelson, Lazarsfeld, and McPhee 1954): in order to participate in politics, you must have enough information to make decisions. Others hold that one acquires information by participating in politics (Pateman 1970). The two camps do not quarrel over whether or not there is a strong correlation between information and participation.

good reasons to be concerned about whether or not we have censored our observations of who participates and why. As chapter 6 shows, models of political participation *are* affected by the act of survey participation. But this is jumping the gun.

CHAPTER 4

Structure of Survey Compliance

So far, all we know about the four relationships between the potential respondent and his or her decision to participate in the survey is that these relationships are plausible and a bit about what influences them. This is useful, but ultimately unsatisfying. We need to understand how these relationships work as a whole. In this chapter, I unite the four relationships into a single structural model of survey compliance.

This is also the time for a disclaimer. As I discuss in the following pages, we have at best weak indicators for the four relationships. Further, the estimation of the structural model is hampered by crude, dichotomous measures for compliance itself as well as for any of the indicators of the relationships. Throughout this chapter, I want to encourage the reader to remain skeptical about the inferences I draw from such fragile models.

Nonetheless, our goals for understanding why people choose or refuse to participate in surveys lead us toward a structural model like those I propose in this chapter. We need the full structural model to gain answers to some useful questions. We don't yet know how successfully the four relationships describe the respondent's decision. How accurately does this model predict who refuses and who agrees to be interviewed? Are these really separate relationships, or all just facets of the same relationship? We don't yet know how important any one relationship is to the full model. Which of the four relationships, if any, dominates the respondent's decision? The last question particularly matters if we want to reduce nonresponse since the relative importance of the relationships tells us something about how to allocate our efforts.

In this chapter, I use the reasons that respondents offer for refusing, resisting, or complying as indicators of the four relationships and incorporate the four relationships in a full structural model of compliance. I then test the structural model in three data sets, the 1986 NES, the 1988 NES, and the 1989 DAS.

Structure of Compliance

In this simple model, I represent compliance as an observed dependent variable, measured without error. Compliance is a function of four unobserved variables: the respondent's relationships to strangers, the interviewer, the interview, and self-image. I measure these four relationships by treating the respondent's reasons for refusing, resisting, or complying as (observed) indicators of the four relationships. A generic version of this structural model appears in figure 4.1.

The respondent's *relationship to strangers* influences whether the respondent is reluctant to confront strangers or, conversely, the respondent enjoys sharing opinions with others or meeting strangers. Similarly, this relationship might induce a respondent to refuse on grounds of privacy or fear of breach of confidentiality.

The respondent's *relationship to the interviewer* affects their rapport. What the interviewer marks as the attitude of the respondent is an indicator of this relationship; in these studies, the interviewer may mark whether the respondent is "polite but firm," "rude," "threatening," or "hostile."[1]

The respondent's *relationship to the interview* affects the respondent's assessment of the value of the interview, interest in the interview, or expected experience of being interviewed. Respondent refusals on grounds of being "too busy," "not interested" or in reference to a prior bad experience with surveys are negative indicators of this relationship. Reasons for compliance such as the respondent was interested or "not too busy" or a reference to some previous good experience with surveys are positive indicators of this relationship.

---

1. One might question whether or not these indicators might also be indicators of the respondent's relationship to strangers. There are two reasons why I treat the interviewer's marks of the attitude of the respondent as indicators of the respondent's relationship to the interviewer, and not of his or her relationship to strangers in general. For one, these are what the interviewer perceives the respondent to be, not necessarily the real attitude of the respondent toward the interviewer. If the inteviewer marks a respondent as rude, we don't really know if that respondent is, in truth, rude. What we do know is that the interviewer perceives the respondent to be rude, and thus that the relationship between the interviewer and respondent was acrimonious. For another, even if we assume that the interviewer correctly assesses the respondent as rude, hostile, or threatening, we don't know if this is the respondent's general attitude toward strangers or just toward the interviewer in particular. The less charitable conclusion about the respondent is that he or she is always this way toward strangers. I prefer to assume that the interviewer is only assessing the immediate situation, and not psychoanalyzing the respondent's general demeanor.

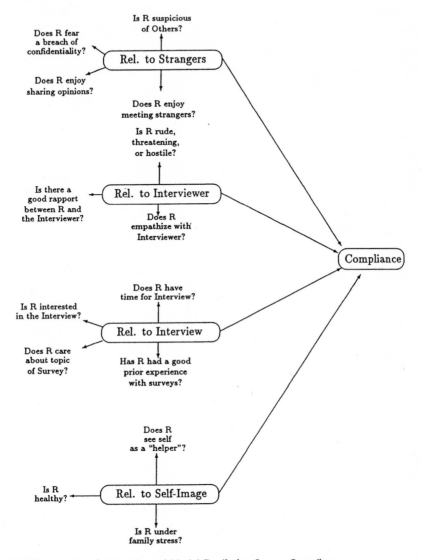

FIGURE 4.1. Generic Structure of Model Predicting Survey Compliance

The respondent's *relationship to self-image* affects the respondent's assessment of his or her health or family situation, and what the respondent sees as his or her usual reaction to requests from strangers. Positive indicators of this relationship include the respondent seeing him- or herself as the sort of person who helps others. Negative indicators of the respondent's relationship to self-image include the respondents refusing on grounds of health or family stress.[2]

We might think of the four relationships as a set of cognitive schemas, tools by which potential respondents break down their decision into manageable routines (cf. Markus and Zajonc 1985). Here, a respondent who recalls a good experience with some prior survey and a refusal remembering a bad experience with a poll are both thinking about their prior experience. Or the respondent who participates because she "isn't too busy" and the refusal who declines because he is "too busy" are both thinking about time. Conceptualizing the potential respondent's decision as a set of schemas becomes particularly useful when we examine the respondents' reasons for complying in comparison to the refusals' reasons for declining.

The indicators for these models vary across three data sets (the 1986 NES, the 1988 NES, and the 1989 DAS), and at least parts of the model may be evaluated in each. The "measurement model" (i.e., the connections between the unobserved independent measures and the reasons for refusal or compliance) may be evaluated in all three data sets. What is probably more interesting than the measurement model is how much the four relationships affect compliance. Because the NES collected reasons for refusal only for the nonrespondents in 1986, it is not possible to use the latent measures to predict compliance for this study. However, we can estimate the full model for both the 1989 DAS and the 1988 NES.

In the previous chapter, I ask the reader to suspend disbelief and to assume that the reasons respondents offer for their actions really are their reasons. I continue to use the respondents' reasons as reasons in this chapter. Some readers may be particularly skeptical about two of the refusals' reasons, "I'm too busy" and "I'm not interested." These may seem to be too close to the refusal's decision not to participate. For these skeptical readers, I estimate variations on the generic model that

---

2. Note that the interviewer has already screened out incapable respondents, so that a respondent who refuses on these grounds is making a subjective statement about health.

treat "Too Busy" and "Not Interested" as proximate to compliance after evaluating the generic form.[3]

There is one additional problem to discuss before proceeding to the actual models: all the indicators are dichotomous. All we have are measures that the respondent complied or not, appeared to the interviewer as rude or not, claimed to be too busy or not. The problems of estimating structural models with latent variables on dichotomous indicators are like the problems estimating simple regression models with dichotomous dependent variables. The point estimates of the coefficients will be unbiased, but the estimates of standard errors will be generally incorrect. Muthén (1978) and Mislevy (1986) suggest applying weighted least squares to the tetrachoric correlation matrix of indicators; that is the approach in the models to follow.[4]

Estimates for 1986 NES Postelection Study

In the 1986 NES Postelection Study, interviewers coded reasons for refusal. While we don't have equivalent measures for the respondents, we can estimate the measurement model for the respondents' relationship to strangers, to the interview, and to self-image.

The indicators for the latent relationship measures are all dichotomous: whether or not the nonrespondent expressed a reason for refusal

---

3. Some readers might wonder why I don't include demographic measures in these models. The reason is simply that including demographics causes the models to fail to converge. In the previous chapter, a few of the particular reasons people expressed displayed consistent demographic patterns. However, these patterns held at the level of the reasons (here, the indicators), not at the level of the four relationships (here, the unobserved variables). Demographic measures just don't help very much in understanding why it is that some people agree and other people refuse to participate in surveys.

4. One could, alternatively, estimate these models on the basis of a variance-covariance matrix of the indicators. I have estimated the models to follow on the variance-covariance matrices, but choose to report the estimation on the tetrachoric correlation matrix instead, for a couple of reasons. For one, what we really want is an estimate of the covariation between continuous indicators, something like a scale of "rudeness" or a probability of claiming to be "too busy." Mislevy (1986) argues that the tetrachoric correlation matrix better approximates the (desired, but unobtainable) variance-covariance matrix for the continuous indicators. For a second (and more immediately practical) reason, the structural model using the variance-covariance matrix of the dichotomous indicators as inputs does not converge in estimation in two cases (the 1986 NES and the 1989 DAS model of refusals). Clearly, what would be the best test of this structural model would be based on a battery of continuous indicators of the four relationships. We don't have the ideal data collection, but I make do with the best data available.

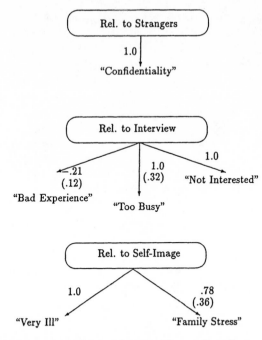

FIGURE 4.2. Measurement Model for Causes of Survey Compliance, 1986 NES, Refusals Only

that could be placed among six broad categories. The categories of reasons for refusal included "Confidentiality," "Not Interested," "Too Busy," references to prior bad experience ("Bad Experience"), "Very Ill," and stressful family situation ("Family Stress"). (The assignment of the open-ended coding of the reasons for refusal for the 1986 NES appears in appendix B.)

I treat the six dichotomous categories as indicators of three of the four relationships in the generic model (omitting the respondent's relationship to the interviewer for lack of relevant measures). I fix three of the six factor loadings to 1, in order to set the scales for the measures ("Confidentiality," "Not Interested," and "Very Ill"). Following Muthén's approach, I conduct a weighted least squares estimate of the measurement model, using the tetrachoric correlation matrix as the input. The estimated coefficients (and their standard errors) appear in figure 4.2.

The measurement model fits adequately to the 1986 refusals.[5] Be-

5. In all figures in this chapter, indicators surrounded by quotes are (catego-

cause three of the six factor loadings are fixed to one, the model estimates only the remaining three. Two of these three are substantially positive: the coefficients on "Too Busy" and "Family Stress." (The two positive coefficients are also statistically significant.) Both of these estimates are close to (or equal to) 1, implying that "Too Busy" and "Not Interested" are approximately equal indicators of the respondent's relationship to the interview, and that "Family Stress" and "Very Ill" are approximately equal as indicators of the respondent's relationship to self-image. The lone negative estimate is the coefficient on "Bad Experience." The sign of this estimate runs contrary to what I expected, but one should also observe that this estimate is not statistically significant at conventional probability levels.

Although we would certainly prefer to have better indicators of the unobserved relationships, these results are somewhat reassuring. Where the coefficients are statistically significant, they have the expected sign and magnitude.

One measure suggests that the overall fit of the measurement model is acceptable: a goodness-of-fit index of .987. (A more appropriate statistic would be the chi-square for the model; however, due to the dichotomous indicators and consequent nonnormality, the chi-square statistic is meaningless [Mislevy 1986].) Without the dependent variable, compliance, the overall fit of the model is less useful to us than the fit of the individual indicators. These estimates on the 1986 NES refusals are really preliminary to the full model. What is surely of greater interest to us is not how individual indicators cohere with the unobserved relationships, but the relative effect of each of the unobserved relationships on compliance.

Estimates for the 1989 DAS

The 1989 DAS interviewers recorded reasons for refusal for all refusals, and reasons for compliance for all respondents. We can either think of the reasons for refusals and compliance as reasons for two totally different acts or as two sides of the same decision. The DAS interviewers recorded the *refusals'* reasons for refusal in two ways: by asking the refusals directly why they did not want to be interviewed, and by noting afterward any reasons the refusals may have expressed during the entire interaction between the refusals and the interviewer. Also, the DAS interviewers asked the *respondents* why they agreed to be interviewed

---

rized) *reasons* offered by the respondent. Indicators without quotes in the figures are *attitudes* toward the interviewer.

at the conclusion of the interview. Because we only have these reasons for compliance after the entire interview, these reasons may well be tainted with the experience of the interview, and not pure measures of the refusals' and respondents' decision. There is some asymmetry to the way in which the respondents' and the refusals' reasons are measured.

In this section, I estimate two separate measurement models tying the reasons to the underlying relationships: one for the refusals, and a separate one for the compliants. Further, I also estimate a structural model of compliance, treating the reasons for refusal and compliance as opposite sides of the same decision.

The 1989 DAS Refusals' Reasons

As with the 1986 NES, I code the nonrespondents' reasons for refusal into six categories: "Confidentiality," "Not Interested," "Too Busy," "Bad Experience," "Very Ill," and "Family Stress." I fix three indicators to one ("Confidentiality," "Bad Experience," and "Very Ill") to set the scale; thus, I estimate factor loadings for only three of the six indicators. Estimates of the measurement model for the 1989 DAS refusals' reasons appear in figure 4.3.

These estimates do not support the model especially well. The signs of two of the three coefficients are in the expected direction, but only one ("Not Interested") is statistically significant. More importantly, the coefficient on "Too Busy" is marginally negative (but not statistically separable from zero). As with the 1986 and 1988 NES, "Too Busy" is one the most prevalent reasons for refusal in the 1989 DAS. But unlike the other studies, the respondents' claims of being "Too Busy" are only weakly associated with the respondents' relationship to the interview. This finding runs counter to what I expected.

The overall fit of the model is, again, reasonable, with a goodness-of-fit index of .98. Given that the estimates of the factor loadings don't support my expectations, we should take this measure of the overall fit with some skepticism (for this model and perhaps for all the models in this chapter).

The 1989 DAS Respondents' Reasons

The interviewers also asked the respondents to the 1989 DAS why they decided to participate in the study. I code respondents' reasons for compliance into six categories: "Openness," "Empathy," "Interest," "Not Busy," "Good Experience," and "Helper." "Openness" is an indicator

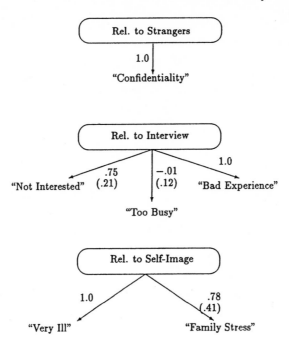

FIGURE 4.3. Measurement Model for Causes of Survey Compliance, 1989 DAS, Refusals Only

of the respondent's relationship to strangers; "Empathy" is an indicator of the respondent's relationship to the interviewer; "Interest," "Not Busy," and "Good Experience" are indicators of the respondent's relationship to the interview; "Helper" is an indicator of the respondent's relationship to self-image.

We can estimate the measurement model for the same four latent survey relationships. There are six indicators, of which four must be fixed to 1 in order to set the scales ("Openness," "Empathy," "Interest," and "Helper"). This means that we only estimate two loadings, the freed coefficients on "Not Busy" and "Good Experience." The estimates for this measurement model appear in figure 4.4.

The signs of the two freed coefficients (the loadings on "Not Busy" and "Good Experience") are in the expected direction, and both coefficients are statistically significant. The magnitude of the two coefficients is slightly smaller than I might have expected. If one expected that the respondents' reasons would parallel refusals' reasons, the importance of time (being "Not Busy") should be roughly equal to that of interest.

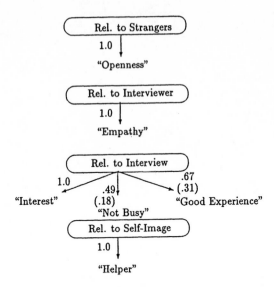

FIGURE 4.4. Measurement Model for Causes of Survey Compliance, 1989 DAS
Respondents Only

Instead, being "Not Busy" is about half as strong. The overall fit of
the model is acceptable, with a goodness-of-fit index of .98, but the
theoretical fit is, again, of greater concern.

But why must we demand that the underlying structure of the respondents' reasons and refusals' reasons mirror each other? For one,
there is a big difference in how the DAS measured the reasons for refusals and respondents. We only learn the respondents' reasons after
they have experienced the interview. After the interview, a respondent
might decide that the interview was fun and interesting, and that the
interviewer is an amiable person; before the interview, the respondent
might be thinking about how to avoid preparing dinner.

Another reason that we might want to be skeptical about a parallel structure of reasons for both refusals and respondents is that the
underlying cognitive structure that leads one person to refuse might be
quite different from the structure that leads another person to comply.
Petty and Cacioppo (1986) suggest that there are two routes to attitude change, central and peripheral. Central routes invoke the explicit
attributes of a decision, akin to a "rational" calculation of costs or benefits. Peripheral routes invoke attributes on the side of the decision such
as the characteristics of the message or the message-giver. It is entirely

possible that refusals depend more on peripheral routes and that respondents rely on central routes. In a way, the peripheral routes give the refusal more opportunities to decline participating. As a refusal, you could bow out of the survey on any of a number of grounds—you dislike the interviewer's appearance, hate nosy questions, just don't feel up to it that day, couldn't care less about surveys, and so forth. As a respondent, you need to be overwhelmingly positive about any of the four relationships and/or not sufficiently negative about all four. Perhaps we should let the respondent's structure of reasons fall into a simple division by whether the reasons are central or peripheral to the task of completing a survey.

A variant of the generic measurement model divides the respondent's reasons into two categories: affective and rational. The affective dimension corresponds to feelings on the part of the respondent about the interview situation, the interviewer or to him- or herself: "Openness," "Empathy," and "Helper" self-perception. The affective dimension corresponds to a peripheral route to the respondent's decision. A rational dimension emphasizes the calculation of the costs or benefits of survey participation: "Interest," "Good Experience," and "Not Busy." The rational dimension parallels the central route.

Figure 4.5 displays the weighted least squares estimates for this revised measurement model. There are now four freed coefficients (as opposed to two in the prior, four-factor model), and all these coefficients are substantial and positive. Note that all four of these coefficients are statistically significant, and substantively large. Among the indicators for the affective dimension, "Empathy" and "Helper" are nearly as large as the scale coefficient ("Openness"). Among the indicators for the rational dimension, "Not Busy" is almost as large as the scale coefficient ("Interest"). The size of these coefficients implies something quite interesting: the value respondents assign to the experience is twice as important as the time constraint. Of course, this finding is especially suspect given *when* interviewers asked the respondent why he or she participated. After the interview, the respondent might well be more likely to devalue any time constraint and inflate his or her assessment of how fun an interview might be.

The overall fit of this revised model is approximately the same (the goodness-of-fit index is .99) as for the generic model (fig. 4.4). The decision about which of the two models better fits the problem rests not with some statistic, but with theory. Throughout this chapter and the previous, I argue that the respondent's decision to participate depends on the state of four different relationships, distinguished from each other

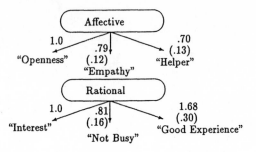

FIGURE 4.5. Measurement Model for Causes of Survey Compliance, Collapsing the Reasons into Affective and Rational Dimensions, 1989 DAS Respondents Only

by the nature of the target (strangers, the interviewer, the interview, and self). The variant of the model suggests that there are really only two relationships, distinguished by the rationality of the respondent's decision.

In the theory, there is quite a distinction between the two models. The model based around the targets asserts that the attributes of the respondent's situation determine whether or not the respondent refuses or complies. What matters is the particular respondent's feelings toward strangers, the particular interviewer, and the survey. Furthermore, this model asserts that the respondent's attitudes toward the four targets refer to very different aspects of the respondent's situation. The alternate model declares that the respondent's style of thinking (affective or rational) determines whether or not the respondent complies or not. Moreover, the second model groups aspects of the respondent's reasons that might seem very dissimilar: whether or not the respondent likes to share opinions with others seems disjoint from whether the respondent likes to help others. I prefer the former model for the reason that it is quite specific to the survey situation, while the latter model is a general model for any act of compliance.

Ironically, the limited set of indicators means that the two models are closer in implementation than in theory. The same three indicators that I use to measure the affective dimension are the same three indicators I use to measure the respondent's relationship to strangers, the interviewer, and self-image. In fact, in the conclusion to chapter 3 I discuss the possibility that these three relationships suggest a nonrational decision by the respondent.

While the affective-rational model seems to serve for the respondents, it does not perform nearly so well for the refusals. An equivalent model might be designed for the reasons for refusal, grouping together the relationships to strangers and to self-image. However, estimates for a two-factor refusal model did not converge for any of the three data sets.

A Full Model of Survey Compliance for the 1989 DAS

We can also estimate the full structural model, with some creative coding. The reasons a respondent has for agreeing and a refusal has for declining might really be references to two sides of the same cognitive structure. Schemas are routines that individuals call upon when making a decision. One schema pertinent to surveys might be prior experience. Two potential respondents recall previous times they had been interviewed. One remembers being impressed with how much she knew about politics: she employs this "experience schema" in a positive way. Another recalls how tedious all those questions were about people he knew nothing about: he employs the experience schema in a negative way.

If one views some categories of reasons as loading on the same set of considerations, some negatively, some positively, it is possible to combine the reasons for refusal and compliance into one of four schema. If the respondent does not mention the schema, the variable for the schema is coded 0. If the reason is for a refusal, the schema is coded −1; if the reason is for a compliance, the schema is coded 1. (The coding of these four schemas appears in table 4.1.) Fears of confidentiality ("Confidentiality") and a desire to express opinions ("Openness") associate with the Confidentiality schema. Being "Too Busy" or "Not Busy" reflect a Time schema. Being "Not Interested" or "Interested" mirrors an Interest schema. Having a prior "Bad Experience" or a "Good Experience" with surveys refers to an Experience schema.

We can use these four schemas to estimate a subset of the structural model. Time, Experience, and Interest become indicators for the respondent's relationship to the interview, while Confidentiality becomes

TABLE 4.1. Coding of the 1989 DAS Respondents' and Refusals' Reasons into Schema

Schema Name	Takes on −1 if *Refusal* Reason is:	Takes on 0 Otherwise	Takes on 1 if *Respondent* Reason is:
Confidentiality	"Confidentiality"		"Openness"
Time	"Too Busy"		"Not Busy"
Interest	"Not Interested"		"Interested"
Experience	"Bad Experience"		"Good Experience"

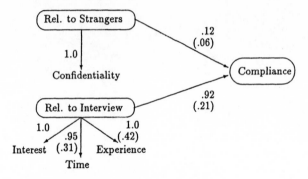

FIGURE 4.6. Full Model of Survey Compliance, 1989 DAS

an indicator for the respondent's relationship to strangers. I fix two of the parameters in the measurement model to 1 (Confidentiality and Interest) and thus estimate only the two coefficients on Time and Experience, and the effect coefficients. The weighted least squares estimates appear in figure 4.6.

The two free parameters in the measurement portion of the model (on Time and Experience) are approximately equal to 1. In other words, for the 1989 respondents and refusals, Time, Experience, and Interest are roughly equal components of the respondents' relationship to the interview.

In some ways the most intriguing aspect of the full model for the 1989 DAS is the size of the effects of the relationships on compliance. Far and away the larger of the two effect coefficients is the relationship to the interview (the "rational") dimension. This is, at the least, partly artifactual. We have but a solitary indicator of the relationship to strangers. As a consequence, the effect of the relationship to strangers is attenuated. But the rational dimension dominates the structure in the 1988 NES data also. I postpone comments on the relationship to the interview until after we consider the model for the 1988 NES.

Estimates for the 1988 NES Pre-Postelection Survey

The 1988 NES interviewers completed a noninterview description booklet for all refusals and for reluctant respondents, marking reasons for refusal or resistance and the general attitude of the respondent toward the interviewer. With the 1988 NES data, we have indicators for all four of the latent relationships, and for both respondents and nonrespondents.

Whether or not the respondent appeared to be Suspicious or referred

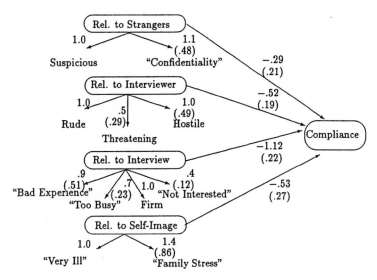

FIGURE 4.7. Structural Model of the Causes of Survey Compliance, 1988 NES

to Confidentiality as a reason for refusal or resistance are indicators of the respondent's relationship to strangers. Whether or not the respondent appeared to be Rude, Threatening, or Hostile are indicators of the respondent's relationship to the interviewer. Indicators for the respondent's relationship to the interview include whether or not the selected respondent was polite to the interviewer and whether or not the respondents refused or resisted on the grounds of a "Bad Experience," "Too Busy, " or "Not Interested." The respondent's relationship to self-image is indicated by whether or not the respondent refused or resisted on grounds of being "Very Ill" or undergoing "Family Stress."

I fix four of the indicators to one (Suspicious, Rude, Firm, "Very Ill"), and estimate with weighted least squares. These estimates appear in figure 4.7.

There are now seven free parameters in the measurement portion of the model. All of these parameters have the right sign (positive), and most are statistically significant. With the 1988 NES, we have measurements pertaining to all four relationships, and the measurement model bears up nicely.

We are probably most interested in the coefficients relating the four relationships to probability of compliance. The signs are in the expected (negative) direction.[6] The respondent's relationship to the interview dominates the other three relationships. The magnitude of the coefficient on the relationship to interview is double those for the relationship to self-image or to the interviewer, and more than three times that of the relationship to strangers. Moreover, the coefficient on the relationship to the interviewer and on the relationship to the interview are statistically significant, while the other two effect coefficients are not. The clear implication of this model is that the way potential respondents feel about the interviewer and the survey is what influences whether or not they agree to be interviewed. The overall fit of the model is quite good: the goodness-of-fit index is .92, and the model correctly predicts 87 percent of the cases (compared to a null model of 72 percent).

With this model, we have answers to two of the questions I pose at the start of this chapter. How well does this model predict survey compliance? Quite well, as it turns out, which is somewhat surprising given the feeble measurement of key concepts. Which of the four relationships dominates the potential respondent's considerations? The respondent's relationship to the interview, where I have been able to test it, far and away overwhelms the other three relationships. Before turning to the implications of the models, let me partially allay some concerns about using reasons as causes.

Treating "Too Busy" and "Not Interested" as No

I ask the reader to suspend disbelief and to assume that the reasons people offer for refusing are, in truth, the causes of their behavior. This request demands a lot, particularly with regard to two of the reasons that people express. Although refusals couch these reasons in terms of time and interest, they may not really indicate that time and interest are the basis of the decision. Perhaps these phrases are merely a polite, culturally acceptable way of saying no. With a little restructuring of the generic model, we can treat "Too Busy" and "Not Interested" as if these reasons are equivalent to the compliance decision.

One might suppose that the reasons "Too Busy" and "Not Interested" come after the respondent's decision and merely serve as culturally acceptable ways to refuse. If this is the case, then one reasonable variant of the generic model is to remove "Too Busy" and "Not Interested" as indicators of the relationship to the interview and to treat the

---

6. Since the reasons here are all reasons to resist or refuse, one would expect that the larger the value of the latent relationship, the less likely the respondent would agree to participate.

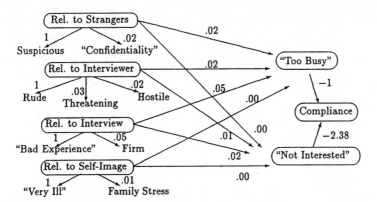

FIGURE 4.8. Model of Survey Compliance with "Too Busy" and "Not Interested" as Proximate to Compliance, Indirect Effects of Relationships on Compliance Only, 1988 NES

two reasons as dependent variables intervening before the decision to comply. In this revised model, if the four relationships have any effect on compliance, the effect comes only indirectly, via the intervening variables "Too Busy" and "Not Interested." An estimate of this alternate model appears in figure 4.8.[7]

Two interesting points arise from the estimates of this revised model. All of the free coefficients (with the exception of the direct effect of "Not Interested" on compliance) have plummeted to near 0. This sudden plunge suggests that either this variant of the model is very poorly measured or that this variant inappropriately rearranges the underlying causal structure. There is evidence for the first point in that the measurement portion of the model should not be as drastically affected as the conceptual model with a change to the indicators to just one relationship. However, if one compares the measurement portion of figure 4.7 with figure 4.8, something clearly happens to the degree to which, for example, concerns about confidentiality influence the respondents' relationship to strangers. Furthermore, we knew at the outset that estimating these models with a battery of dichotomous indicators was working from crude measures. There is also the possibility that this is an inappropriate change to the causal structure. The simpler models, treating "Too Busy" and "Not Interested" as indicators of the respon-

---

7. I omit the standard errors for this model and the next for two reasons. For one, *none* of the estimated coefficients are statistically significant. For another, the coefficients are already difficult to read without including standard errors that provide no additional information.

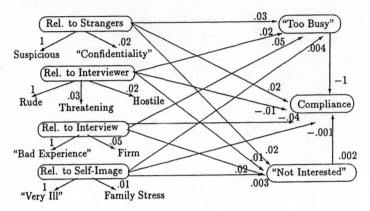

FIGURE 4.9. Model of Survey Compliance with "Too Busy" and "Not Interested" as Proximate to Compliance and Direct Effects of Relationships on Compliance, 1988 NES

dents' relationship to the interview, worked for all three of the data sets, and produced sensible coefficients.

The other point of interest is that the respondent's relationship to the interview continues to dominate over the other three relationships. The indirect effects on compliance of the relationship to the interview are at least twice those of the other indirect effects.

Of course, we aren't required to assume that the four relationships affect compliance *only* via the intervening variables "Too Busy" and "Not Interested." Perhaps claiming to be "Too Busy" or "Not Interested" is very close to compliance, but there are still direct effects of the four relationships on the respondent's decision. We can re-estimate this variant of the model with these direct effects, and this appears in figure 4.9.

The measurement part of this model is identical to the model in figure 4.8 (and therefore suffers from the same problems). The most interesting aspect of this new model is the effects of the respondent's relationship to the interview on compliance. The direct effect of the relationship to the interview (−.04) is about the same as its indirect effect via "Too Busy" (−.05). The indirect effect of the relationship to the interview via "Not Interested" is essentially 0.

There are two possible conclusions to draw from these respecifications. One is that this model is poorly measured, and that even if it makes more sense, we aren't in a position to determine so. The other possibility is that the improvement doesn't really increase our understanding of compliance. The respondent's relationship to the interview remains the most important of the four relationships for predicting compliance. Given that the simpler specification without intervening variables fares reasonably well (fig. 4.7), I prefer the latter conclusion.

Summarizing the Findings

The models estimated over the three data sets provide provisional support for the general structure proposed at the start of this chapter. Given that the unobserved variables are crudely measured and that the estimation of the model must depend on unorthodox techniques, the degree of similarity across the data sets is striking, or lucky. We do have to be restrained in drawing too much from such weak data. With this caveat in the background, some implications are possible.

The implications of the common structure of reasons for participating in the survey are several. The general strength of the overall structure over the separate data sets suggests that reasons for refusal are a useful and powerful explanation of responsiveness. Prior approaches to the study of nonresponse emphasized demographic characteristics. The reasons offered by the respondents for their actions provide new leverage. We need to pay attention to the reasons respondents offer for their actions. For one, survey organizations should attend to and record the reasons refusals express. For another, survey organizations should also ask respondents why they agreed to participate. Not only does this information help us better understand the causes of survey participation, but as I demonstrate in chapter 6, this information permits methods of correcting for the damage nonresponse causes to our analysis.

The dominance of the respondent's relationship to the interview suggests that there may be ways for survey organizations to boost response rates. It is doubtful that any survey organization could influence the respondent's relationship to strangers, much less the respondent's relationship to self-image. It is possible that the organizations could improve the respondent's relationship to the interviewer, but nurturing the rapport between interviewer and respondent is already a high priority.

But if there is anything that survey organizations might be able to alter, it is the respondent's relationship to the interview. Interest, Time, and Experience are some of the factors that influence this relationship that I discuss in this chapter. Is it possible to boost respondents' interest in surveys? The NES and DAS send letters to selected respondents who initially refuse attempting to persuade these people to agree to be interviewed. These letters are typically very dry, trying to explain to the selected respondents that the study really needs to talk with people like them. This is an opportunity to raise interest in the study, and one that needs more attention by survey staff. We ought to consider compensating for the respondent's time, as well as shortening the interviews. We have to be reflective about the content of the studies. What is fascinating to a political scientist may be utter tedium to respondents. It's counterproductive to insist on a battery of questions that even well-informed respondents have difficulty answering, even if that battery is part of the established core collection. Surveys can either be fun, interesting, and informative or painful and boring, but the choice belongs to the survey researcher.

CHAPTER 5

How Survey Nonresponse Damages Scientific Research

[A] Congressional appropriations committee unexpectedly killed another Federal study on sexual behavior. Senator Jesse Helms, a Republican from North Carolina, and Representative William Dannemeyer Dannemeyer, a Republican from California, had contended that heterosexuals would shrink from the survey as intrusive, while gay men would respond to it, thus distorting its results.
—*New York Times*, September 27, 1989

Legislators are not usually thought to be philosophers of science, but the preceding quotation strikes straight to the problem of nonresponse for scientific research. While their concern about which groups would shy away from surveys on sexual behavior might or might not be correct, nonresponse is a problem whenever some groups systematically refuse to participate in the surveys. Typically, we want to extrapolate from the obtained sample to some population. However, if the respondents differ from the nonrespondents in important ways, then the obtained sample is a biased representation of the population.

Every conceivable method of analyzing survey data is at risk because of nonresponse. Whether the analyst produces scatterplots, means, proportions, regressions, probits, or logits, survey nonresponse biases statistics.

First, I show how survey nonresponse undermines statistical inference. Well-known research by Kalton and Platek demonstrates that nonresponse biases estimates of univariate statistics such as means, proportions, or variances. Further research by Tobin and Heckman establishes how nonresponse also biases estimates of multivariate relationships. I contribute to this literature by demonstrating, with Monte Carlo simulations, where nonresponse is likely to be most damaging. Next I illustrate how one can repair the damage caused by nonresponse. I again use Monte Carlo simulation to show the consistency of statistical corrections for nonresponse and the sensitivity of these corrections to different kinds and amounts of nonresponse.

The first section discusses bias in univariate and bivariate statistics arising from nonresponse. The second section demonstrates inconsistency to estimates of multivariate relationships caused by nonresponse. The third section demonstrates general strategies for correcting for nonresponse.

How Nonresponse Biases Univariate Estimates

Nonresponse causes bias in univariate statistics (e.g., means, proportions, and variances) if response rates are imperfect *and* respondents differ from nonrespondents. That nonresponse bias arises from this combination makes intuitive sense: if the nonresponse rate is high, but respondents are identical to nonrespondents, then there is little nonresponse error; if the respondents differ from the nonrespondents to a great extent, but the nonresponse rate is close to zero, again there is little nonresponse error.

Bias to a Sample Mean

Suppose we are interested in how close the sample mean $\bar{y}$ (lowercase) comes to the population mean $\bar{Y}$ (uppercase).[1] I use the subscript r to denote respondents and m (for missing) to denote nonrespondents; R to denote the number of respondents and M to denote the number of nonrespondents. The total sample size is $R + M$. The true population mean $(\bar{Y})$ is related to the population mean for respondents $(\bar{Y}_r)$ and the population mean for nonrespondents $(\bar{Y}_m)$ as a weighted sum:

$$\bar{Y} = \frac{R}{R + M}\bar{Y}_r + \frac{M}{R + M}\bar{Y}_m \qquad (5.1)$$

---

1. Kalton's calculations proceed from the assumption that nonrespondents will always be nonrespondents and that respondents will always be respondents (Kalton 1983). This assumption permits Kalton to identify *population* statistics for both respondents and nonrespondents. Of course, as chapters 3 and 4 argue, any individual's responsiveness to a survey is not fixed—it varies. Certainly, some people will always refuse to participate, and others will always cooperate, but most refuse or comply depending on circumstances. Platek (1977, 1980) proves that Kalton's calculations hold when one assumes that responsiveness varies continuously, and thus little generality is lost by accepting Kalton's assumption of hard-core respondents and nonrespondents.

The two fractional components are the response rate $[R/(R+M)]$ and the nonresponse rate $[M/(R+M)]$. In words, the population mean $(\bar{Y})$ is nothing more than the population mean for respondents times the proportion of respondents plus the population mean for nonrespondents times the proportion of nonrespondents.

Because I define the population of respondents as independent of the population of nonrespondents, the expected value of the *sample* mean for respondents $(\bar{y}_r)$ is the *population* mean for respondents:

$$E(\bar{y}_r) = \bar{Y}_r \qquad (5.2)$$

Similarly, the expected value of the sample mean for nonrespondents is the population mean for nonrespondents:

$$E(\bar{y}_m) = \bar{Y}_m \qquad (5.3)$$

The bias in the sample mean for respondents $(\bar{y}_r)$ is simply the difference between the expected value of the sample mean $[E(\bar{y}_r)]$ and the population mean $(\bar{Y})$:

$$
\begin{aligned}
B(\bar{y}_r) &= E(\bar{y}_r) - \bar{Y} \\
&= \bar{Y}_r - \left(\frac{R}{R+M}\bar{Y}_r + \frac{M}{R+M}\bar{Y}_m \right) \\
&= \frac{M}{R+M} (\bar{Y}_r - \bar{Y}_m) \qquad (5.4)
\end{aligned}
$$

In other words, the difference between a sample mean (in a survey with nonresponse) and the true population mean is the nonresponse rate $[M/(R+M)]$ times the difference between the population mean for the respondents and the mean for the nonrespondents $(\bar{Y}_r - \bar{Y}_m)$. Obviously, if either the nonresponse rate goes to zero *or* there is no difference between respondents and nonrespondents, then there is no bias in the sample mean.

Typically, we will use the nonresponse rate $[M/(R+M)]$ as a proxy for the nonresponse error $[B(\bar{y}_r)]$, but this is an obvious mistake. Clearly, the nonresponse error depends on *both* the proportion of respondents that are missing and how different the missing respondents are from those that were actually interviewed. Figure 5.1 displays the interrelationship between nonresponse rates, differences between the respondents and nonrespondents, and the nonresponse error.

The horizontal axis represents the difference between the respondent

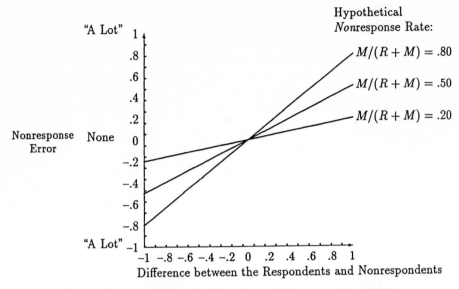

FIGURE 5.1. Relationship of Nonresponse Rate to Nonresponse Error of Mean

and nonrespondent population. The vertical axis displays the total non-response error $[B(\bar{y}_r)]$. The three lines plotted are the nonresponse error for three hypothetical levels of *non*response. The relationship is mono-tonically positive with respect to nonresponse rate and the difference in the two populations: i.e., an increase in either the nonresponse rate *or* the difference between the respondents and nonrespondents means an in-crease in the overall error. Note that the nonresponse error can produce the sample means based on respondents that are either underestimates *or* overestimates.

A concrete example is in order: nonresponse is one reason why sur-veys overestimate the proportion of people who vote in general elections. As most observers of elections know, polls consistently report a higher proportion of people voting than in fact turn out for an election. There are three explanations. One is that people fib—claim voting when they haven't. A second is that some polls stimulate turnout. In a study where the interviewer contacts the respondent before *and* after the election, the survey may have piqued the voter's interest in the election. But a third explanation is that surveys oversample voters. Recall from table 3.12 that people who participate in politics more frequently also participate in surveys more frequently. One can easily show that the respondents who were most amenable to being interviewed voted more frequently than those who resisted. In the 1988 NES, 59 percent of those who resisted being interviewed voted in the general election, while 70 percent of those who did not resist being interviewed voted.[2] I return to the problem of correcting for overestimating turnout in the next chapter.

Bias to Sample Variance

Nonresponse also biases estimates of variance. In statistical inference, we are interested in "differences" of various sorts: that a mean, for example, is statistically different from zero, or that a mean for Group A is statistically different from the mean for Group B. Combined with biased estimates of sample means, biased estimates of variances may lead us to both Type I and Type II errors in our statements about these differences. That is, one may discover differences that, in truth, don't exist (Type I errors or "false positives"). Or one may fail to find differences where, in truth, differences are present (Type II errors, or "false negatives"). In order to see how both errors may occur, one needs to understand how nonresponse causes underestimates of sample variance.

Again, following Kalton (1983), I use lowercase to denote sample statistics and uppercase to denote population properties. The *total* population variance (S^2) across the population of individuals i is:

$$S^2 = \frac{\sum_{i=1}^{R+M}(Y_i - \bar{Y})^2}{(R+M)-1} \tag{5.5}$$

The expectation of the sample variance for *respondents* (s_r^2) is the population variance for respondents (S_r^2), which may be computed as:

$$S_r^2 = \frac{\sum_{i=1}^{R}(Y_{ri} - \bar{Y}_r)^2}{R-1} \tag{5.6}$$

---

2. These numbers are based on the so-called validated vote measures collected by the NES. The NES systematically checks the registration and voting records of the respondents. There are inevitable implementation problems: city clerks sometimes refuse to give access to the NES, voters may be registered in a district other than where the interview took place, the city clerks may make administrative errors in recording the names, and so forth. But the validated voting measures are a significant improvement over a respondent's self-report in determining whether or not the respondent voted.

The numerator of the population variance expression (5.5) may be expanded as:

$$\sum_{i=1}^{R+M} (Y_i - \bar{Y})^2 = \sum_{i=1}^{R}(Y_{ri} - \bar{Y}_r)^2 + R(\bar{Y}_r - \bar{Y})^2$$

$$+ \sum_{i=1}^{M}(Y_{mi} - \bar{Y}_m)^2 + R(\bar{Y}_m - \bar{Y})^2$$

$$= (R-1)S_r^2 + (M-1)S_m^2 \frac{RM}{R+M}(\bar{Y}_r - \bar{Y}_m)^2 \quad (5.7)$$

If the number of respondents is large, then $R \approx R - 1$, $M \approx M - 1$, and $R + M \approx (R + M) - 1$, which leads us to the following expression for the population variance:

$$S^2 \approx \frac{(R-1)S_r^2 + (M-1)S_m^2 + \frac{RM}{R+M}(\bar{Y}_r - \bar{Y}_m)^2}{R+M}$$

$$\approx \frac{R}{R+M}S_r^2 + \frac{M}{R+M}S_m^2 + \frac{RM}{(R+M)^2}(\bar{Y}_r - \bar{Y}_m)^2 \quad (5.8)$$

Consequently, the bias of the variance calculated only upon respondents (s_r^2) is:

$$B(s_r^2) \approx E(s_r^2) - (S_r^2)$$

$$\approx S_r^2 - \left[\frac{R}{R+M}S_r^2 + \frac{M}{R+M}S_m^2 + \frac{RM}{(R+M)^2}(\bar{Y}_r - \bar{Y}_m)^2 \right]$$

$$\approx \frac{M}{R+M}(S_r^2 - S_m^2) - \frac{RM}{(R+M)^2}(\bar{Y}_r - \bar{Y}_m)^2 \quad (5.9)$$

Unlike estimates of the sample mean for respondents, the sample variance based only on respondents will generally underestimate the population variance. There are three "moving parts" to the nonresponse error for sample variance: the nonresponse rate $[M/(R+M)]$, the difference between the population variance for respondents and nonrespondents $(S_r^2 - S_m^2)$ and the squared difference in sample means $[(\bar{Y}_r - \bar{Y}_m)^2]$. The first term of this expression may be positive or negative, depending only on whether the population variance for respondents (S_r^2) is greater than or less than the population variance for nonrespondents (S_m^2). Because R and M are both non-negative integers, the nonresponse rate $[R/(R+M)]$ will always be positive. The second term will always be

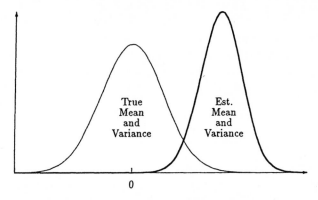

0

FIGURE 5.2. Survey Nonresponse and False Confidence Intervals

positive: the difference in the means is squared, and the product of the nonresponse rate and response rate is a product of nonnegative integers. If the second term is larger than the first, we will underestimate variance. Specifically, we will underestimate variance if any of the following are true. (1) If S_m^2 is greater than S_R^2, then the first term will be negative. In other words, if the nonrespondent population is more variable than the respondent population with respect to the attribute of interest, we will underestimate sample variance. This situation is especially likely if we are interested in the variance of an attribute that is associated with participation in the survey. (2) If the difference in the sample variance $(S_r^2 - S_m^2)$ is less than the response rate times the squared difference in the sample means:

$$\frac{R}{R+M}(\bar{Y}_r - \bar{Y}_m)^2 \tag{5.10}$$

In other words, if the sample mean for respondents is quite different from the mean for nonrespondents and the populations are distinct (both variances are small), we will underestimate sample variance.

Nonresponse leads to an irony. From the previous section, we know that nonresponse causes estimates of the mean to be above *or* below the true value. From this section, we know that nonresponse causes us to underestimate the true population variance. Suppose that the true population mean is zero, that the estimated sample mean is greater than zero, and that the population variance is significantly underestimated (see fig. 5.2). If nonresponse merely shifted the mean, the wider (true) variance would cause us to reject the hypothesis that the mean is nonzero. Instead, not only will we wrongly conclude that the mean is different from zero, but also this researcher will be more confident about the difference! In this figure, survey nonresponse induced a false positive (concluding that the mean is nonzero when it is not), but a false negative is just as possible. In the same picture, just shift the zero to the right, under the estimated mean.

How Nonresponse Biases Multivariate Relationships

Nonresponse not only undermines the validity of a sample's description of the population, it also distorts the relationships between attributes of the population. The way in which nonresponse affects multivariate analyses depends on what information we have about the nonrespondents. In some circumstances we may have no information at all about the nonrespondents. Such samples are "truncated." Alternatively, we may have some information about the nonrespondents but lack information on other important variables. These samples are "censored." In this section, I review the literature demonstrating how truncated and censored samples undercut scientific research.

A *truncated* sample is one where observations are missing for *both* exogenous and endogenous variables. Suppose that some groups systematically refuse to participate in surveys. What happens to our inferences about the population given that some groups drop out of the analysis? Sample truncation damages the *external validity* of our research—the degree to which we may generalize from the sample to the population as a whole. As I show, sample truncation also jeopardizes *internal validity:* the degree to which we can draw reliable inferences even about the obtained sample itself.

One way that truncation of the sample affects multivariate analyses is that truncation obscures the true functional form of a relationship between the variables. In an extreme way, figure 5.3 displays how truncation may prevent us from observing the "true" functional form of a relationship between variables. The "true" relationship between X and Y is the dotted curve. However, we only observe those cases to the right of the dashed vertical line. By looking only at these cases, we might mistakenly estimate a linear relationship. At the extreme of this particular functional form, the effect of truncation would cause an underestimate of the effect of X on Y. There is little that we can do to cope with this particular problem.[3]

---

3. Although unlikely, perhaps we might notice the heteroskedasticity of the

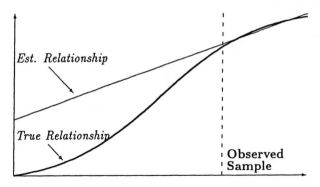

FIGURE 5.3. How Truncation Affects Regression Estimates of Obscured Functional Form

If we have information about why the nonrespondents drop out of the study, remedies are possible. The key to handling nonresponse in multivariate analyses is to use information about why the nonrespondents are missing, in order to model the process by which we obtain respondents in our samples. Does nonresponse arise from *explicit selection?* That is, do the sample persons have to satisfy some minimum threshold on the very dependent variable of interest in order to become respondents? If survey participation were exactly like political participation, a sample person would have to be a participant even to be make it into the analysis. Or does nonresponse arise due to *implicit selection,* where a sample person becomes a respondent due to factors potentially unrelated to the real variables of interest?

Explicit Selection

The most extreme formulation of censored samples arises from explicit selection on the dependent variable. In other words, we observe values for the dependent variable only if the variable crosses some minimum threshold. Suppose we want to use survey data to study why workers take jobs at particular wages. The problem will be that jobs must pay some amount before making it worthwhile for any worker to accept a

---

residuals within the observed sample, which might lead us to fit a simple polynomial function. It is extremely unlikely that we would estimate the model on a sigmoidal function. We would miss the key features of the model: that there is a transitional phase between relatively flat phases. In situations where the sample is truncated on both X and Y, the only recourse is theory.

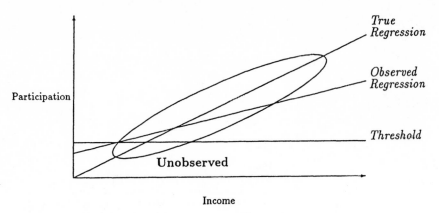

FIGURE 5.4. How Censoring Attenuates Regression Estimates

job. The value of the dependent variable is "censored": we don't know the minimum acceptable wage for respondents who don't accept the job. Consequently, we will underestimate the influence of other factors (e.g., status of the job, working conditions, income of other members of the household, etc.) that might also influence whether or not a worker accepts a job. While the connection to survey nonresponse requires another step, this formulation—censoring on the dependent variable—lays the foundation.

For purposes of illustration, suppose that survey participation is a linear function of income (fig. 5.4). The oval represents all sample persons, including respondents and nonrespondents. The true relationship between survey participation and income in this example would be a line straight through the center of the oval. However, we only observe those people who are sufficiently motivated to participate in the survey: only those cases above the threshold actually become respondents. If we estimate the relationship between participation and income only on the respondents, we obtain the flatter line. Censoring based on explicit selection causes estimates to become *attenuated,* or flattened. Tobin (1958) developed the explicit calculations for the consequences of selection on the dependent variable.

Suppose that the underlying, "true" model is a simple linear equation, relating the true dependent variable Y (uppercase) and the independent x (lowercase).

$$Y = x'\beta + u \tag{5.11}$$

Suppose that the error term, u, is distributed normally with mean 0 and variance ω^2:

$$u \sim N(0, \omega^2) \tag{5.12}$$

However, we only observe y (lowercase), where y is equal to c below some cutoff, and equal to Y above the cutoff:

$$y = c \text{ when } Y < c \tag{5.13}$$
$$y = Y \text{ when } Y \geq c \tag{5.14}$$

What happens to estimates of Y, given that we observe y only above the threshold c? The expected value of y given that $Y \geq c$ is:

$$E(y|Y \geq c) = E(x'\beta + u|x'\beta + u \geq c) \tag{5.15}$$

Because the sample selects only on Y, and the x are independent of Y

$$E(y|Y \geq c) = x'\beta + E(u|x'\beta + u \geq c) \tag{5.16}$$

Move $x'\beta$ to the right-hand side of the inequality, to yield an expression strictly in terms of u :

$$E(y|Y \geq c) = x'\beta + E(u|u \geq c - x'\beta) \tag{5.17}$$

Recalling that u is distributed normally with mean zero and variance ω^2, one can compute the probability that $u \geq c - x'\beta$:

$$\Pr(u \geq c - x'\beta) = 1 - \Phi\left(\frac{c - x'\beta}{\omega}\right) \tag{5.18}$$

(where Φ is the cumulative normal probability function). This is simply the area under the normal distribution to the right of the cutoff (c).

We can move from the probability to the expected value of the continuous distribution. The expected value of a continuous distribution is the integral of the probability that u is over the threshold $[\Pr(u)]$ times the value of u, over the area above the threshold $(c - x'\beta \to \infty)$:

$$E(u|u \geq c - x'\beta) \quad = \quad \int_{c-x'\beta}^{\infty} u \Pr(u)du \qquad (5.19)$$

$$= \quad -\omega \frac{\phi\left(\frac{c-x'\beta}{\omega}\right)}{1 - \Phi\left(\frac{c-x'\beta}{\omega}\right)} \qquad (5.20)$$

(where ϕ is the normal probability density function).

We can substitute the conditional expected value of u (5.20) back into the calculation of the conditional expectation of y (5.17) to get:

$$E(y|Y \geq c) = x'\beta - \omega \frac{\phi\left(\frac{c-x'\beta}{\omega}\right)}{1 - \Phi\left(\frac{c-x'\beta}{\omega}\right)} \qquad (5.21)$$

In words, the expected value of the y censored above the threshold c is the true value $(x'\beta)$ less some bias. In order for the bias to go to 0 $[\omega\phi()/\Phi() \rightarrow 0]$, one of two things must happen. If the variance in the model goes to 0 $[\omega \rightarrow 0]$, then the bias term becomes 0. That is, if our model perfectly predicts y, then the variance in the error term is 0, and there is no bias due to explicit selection. Of course, we have yet to see a perfect model in any discipline. The bias goes to 0 as the probability of selection into the sample becomes perfect [i.e., as $\Phi() \rightarrow 0$]. In other words, explicit selection is less of a problem for us if we perfectly model the problem of interest and we obtain 100 percent response rates. Anything less than perfect modeling and perfect response rates and we will see some selection bias.

One can deduce some interesting consequences from the Tobin formulation of censored samples, selected on the value of Y. First, the expected value of y will be attenuated—always less in absolute value than the true value of Y. The second term $[\omega\phi()/\Phi()]$ in the Tobin expression (5.21) will always be nonnegative. The standard deviation (ω) and the probability functions (ϕ and Φ) will always be negative. Because this second term is *subtracted* from the true value, the latter term will reduce the expectation of y.

Second, if we assume that all of the regressors (x) are drawn from a multivariate normal distribution, the bias in the constant is *proportional* to the bias in the slope (Goldberger 1981). The proportionality constant (λ) is given by the expressions:

$$\lambda = \frac{\theta}{1 - \rho^2(1 - \theta)} \tag{5.22}$$

$$\theta = \frac{var(y)}{\omega^2} \tag{5.23}$$

Where ρ is the coefficient of determination from the underlying model.

Tobin's construction of the problem of censored samples is the first of many important variations. However, Tobin models a version of sample selection that is too simplified for understanding how survey nonresponse biases multivariate estimates. Heckman (1976, 1979) devised a very clever way of generalizing beyond selection strictly on the dependent variable. Heckman's more general and certainly more applicable formulation is the problem of *incidental selection.*

Incidental Selection

From the discussion in chapters 2 through 4, we know that many factors influence survey participation: income, race, interest, information, and time are but a few of the causes. Furthermore, we more often estimate models where the dependent variable is something besides survey participation. Our models and the causes of nonresponse may be related in any of three ways. First, the dependent variable in the equation of interest determines sample selection; Tobin models this situation. Second, one or more independent variables in the equation of interest determine whether the sample person responds. Third, sample selection is wholly unrelated to the variables in the equation of interest. Heckman (1976, 1979) develops a model that incorporates all three.

Suppose that the model of interest (outcome equation) is a simple linear model:

$$Y_i = \beta' X_i + \epsilon_i \tag{5.24}$$

(That is, Y is a linear function of the exogenous X's and some error ϵ.) Suppose that Y is observed if and only if a second linear model exceeds 0:

$$\delta' Z_i + u_i > 0 \tag{5.25}$$

Suppose further that the errors (ϵ and u) are distributed normally:

$$\begin{pmatrix} \epsilon_i \\ u_i \end{pmatrix} \sim N \left[\begin{pmatrix} 0 \\ 0 \end{pmatrix}, \begin{pmatrix} \sigma^2 & \rho\sigma \\ \rho\sigma & 1 \end{pmatrix} \right] \tag{5.26}$$

That is, ϵ and u have a covariance $\rho\sigma$, where σ is the standard deviation of ϵ. The key feature of Heckman's construction is this covariance $\rho\sigma$. This covariance represents the extent that other causes of the outcome, not explicitly appearing on the right-hand side of the outcome equation, are related to the other causes of selection into the sample.

The selection mechanism (5.25) causes inconsistency in estimates of the the outcome model (5.24):

$$\begin{aligned} E(Y_i | Y_i \text{ observed}) &= E(\beta' X_i + \epsilon | \delta' Z_i + u_i > 0) \\ &= \beta' X_i + E(\epsilon_i | \delta' Z_i + u_i > 0) \\ &= \beta' X_i + E(\epsilon_i | u_i > -\delta' Z_i) \\ &= \beta' X_i + \rho\sigma \frac{\phi(-\delta' Z_i)}{1 - \Phi(-\delta' Z_i)} \\ &= \beta' X_i + \rho\sigma \frac{\phi(\delta' Z_i)}{\Phi(\delta' Z_i)} \end{aligned} \tag{5.27}$$

where $\phi()$ is the normal probability density function and $\Phi()$ is the cumulative normal probability density function.

The net effect of censoring may be thought of in three parts: ρ, σ, and $\phi()/\Phi()$ (the hazard rate).[4] The *direction* of bias of Y depends solely on the sign of ρ, because both σ and $\phi()/\Phi()$ are positive. The *magnitude* of bias of Y depends primarily on σ and $\phi()/\Phi()$. If the error in the outcome equation (5.24) is not correlated with the error in the selection equation (5.25), $\rho\sigma = 0$, and there is no bias. If the error in the outcome equation (5.24) is *negatively* correlated ($\rho < 0$) with the error in the selection equation (5.25), then the expected value of Y will underestimate the true value of Y. If the variance in the outcome equation is large, then σ^2 will be large and again $E(Y_i | Y_i \text{ observed})$ will underestimate Y. Finally, if the likelihood of the observations entering the sample is low (i.e., low response rate), the hazard rate $[\phi()/\Phi()]$ will be large and positive, and again the expected value of Y will underestimate the true value of Y. The hazard rate is an inverted expression of

---

4. The "hazard rate" describes the probability that an event will occur at that instant. It is commonly applied in actuarial analysis to describe the probability of death at a given age. Here, the hazard rate refers to the probability of a case dropping out of the sample (i.e., nonresponse). This particular specification of the hazard rate is also known as the Inverse Mill's Ratio.

the response rate, referring to the likelihood of a *case* being in the sample, rather than to the absolute proportion of obtained cases. Note that the response rate does not explicitly enter into the formulation of the problem in either the outcome equation (5.24) or the selection equation (5.25), but in the calculation of the bias.

When should we be wary of how survey nonresponse affects our research? What, exactly, happens to multivariate estimates when nonresponse occurs as a result of incidental selection? Some simulations make the problem concrete.

Monte Carlo Simulation of Selection Bias

Simulations are valuable because, unlike the real world, in a simulation we can impose true values and vary the conditions of selection into the sample. To clarify the presentation of these simulations, I use a standard typeface to refer to the theoretical parameters (e.g., ϵ or u) and typewriter face to refer to the simulated variables (e.g., EPSILON and U).

Begin by constructing the error terms (u and ϵ). Draw the error term on the selection equation (u) from a normal distribution with mean 0 and variance of 1.[5] To construct the error term on the outcome equation (ϵ), proceed in three steps. First, draw an intermediary variable (E) from a normal distribution with mean 0 and variance 1. Second, draw a "mixing" parameter R from a uniform distribution from 0 to 1. Third, produce EPSILON as a linear combination of U and a uniform random number:

```
EPSILON=R*U+(1-R)*[-.5+UNI(1)]
```

Because a linear transformation of a normally distributed variable yields a normally distributed variable, this process produces ϵ with some covariance with u.[6] The covariance $\rho\sigma$ between U and EPSILON may be

---

5. The subject of generation of random distributions raises concerns about serially correlated errors. At some level, *every* algorithm for the generation of uniform random numbers will be serially correlated (Mitriani 1982). Random number generators, since they typically depend upon a combination of two uniform random numbers, can be especially susceptible. In lieu of better random variate generation, the simulations in this chapter rely upon the package of generators in SHAZAM (White 1978).

6. Strictly speaking, the error term generated here is not a linear combination of normal variations. When the mixing parameter is zero, the distribution is uniform. Except at this extreme, however, the distribution of EPSILON passes a Kolmogorov-

calculated separately.

The true outcome equation is a linear combination of some X and β, where the X are normally distributed. Here, the simulation fixes the β vector to $\{1, 1, 2\}$. The true Y may be then generated from the randomly drawn X and the fixed β such that:

```
X1=NOR(1)
X2=NOR(2)
Y=1+1*X1+2*X2+EPSILON
```

We can then estimate the simulated Y by regressing on X1 and X2, saving the estimated coefficients. These are the "true" values—values before any selection. The next step is to observe how sample selection affects estimates on the censored data.

Sample selection might sensibly vary by the trichotomy mentioned: selection on the dependent variable (i.e., $Y = Z$), selection on some independent variable ($X \in Z$), and selection on some variables unrelated to the outcome model ($X,Y \notin Z$). In all three variants, the procedure is similar: generate a temporary variable Y2 as a function of Z and U, then select out all cases where Y2 is less than or equal to zero.[7] Note that the one element common in the selection process is the error term (U), which has some covariance with the error in the outcome equation (EPSILON). I take these variations up in turn.

Selection on Y

To simulate selection on Y, we simply generate a Y2, which is a function of Y and U, and select only those Y2 greater than 0:

```
Y2=Y+U
SELECT IF Y2 IS GREATER THAN 0
```

We may then regress Y on X1 and X2, to simulate the effects of selection on Y. We can then save the difference between the estimated coefficients for the models with and without selection. Repeating the simulation over 1,000 replications with 1,000 cases in each replication, allowing ρ (the amount of covariance between the error terms from the structural equation and the selection equation) to vary from zero to one,

---

Smirnov test with $p < .01$.

7. One may also compute a response rate as the proportion of Y2 that is greater than zero.

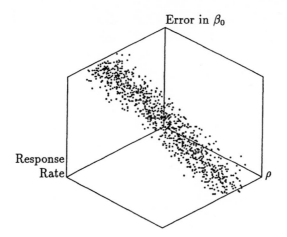

FIGURE 5.5. 3-D Scatterplot of Error in β_0 against ρ and Response Rate, Data Selected on Y

yields a data set of errors in estimated coefficients. The response rates for these replications range from 50 to 86 percent, quite representative of response rates for respectable surveys.

Figures 5.5, 5.6, and 5.7 display representations of three-dimensional scatterplots of the error in the coefficients (B_0, B_1, and B_2, respectively) on the vertical axis against the correlation in the error terms (ρ) and the response rate on the horizontal axes. All three figures make clear that the key to the error in the estimates is ρ. As ρ increases, the error in the estimated coefficient becomes worse (underestimating the constant and overestimating the slope coefficients). The response rate also affects the error in the estimated coefficients: as the response rate declines, the estimates are further off the mark. The relationship is close to linear in all three scatterplots.[8] An OLS regression provides a more precise handle on the relationship between the error in the estimates, ρ, and the response rate.

The strategy here is to examine how sensitive errors in the estimates of a coefficient (B_0, B_1, B_2) are to the response rate and the correlation of the errors across the selection and outcome equations (ρ). If the coefficients are insensitive to the response rate and ρ, then a regression of the error in the estimates of B_0, B_1, and B_2 on ρ and the response rate should be zero. Table 5.1 displays an ordinary least squares regression of

---

8. There is a slight curvature apparent in all three of the scatterplots, but the curve is so slight that a linear model does little damage.

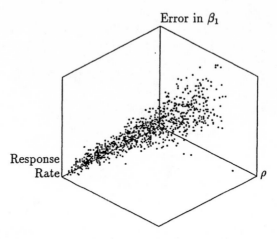

FIGURE 5.6. 3-D Scatterplot of Error in β_1 against ρ and Response Rate, Data Selected on Y

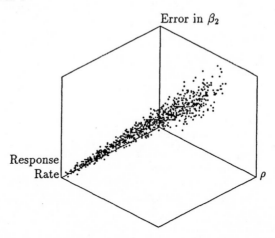

FIGURE 5.7. 3-D Scatterplot of Error in β_2 against ρ and Response Rate, Data Selected on Y

the errors in the coefficients (absolute value of the true coefficient minus the coefficient estimated on the data contaminated by selection bias) as a function of ρ and the response rate.

The constant term is the most sensitive to the selection properties (ρ and response rate). For each percent that we lose from the response rate, the constant term drops by a little more than half a percent. If the error in the equation of interest is perfectly related to the error in the selection model, we would underestimate the constant term by 50 percent. Not only is the R^2 term for the regression of error in B_0 nearly perfect but all the OLS coefficients are larger than equivalent coefficients for the other error terms. This is a relationship that holds through the different forms of selection, as shown in the following. The relationship between the covariance and the error terms and the error in the constant term is negative. That is, as the covariance of the errors approaches one, the constant term estimated from the data with nonresponse is *overestimated* by nearly 50 percent.

Response rate works in the opposite direction: the coefficient on response rate is opposite in sign to the coefficient on ρ. In fact, throughout all the variations on the selection mechanism, the coefficients on the covariance in the error terms are opposite to the coefficients on response rate. This makes sense: the damage due to response rate occurs when response rate is *low,* the damage due to covariance between the error terms occurs when ρ is *high.*

The slope coefficients (B_1 and B_2) are also biased due to selection on the dependent variable. Note that the ρ coefficients are positive, so that as the covariance in the error terms approaches one, the model suffering from selection bias will tend to *underestimate* the true coefficients. Also notice that as the response rate rises, the error in the slope coefficients decreases.

TABLE 5.1. OLS Regressions of Error in OLS Estimates of Models with Data Selected on Y

	Error(B_0)		Error(B_1)		Error(B_2)	
	B	SE	*B*	SE	*B*	SE
ρ	−.48	.004	.19	.01	.40	.01
Response Rate	.57	.030	−.21	.06	−.35	.06
(Constant)	−.42	.020	.18	.04	.31	.04
R^2	.94		.31		.68	

Dependent variable is error in the OLS regression, true value−estimate after selection for the model $Y = B_0 + B_1 X_1 + B_2 X_2$.

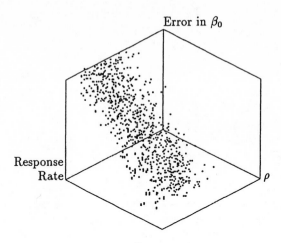

FIGURE 5.8. 3-D Scatterplot of Error in β_0 against ρ and Response Rate, Data Selected on X_1

Selection on X

Simulation of selection on some X (in this case, X1) follows the same pattern. I generate Y2 as a function of X1 and U:

```
Y2=X1+U
SELECT IF Y2 IS GREATER THAN 0
```

Again regressing Y on X1 and X2 and saving the error in the estimated coefficients, we have a data set of error as a function of ρ and the response rate. In figures 5.8, 5.9, and 5.10 we again see a representation of the three-dimensional scatterplot of errors in B_1, B_2, and B_3 as a function of ρ and response rate. Note that the errors to B_0 and B_1 are still nearly linear, but that the error in B_2 is a formless cloud. B_2 is not affected by selection on X_1 because X_1 and X_2 are statistically independent. (The mean correlation between X_1 and X_2 across the 1,000 replications is 0, with a minimum of $-.11$ and a maximum of .11.) If X_2 were related to X_1, we would see that the error in the estimate of B_2 would also be sensitive to ρ.

Table 5.2 displays the OLS regressions of the errors in the coefficients as a function of ρ and response rate. Again, the strongest effects in the error are in the constant term. The fit of the OLS regressions of error on the response rate and ρ is much stronger than the fit on the other

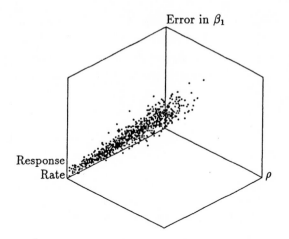

FIGURE 5.9. 3-D Scatterplot of Error in β_1 against ρ and Response Rate, Data Selected on X_1

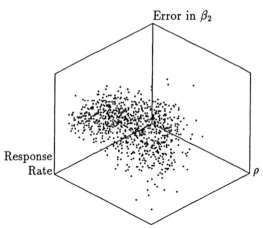

FIGURE 5.10. 3-D Scatterplot of Error in β_2 against ρ and Response Rate, Data Selected on X_1

parameters. Also, the size of the coefficients on response rate and ρ for error on B_0 dwarfs the other coefficients in the table. Heckman (1976, 1979) demonstrates that inconsistent estimates may be found even in variables unrelated to the process of selection, but *biased* estimates occur when the variables are part of the selection process.

Selection on Z

Finally, we may simulate selection on a variable *not related* to Y. Generate Y2 as a function of some X3 and U:

```
X3=-1+UNI(2)
Y2=X3+U
SELECT IF Y2 IS GREATER THAN 0
```

In figures 5.11, 5.12, and 5.13, I display representations of the three-dimensional scatterplots of the error in B_0, B_1, and B_2. The only one of the three coefficients that is biased in a systematic way due to ρ and the response rate is the constant term B_0. The three-dimensional scatterplots for B_1 and B_2 are both formless clouds, but there is still error.

Table 5.3 displays the OLS regressions of the errors in the estimated coefficients as a function of ρ and the response rate, applying the same procedures for computing errors. Even though selection is based entirely on variables not related to the dependent variable in the outcome equation, one can still see a systematic bias to the constant term in table 5.3. This makes sense: the problem emerges from a variable (Z), which is not included in the outcome equation, but is related to selection, explaining some of the variation in u. In other words, what is missing from our primary analysis hurts twice: once in excluding the observation (and reducing our degrees of freedom), again by introducing a misspecification

TABLE 5.2. OLS Regressions of Error in OLS Estimates of Models with Data Selected on X_1

	Error(B_0)		Error(B_1)		Error(B_2)	
	B	SE	B	SE	B	SE
ρ	−.81	.02	.39	.05	−.09	.04
Response Rate	.73	.11	−.04	.26	−.21	.21
(Constant)	−.38	.06	.11	.13	.14	.11
R^2	.95		.43		.07	

Dependent variable is error in the OLS regression, true value−estimate after selection for the model $Y = B_0 + B_1 X_1 + B_2 X_2$.

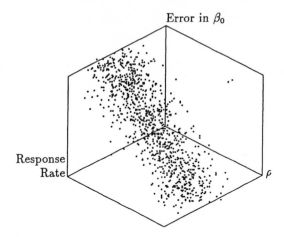

FIGURE 5.11. 3-D Scatterplot of Error in β_0 against ρ and Response Rate, Data Selected on Unrelated Z

error. However, the bias to the slope coefficients is not evident: none of the coefficients in the latter columns of the table are statistically distinguishable from zero. There is still additional error in these estimates due to nonresponse, but the error is unbiased.

In other words, we will have systematic bias to the estimates of the constant term alone if the process of selection is not related to the dependent variable and all of the independent variables. To the extent that our research is about problems that are wholly unrelated to sample selection, only our estimates of the constant term will be systematically incorrect because of nonresponse. However, our estimates of the other coefficients will also contain error, but we will not be in a position to say which direction the error will go.

While Tobin and Heckman make the *inconsistency* introduced by

TABLE 5.3. OLS Regressions of Error in OLS Estimates of Models with Data Selected on Unrelated Z

	Error(B_0)		Error(B_1)		Error(B_2)	
	B	SE	B	SE	B	SE
ρ	−.64	.01	.02	.04	.04	.03
Response Rate	.79	.08	−.05	.24	−.13	.19
(Constant)	−.42	.04	.01	.12	.06	.10
R^2	.96		.00		.02	

Dependent variable is error in the OLS regression, true value–estimate after selection for the model $Y = B_0 + B_1 X_1 + B_2 X_2$.

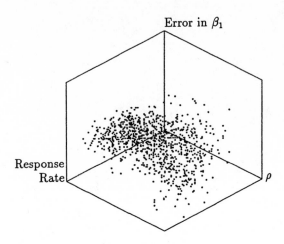

FIGURE 5.12. 3-D Scatterplot of Error in β_1 against ρ and Response Rate, Data Selected on Unrelated Z

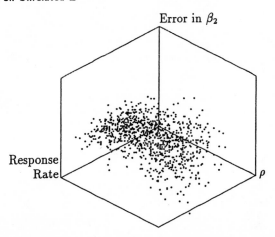

FIGURE 5.13. 3-D Scatterplot of Error in β_2 against ρ and Response Rate, Data Selected on Unrelated Z

nonresponse explicit, these simulations add to our understanding of the nature of *bias* and *inefficiency* due to nonresponse. The problem is that estimates of certain variables will be systematically wrong no matter what the sample size. If a variable in the equation of interest is related to why people participate in our surveys, our estimates of that variable will be biased. In chapters 3 and 4 I explain that nonresponse is related to how respondents feel about strangers, the interviewer, the interview, and themselves, and that these relationships manifest themselves in aspects like the respondents' level of interest and information, fear of crime, and general participativeness. The implication of these simulations is that if our model includes interest, information, fear of crime, or general participativeness on either the right- or left-hand side of the model our estimates will be biased due to nonresponse. Fortunately, we need not rest with such a gloomy observation.

Modeling Corrections for Nonresponse

The preceding sections warn of the dangers nonresponse wreak upon analysis of survey data. Univariate statistics—means, proportions, variances—will be biased, in ways that lead to both false positives and false negatives. Multivariate relationships will be inconsistently estimated to the extent that what determines entry into the sample is also part of the phenomenon under study. The foregoing algebra also leads to potential solutions to nonresponse, namely, modeling entry into the sample as part of the process under study. Before getting to the solutions, we need to consider a popular approach to the problem—weighting—and show it not only fails to solve the problem but may even make matters worse.

Weighting

The most common strategy of coping with nonresponse is to weight cases for which one has data to compensate for the cases that are missing. While weighting may be an appropriate tactic for correcting *some* univariate statistics, there are a variety of problems in the use of weights in many univariate analyses.[9] And weights used in multivariate analyses can lead to colossal errors.[10]

---

9. Strictly speaking, weights are used for other purposes besides correcting for nonresponse. Poststratification weights are also used to reduce sampling variance.

10. An alternate approach to repair data for nonresponse is imputation. Instead of multiplying the cases one has to compensate for the cases one is missing, imputation uses the data one has to generate values for the missing cases. As such, imputation is particularly appropriate for *item* nonresponse, since one has quite com-

There are three approaches to generating weights for nonresponse: population-based weights, sample-based weights, and probability of response weights. Population weighting adjustments employ data from an external benchmark to correct the marginals in the sample so they correspond to "known" population estimates. The CPS is corrected with population weights, derived from demographic formulas of births, deaths, and migrations.[11] Population weights require knowledge about the population distribution over weighting classes.

Sample weighting adjustments apply the inverse of the response rate for a class of respondents to make the distribution of classes of respondents identical to the distribution of classes of nonrespondents and respondents in the general population.

Probability of response weighting adjustments produces weights derived from the likelihood of obtaining a response from each class of respondents. One response probability adjustment is the Politz-Simmons procedure of accounting for no contacts. The idea behind the Politz-Simmons adjustment is to ask the respondents how often they would be at home over different periods, and to use this information to compute a probability of finding that respondent at home in general. The Politz-Simmons adjustment accounts only for no contacts, and not for refusals. Another probability of response adjustment is to regress a dummy variable measuring response onto factors explaining participation in the survey. The adjustment employs the predicted values of this regression to generate a probability of response weight. This procedure at first glance may appear similar to, but is fundamentally different from, the modeling-based approaches discussed in the following.

Weights may be able to repair some univariate estimates. If we have the information required by population weighting, we can repair the sample distribution of a class to be identical to the population distribution *on that weighting variable*. If we know how many blacks or Hispanics there should be in the sample, we *can* weight the data such that the sample correctly represents the population proportions. The problem is that we may want to infer from the sample to the population on measures for which we have no external population distributions. In

---

parable data for the nonrespondents and respondents on some other items. Because this research is concerned with *unit* or total nonresponse, I omit further discussion of imputation, other than to point to two sources of further information. Kalton (1983) provides a thorough introduction to most varieties of imputation. Rubin (1987) and Little and Rubin (1987) provide state-of-the-art details on multiple imputation techniques.

11. The demographic formula is that change in population is the sum of births and immigrations, less the sum of deaths and emigrations, over the same period.

these circumstances, weights are as likely to mislead as correct, even in univariate distributions.

Suppose that we want to identify the proportion of people who actually turned out to vote in an election, but that we only have weighting class information on race and income. Are the respondents of a particular race and income good proxies for the nonrespondents of the same race and income? Maybe, but maybe not: there is certainly no guarantee that other factors would make respondents differ from nonrespondents of the same weighting class. The problem comes down to unmeasured factors causing survey participation, and on how closely associated the weight class variable is to other variables of interest. If income and general social participation are related to survey participation, as chapter 3 strongly suggests, the few poor people who do participate in a survey will be in many ways quite unrepresentative of poor people in general. If we used poor respondents as proxies for poor nonrespondents, we would most likely overstate the rate poor people participate in politics.

Worse problems arise when one hopes to use weights to correct for nonresponse in multivariate analyses. Problems emerge if we inappropriately use respondents as proxies for nonrespondents, as in the case of correcting univariate statistics. But additional problems emerge because weighting on some classes will reduce the covariances between nonweighting class variables (Kalton 1983). That is, if we are analyzing the relationship between participation, education, and race, and we weight for race, we will reduce the covariance between participation and education. Since regression coefficients are determined by covariances, this means that weighting causes us to underestimate the effect of nonweighting class variables.

Simulation can show how poorly weighting corrects for selection bias. As a simple test, in the simulation of the effects of selection on the dependent variable, we can apply weights to all the variables and see what happens to the error in the estimates. In some ways, the most attractive weighting scheme is to weight by the inverse of the probability of response. Unlike weights by arbitrary demographic categories, there seems to be some sense in weighting the cases by their likelihood of actually participating in the sample. After applying these weights, we can examine how different the weighted variables are from their true means, and how far off the regression coefficients based on the weighted variables are from the true coefficients.

In table 5.4, we observe the differences between the true values and the estimated values for the means of the variables and for their coefficients. The upper panel of this table displays the unweighted and

TABLE 5.4. Simulated Error in Unweighted and Weighted Variables, when Selected on Y, Weighted by Probability of Selection

Error in:	True Mean— Mean for Replication	Std. Dev. of Mean for Replication	Different from Zero?
Y (unweighted)	−.63	.15	YES
Y (weighted)	−.79	.41	NO
X_1 (unweighted)	−.08	.04	YES
X_1 (weighted)	.02	.05	NO
X_2 (unweighted)	−.18	.05	YES
X_2 (weighted)	.08	.06	NO
B_0 (weighted)	−.26	.17	NO
B_1 (weighted)	.15	.15	NO
B_2 (weighted)	.29	.18	NO

weighted means of the three variables in the simulation. *All* of the unweighted variables have averages that exceed the true average. In other words, if the data are selected on the dependent variable and if we do not weight for selection, we will overestimate the means of all the variables. *None* of the weighted variables have averages that are significantly different from zero at conventional levels. The reader should notice that Y has not really been "fixed": the mean of the weighted variables is larger than the mean of the unweighted variables, only the average standard deviation of the means in each replication is larger.

In the lower panel, we can observe in a superficial way what happens to the regression coefficients when we estimate the model with weighted data. In some sense, we appear to be all right by weighting the data: to be sure, the mean error in the estimates of each coefficient is not that close to zero, but the standard deviation is wide enough so that the mean error is not significantly different from zero.[12] To stop at this conclusion is a mistake. The error itself is highly sensitive to the correlation between the error terms in the outcome and selection equations (ρ).

Table 5.5 displays OLS regressions of the error in the estimated coefficients on the response rate and the correlation between error (ρ). The critical point to notice from these regressions is that the error is highly sensitive to the size of ρ. As ρ goes to one, we will overestimate the constant term and underestimate both slope coefficients. What this means is quite simple: weighting by the probability of selection did not help the fundamental problem *one bit.* Our problem is that the

---

12. This is at the conventional probability levels of $p < .05$ or .01. The estimates of B_0, B_1 and B_2 may be far off the mark: the error in the coefficients is statistically distinguishable from zero at $p < .20$.

regression coefficients are biased to the extent that the error in our model is correlated with the error in the selection (ρ). The regression coefficients on the weighted, censored data are also biased with respect to ρ, *exactly* the same problem as the unweighted, censored data. Moreover, the damage to the slope coefficients goes exactly counter to what we would prefer. Because the error here is true value−estimated value, a *positive* error means that the estimated value *underestimates* the slope. That means that weighting the data dampens down the estimated values, causing scientists to miss findings they would have detected had they not attempted to repair the data by weighting. And this weighting scheme has some intellectual backbone: the respondents are weighted by their likelihood of participating in the survey. Weighting is emphatically *not* a solution to the problem of nonresponse in multivariate analyses.

Modeling Nonresponse

Heckman's formulation of the selection bias problem leads to a solution based on modeling the process of nonresponse. If we can model why people participate in surveys, then we have the means to correct for the model misspecification. Heckman's articles lay out a two-stage approach to modeling nonresponse. The prerequisite for adopting Heckman's correction is that we identify at least one variable that is a cause of selection that is not also in our model of interest. (This is a problem of identification in any system of equations, not unique to Heckman's two-stage correction for sample selection.)

The two-stage approach derives directly from Heckman's construction of the problem. (This procedure is for *continuous* dependent variables in the outcome model. I explain a variant of this procedure is necessary for *dichotomous* dependent outcome variables.) The first step is to identify the causes of participation in the survey (Z). It is impor-

TABLE 5.5. OLS Regressions of Error in OLS Estimates of Models with Data Selected on Y, Weighting the Data by the Probability of Selection

	Error(B_0)		Error(B_1)		Error(B_2)	
	B	SE	B	SE	B	SE
ρ	−.53	.02	.26	.04	.43	.04
Response Rate	−.56	.11	.34	.29	−.09	.28
(Constant)	.02	.08	−.21	.13	.15	.20
R^2	.92		.29		.57	

Dependent variable is error in the OLS regression (true value−estimate) after selection for the model $Y = B_0 + B_1 X_1 + B_2 X_2$.

tant to emphasize that the Z must include data on all the cases—that is, data on both respondents *and* nonrespondents. The second step is to include an additional regressor in the outcome model (the equation of interest) as a proxy for the correlated error between selection and outcome equations. Heckman (1976, 1979) and Achen (1986) suggest two different approaches to obtain the proxy regressor.

Heckman advocates a probit analysis of the likelihood of response given Z, variables predicting response. The dependent variable in this first step is a dummy variable coded 1 if there is a response, and coded 0 otherwise. The probit coefficients on Z are δ_P. Multiply the δ_P by the Z_i to generate predicted values ($\delta_P' Z_i$). From these predicted values, generate the Inverse Mill's Ratio of the predicted values:[13]

$$\text{IMR} = \frac{\phi(\delta_P' Z_i)}{\Phi(\delta_P' Z_i)} \tag{5.28}$$

The second step of Heckman's correction is to include the Inverse Mill's Ratio as an additional regressor in the outcome equation. I.e.,

$$Y_i = \beta' X_i + \rho\sigma\text{IMR}(\delta_P' Z) \tag{5.29}$$

The coefficient on the Inverse Mill's Ratio ($\rho\sigma$) is an estimate of the covariance between the error in the outcome model and the selection model. The magnitude of this term provides a direct estimate of the size of the selection bias.

Achen's correction is strategically similar but uses a linear probability model to generate the estimate of the likelihood of nonresponse. The dependent variable in the first step is again a dummy variable for response, coded 1 if there is a response, 0 otherwise. He advocates using ordinary least squares to regress this dummy variable on the Z, producing linear coefficients δ_L. (One may then repeat the procedure, using generalized least squares to produce better estimates of the δ_L.) Save the *residuals* from this first step ($\hat{u}_i$), and restrict the residuals to the bounds $.001 \leq \hat{u}_i \leq .999$.

The second step of Achen's correction includes the corrected residual estimates as an additional regressor in the outcome equation. Again, the

---

13. Many statistical packages compute the Inverse Mill's Ratio as an option in the probit procedure (e.g., SHAZAM and LIMDEP). If it is not available as an option, one may compute the Inverse Mill's Ratio with the normal density and cumulative density functions.

coefficient on the corrected residuals is an estimate of $\rho\sigma$, the covariance between the error in the outcome and selection models.

Heckman's and Achen's methods work only if the dependent variable in our equation of interest is continuous. If the outcome equation models a dichotomous dependent variable (e.g., voting or not voting, voting Democrat or Republican), then a straightforward application of the preceding techniques will *not* yield consistent estimates. The reason is that the corrections assume a joint normal distribution of the error terms. If the outcome equation is dichotomous, the error (ϵ) will not be normally distributed. Achen advocates a nonlinear least squares correction. The first step is identical: compute an estimate of the residuals ($\hat{u}_i$) as a function of the Z, correcting to zero to one bounds. The second step is to estimate the function:

$$Y_i = \beta' X_i + \rho\hat{u}(\beta' X_i)(1 - \beta' X_i) \tag{5.30}$$

The final, squared term in the nonlinear expression is a proxy for the variance of u. Appropriate starting estimates of the β are the coefficients from an ordinary least squares estimate of the outcome model, omitting the correction for nonresponse.

Achen and Heckman prove that these procedures yield consistent estimates. I do not repeat their algebra here; instead, I refer the reader to their separate works.

The reader may find a cookbook summary of the steps in the two methods helpful; this appears in appendix C.

All of these two-stage procedures require some elaborate calculations to generate the standard errors of the outcome model. In general, the standard errors produced by the second step are not correct. Complete details for calculation of the standard errors for the Achen estimators, including a SHAZAM setup, are included in appendixes D, E and F.

There is an alternate approach to the problem of correction for censored samples, namely a Maximum Likelihood approach. (Amemiya [1985] and Maddala [1983] lay out extensive details on such an approach.) The Maximum Likelihood techniques share a common strategy with the two-stage approaches: correct the model for nonresponse; don't correct the data. One reason to favor the simpler two-stage approach is that Maximum Likelihood approaches entail considerable computational complexity and are not feasible in the most commonly used statistical packages (such as SPSS-X or SAS). Both approaches are efficient, while the Maximum Likelihood approach may be more efficient in the asymptote, however distant the asymptote may really be. The two-stage correction is easily estimated with any statistical package that supports probit. Indeed, the Achen corrections may be run on any statistical package that conducts ordinary least squares regression (assuming a continuous dependent variable in the outcome equation).

Monte Carlo Simulation of the Corrections for Nonresponse

Heckman and Achen demonstrate that their corrections yield consistent estimates *in the asymptote.* How many cases do we have to obtain to reach asymptotic efficiency? How sensitive are these corrections to response rate and the correlation of the error terms? One's confidence in the robustness of these corrections depends on the answers to these questions. Fortunately, the Monte Carlo simulations developed earlier provide a splendid way to provide answers to these questions and to compare the relative efficiency of the two approaches.

A simple addition to the simulations of selection bias adds two additional correction steps. First, create a dummy variable that corresponds to selection:

```
Y2DUM=0
IF Y2 IS GREATER THAN OR EQUAL TO 0 THEN Y2DUM=1
```

Then (for both the Heckman probit correction and the Achen linear correction) use the selection variables to generate an estimate of the likelihood of response. In the Heckman case, save the predicted values from the probit analysis of Y2DUM, and compute the hazard function (Inverse Mill's Ratio) of the predicted values. In Achen's correction, save the residuals from a linear regression of Y2DUM on the selection measures. As with the estimates of the error due to selection bias, we can record the error after correction by subtracting the corrected value from the true value. Repeating over 1,000 iterations, we have a nice data set documenting the effect of correction for nonresponse.

Figures 5.14 and 5.15 display the error in the constant term after correction for the Heckman probit and Achen linear correction methods. (Similar distributions occur with the slope coefficients also; I choose the constant term arbitrarily.) Three features are readily apparent from these scatterplots. First, both methods generate efficient and unbiased estimates. The mean error is 0, indicating that the methods are unbiased. The errors are clustered tightly around 0 for both Heckman and Achen corrections, indicating that these methods are efficient. The second feature is that the corrections are relatively more efficient when

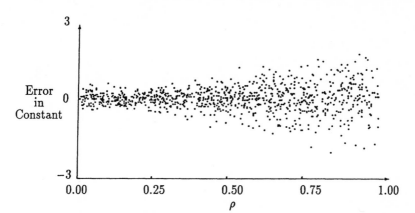

FIGURE 5.14. Error in Constant after Heckman Correction

ρ is small than when ρ is large. The spread of the error increases as ρ increases, accounting for the trumpet shape of the distribution. In other words, as the underlying problem worsens, the corrections are less reliable. The third feature is that both corrections may yield wildly inaccurate estimates, especially as ρ approaches 1: notice how many of the error terms are clustered towards the extremes $(-3, +3)$ on this graph. Lest the reader take this last feature to mean that the analyst might be better off not applying the corrections, take notice of the three-dimensional scatterplots earlier in the chapter. While it is true that the Heckman and Achen corrections may occasionally produce erroneous estimates, we are on balance better off using these corrections (since the mean of the corrected error is 0). In contrast, the uncorrected estimates are seriously biased when ρ is 0.

The Heckman and Achen corrections are approximately equal in their sensitivity to ρ. A statistical analysis of the sensitivity and efficiency of the two correction approaches appears in appendix G. The Heckman approach is marginally less sensitive to ρ in the case of selection on Y, while the Achen approach is less sensitive to ρ in the case of selection on X.

The corrections provided by Heckman and Achen, in general, work well. The error in the estimates after correction is generally less than the error in the uncorrected models. More importantly, the error in the corrected estimates is efficient and consistent—centered tightly about zero—even as the covariance increases between selection errors and the error in the outcome equation. But the overall spread of the error in-

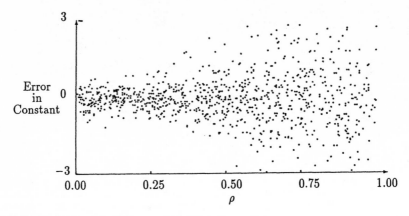

FIGURE 5.15. Error in Constant after Achen Correction

creases as ρ increases. Heckman and Achen provide useful methods to handle selection bias, but the methods are not magic tricks. If the error in the outcome equation is strongly correlated with the error in the selection process, then the corrections themselves will yield unreliable estimates.

Nonresponse will bias our understanding of politics to the extent that our models are related to why people participate in surveys. But we need not leave our analysis at risk because of nonresponse: we now have corrections for nonresponse bias in multivariate analyses. The reward for the reader who perseveres through the algebra, calculus, and Monte Carlo simulations in this chapter is imminent: the next chapter applies the corrections for selection bias to a diverse set of models of politics.

CHAPTER 6

Applications of Corrections for Nonresponse

The theme of the last chapter is that survey nonresponse threatens scientific research. In particular, multivariate analyses will be biased if either the dependent variable or the independent variables are related to the causes of nonresponse.[1] Is this just playing methodological Chicken Little ("The response rates are falling! The response rates are falling!"), or is there reason for concern? What we don't know is *how much* damage survey nonresponse causes to social science estimates or what sorts of conclusions are altered by nonresponse.

If we could compare our estimates with the "true" values, we would have a sense of how nonresponse affects our models. Outside of the realm of simulation, we never know a true value. What we can do is to apply Heckman's and Achen's corrections for nonresponse to some well-regarded and influential political science models and to see what difference the corrections make. The approach of this chapter is to compare corrected and uncorrected estimates.

Is this a fatuous comparison? After all, the Heckman and Achen approaches are statistical remedies, not statistical cures. Their two-stage corrections yield consistent estimates, but not guaranteed, ironclad true values. In some instances (namely, when ρ, the correlation between the error terms in the outcome and selection equations, approaches one), the remedy may be no better than the disease: although the corrections are consistent and unbiased, they are less efficient and may have considerable error. What I ask the reader is not to suspend disbelief—instead, I wish exactly the opposite. The key here is to ask whether or not the corrections yield differences that make sense. Do the corrections cause estimates to change in sensible ways? Do these changes inform us about the sorts of people who don't respond to surveys? Do these changes cause us to draw different conclusions from our data?

First, I develop three selection mechanisms, equations predicting whether or not the selected sample person is likely to become a full-

---

1. Also, if there is no error in the selection mechanism and there is no problem with the functional form, then they will be unbiased.

fledged respondent. I then apply the two-stage corrections to a diverse set of models.

A Selection Mechanism

One goal of this chapter is to devise corrections. If one knows why people are part of a sample, one has the means to model how entry into the sample affects the coefficients in equations of interest. Two approaches follow from the discussion in previous chapters: an *administrative approach* modeling the survey process as a function of persuasibility and contactability, and a *behavioral approach* that treats the sample person's reasons for refusing, resisting, or complying as indicators of the causes of their decision. A third approach is to model survey compliance on the basis of demographic characteristics.

The simplest way to model the survey process is to treat response as a function of study administration, the amount of persuasion and the number of contacts needed to draw a respondent into the sample. Specifically, one can produce a very effective, very simple, model of survey participation as a function of the number of calls to the household and whether or not the organization sent a persuasion letter to the respondent or attempted to convert a refusal. Whether or not the organization sent a persuasion letter or tried to convert a refusal reflects whether or not the interviewer felt additional persuasion was needed to get the respondent to agree.[2] The number of calls measures the accessibility of the respondent.[3] Sending a persuasion letter or attempting a refusal conversion substitutes for the compliance stage, while the number of calls substitutes for the contact stage.

This administrative approach has several virtues. One could argue that the independent variables are treatments applied to the respondents. These treatments causally precede the final decision by the respondent to participate.[4] Whether these treatments were applied or not is arguably exogenous from any model of interest. Furthermore, these

---

2. A "refusal conversion" refers to more than merely attempting to convince a reluctant respondent to participate. The Survey Research Center (the organization conducting NES interviews) will send out a specially trained, highly skilled interviewer to convert some refusals. The interviewer making a refusal conversion is, in general, *not* the original interviewer.

3. Specifically, I use the natural logarithm of the number of calls. The reason is that one might suspect that the marginal effect of additional calls declines with each additional call. The difference between a small number of calls (say 1 or 2 calls) is more important than the difference between a large number of calls (say 10 or 11 calls).

4. They are not *experimental* treatments, since there is no random assignment

treatments are applied to all respondents (although not equally). If it takes X calls to obtain an interview from a certain respondent and it takes Y calls to obtain an interview from another respondent, X and Y are independent measures of how accessible the respondent is. There is no missing data on the survey process with this approach. The behavioral approach is much more susceptible to problems of missing data. That behavioral data are available for a respondent indicates that the interviewer was able to contact the respondent and that the respondent was forthcoming with at least a reason for refusal.

The administrative approach has an important flaw. While the administrative measures are arguably exogenous from any model of interest, they are *endogenous* to the model of survey participation.[5] As a result, the estimates of the residuals will be inconsistent. In practice, the inconsistency in the estimates of the residuals produces only slight differences between corrections due to the alternative approaches.

Probit estimates of likelihood of obtaining an interview as a function

---

of treatments and subjects, nor a control.

5. Specifically, the correction detailed in this chapter employs the *residuals* from the selection mechanism. The selection equation represents y_1 (compliance) as a function of some other endogenous measure y_3:

$$y_1 = \alpha_1 + \beta_1 y_3 + u_1$$

We want the residual (u_1):

$$u_1 = y_1 - (\alpha_1 + \beta_1 y_3)$$

The expected values of α_1, $\beta_1 y_3$, and u_1 may be calculated to the simple expressions:

$$
\begin{aligned}
E(\alpha_1) &= \alpha_1 - \frac{\sigma_{13} \bar{y}_3}{\sigma_{y_3}^2} \\
E(\beta_1 y_3) &= \beta_1 + \frac{\sigma_{13} y_3}{\sigma_{y_3}^2} \\
E(u_1) &= y_1 - E(\alpha_1) - E(\beta_1 y_3) \\
&= u_1 + \frac{\sigma_{13}}{\sigma_{y_3}^2} (\bar{y}_3 - y_3)
\end{aligned}
$$

Where $\sigma_{y_3}^2$ is the covariance between y_1 and y_3. In other words, the expected value of a residual (u_{1i}) is inflated by the correlation between y_1 and y_3 times the absolute deviation of that residual from the mean. If y_3 is not strongly correlated with y_1, the additional term will be close to zero. Similarly, if the residuals tend not to vary much from the mean, the additional term will again be close to zero. I thank Chris Achen for pointing out the endogeneity problems of the administrative approach, and providing me with these calculations.

TABLE 6.1. Probit Estimates of "Administrative" Selection Mechanism, 1986 and 1988 NES, and 1989 DAS

	NES		DAS
	1986	1988	1989
Persuasion Letter Sent?	−2.263	−2.236	−1.122
Refusal Conversion Tried?	−.263	−.217	
Log of Number of Calls	−.164	−.365	−.358
(Constant)	1.179	2.353	1.673
% Correct	90	91	73

Dependent variable is "Response," where respondents are coded 1, and nonrespondents are coded 0. Cell entries are probit coefficients. All coefficients are statistically significant at $p < .01$.

of the administrative measures appear in table 6.1. The dependent variable is "Response," coded 1 if an interview was obtained, 0 otherwise. (I discard only nonsample cases from the analysis.) This selection model does quite well in predicting likelihood of a response for all three data sets (1986 and 1988 NES, 1989 DAS).

The largest treatment effect is the persuasion letter, followed by refusal conversion and number of contacts. There are two points worth pursuit. The first is that the signs on all the treatments are negative (with the exception of the constant term). On casual inspection, the negative signs on additional attempts to elicit an interview seem surprising. It would be a mistake to follow such casual inspection and conclude that persuasion letters or refusal conversion attempts *decrease* the likelihood of obtaining an interview. While it is true that most persuasion letters or refusal conversion attempts fail, these methods do work for some individuals. Whether or not the cost of administering these methods is worth the gain in response rate or improvement in the study is a separate matter. A more appropriate way to interpret these variables is as a sign of "needing additional persuasion" (less compliant) or "needing additional contact" (less contactable). With this interpretation, the negative signs should be expected.[6]

The second point of note from these coefficients is the substantial size of the constant term. A respondent who was contacted on the first call (log = 0), without being sent a persuasion letter or a refusal conversion, is very likely to respond. The probit constants all exceed 1.67,

---

6. The negative signs here are also indicative of the endogeneity problem I mention in the preceding note. If one's interest lies in how effective these techniques are, the appropriate dependent variable would be marginal gain in response. Furthermore, the persuasion letters and refusal conversions would have to be randomly assigned treatments, not treatments assigned on the basis of an initial refusal.

which corresponds to a 95 percent on the normal probability distribution.

The behavioral approach to the selection mechanism is to treat survey participation as a consequence of the context of the interview and the attributes of the respondent.

One version of such a behavioral approach employs the reasons for refusal or compliance offered by the respondents in the 1988 NES and the 1989 DAS. One may proceed from the factor loadings in the measurement portions of these models to generate indexes of the four relationships. Compliance (a dichotomous variable with 1 = response, 0 else) may be regressed on the four indexes in a probit model. Table 6.2 displays the probit coefficients for this model for the 1988 NES.

The coefficients for the probit selection equation based on the reasons for refusal or resistance are similar to the LISREL coefficients for the structural model in the two most important details. The coefficients on the respondent's relationship to the interview dominates the other coefficients: the probit coefficients on the relationship to the interview are nearly double those of the nearest coefficients. Secondly, the signs on the coefficients for relationship to the interview and to the interviewer are negative, as expected. (Note, however, that the coefficient on the respondent's relationship to self-image is not statistically distinguishable from zero.)

We don't escape the endogeneity problem with these measures of reasons for refusal or compliance. In the 1988 NES, the only respondents for which there are nonzero measures of these relationships are the refusals and reluctant respondents. These are the very same people who would have been sent a persuasion letter or a refusal converter. With the 1989 DAS, there is some improvement in that all refusals and respondents were asked (or at the least, marked for) reasons for compliance or refusal.

TABLE 6.2. Probit Estimates of "Behavioral" Selection Mechanism, 1988 NES

Rel. to Strangers	.174
Rel. to Interviewer	**−.561**
Rel. to Interview	**−.998**
Rel. to Self-Image	.034
(Constant)	1.719
% Correct	86

Dependent variable is "Response," where respondents are coded 1, and nonrespondents are coded 0. Cell entries are probit coefficients. **Boldfaced** coefficients are statistically significant at $p < .01$.

A partial escape from one version of the endogeneity problem would be to choose demographic measures as elements of a behavioral model of compliance. After all, the third chapter details patterns among those who are contactable and those who are amenable to participate by demographic categories. Table 6.3 displays the probit estimates for a demographic model of selection for the 1988 NES.

The probit make sense. Income is strongly associated with the probability of compliance, as is being black or Hispanic. Situations where the interviewer and respondent are of different races reduce the likelihood of compliance. These models also perform quite well, predicting 84 percent of the cases correctly.

However, we only partially elude the endogeneity problem. At one level, there is at least some interaction between availability of demographic information and likelihood of compliance. We have presumably better measures of age and income for the respondents to the study than for the nonrespondents, even on the basis of information supplied by others. In addition, information will not be available at all for some fraction of the "no contact" respondents. Worse, even if we were able to obtain demographic information about all the respondents and nonrespondents alike, the model may not prove all that useful to us. As the previous chapter explains, the selection model corrects for nonresponse bias as the first equation in a system of equations. The subsequent equations may well depend on the very independent demographic measures used in the selection model. Hence the system of equations becomes underidentified (or completely *un*identified if the overlap between independent variables is complete).

The researcher's choice of the appropriate selection equation will depend on the researcher's agenda. If the information about the nonre-

TABLE 6.3. Probit Estimates of "Demographic" Selection Mechanism, 1988 NES

R's Income	.088
Male?	.157
Hispanic?	.589
Black?	.544
White Respondent, Black Interviewer?	−.022
Black Respondent, White Interviewer?	−.522
(Constant)	.717
% Correct	84

Dependent variable is "Response" where respondents are coded 1, and nonrespondents are coded 0. Cell entries are probit coefficients. **Boldfaced** coefficients are statistically significant at $p < .01$.

spondents is available (demographic or about the survey itself), and does not affect the model of interest (i.e., the variables in the selection mechanism are not also properly part of the model of interest), the researcher would be on stronger grounds to prefer the behavioral models. However, most of the time, the researcher will not have information about the nonrespondents other than what was recorded during the course of administering the study, and the field administration model is preferable. (It is also easier to collect the field administration measures.) If the researcher plans to study the effects of demographic measures on social or political variables, then the field administration model is vastly preferable.[7]

Why not use a combination of all three? There are two answers. One answer is somewhat evangelical: the regressors in two of the selection models are relatively inexpensive to collect. As a matter of fact, most survey organizations collect the field administration measures as a matter of course. The second answer is treating these as three separate models permits a test of the robustness of the corrections. By approaching nonresponse three different ways, we can triangulate a better sense of the effect of the corrections. Armed with models for sample selection, the next task is to choose models to evaluate for the consequences of nonresponse.

Selecting Models for Evaluation

Now that we have a variety of models of sample selection, we are in a position to evaluate the effect of the Heckman and Achen corrections. There are two criteria for choosing the models to evaluate. First, the models should be a fair representation of the type of models that political scientists estimate with survey data. Secondly, the models should vary with respect to susceptibility to nonresponse bias. From the previous chapter, we know that nonresponse affects multivariate analyses differently depending on the relationship of the variables in the model of interest to the process of selection. And chapters 3 and 4 suggest that the process of selection into the sample is influenced by such factors as the respondent's level of interest and information, and political participativeness. We can use the information from chapters 3 and 4 to make informed hunches about whether or not a model might be susceptible to nonresponse. As a guide to determining whether or not the models might be affected by nonresponse, I use the structural model

---

7. The fits of the behavioral and field administration approaches are about the same in terms of the percent of cases correctly predicted.

in chapter 4: are any of the variables in the model of interest aspects of the respondent's relationship to strangers, interviewer, interview, or self-image?

Political scientists commonly estimate four broad classes of models with survey data: political participation, vote choice, candidate evaluation, and policy position. Of course, political scientists do not hold hegemony over uses of survey data. Since the data sets for which we have sufficient data on the nonrespondents with which to construct selection models are heavily oriented toward political science, we are somewhat constrained toward evaluating political science models. However, in an effort to be pan-disciplinary, this chapter also assays the effects of correction for nonresponse on a model of family income.

Models of *political participation* strive to explain such phenomena as why people vote, join in campaigns, work toward solving community problems, or contact government officials. As I discuss in the conclusion to chapter 3, there are good reasons to suspect that survey participation and political participation share common causes. Survey participation and political participation may both be influenced by the respondent's informedness and interest, or they may both be products of general social participation. Therefore, we might guess that turnout models will be affected by nonresponse. This chapter looks at two types of models of turnout in the general election: one based on demographic situation (Wolfinger and Rosenstone 1980). and one based on residency and mobility (Squire, Wolfinger, and Glass 1987).

Models of *vote choice* proliferate throughout the political science literature, explaining why people vote for particular presidential or congressional candidates. The dependent variable of these models—who one has decided to vote for—is unlikely to influence whether or not one agrees to be interviewed. However, some of the independent variables of these models may well influence survey participation. Some models rely on political information as part of the explanation for vote choice (e.g., Jacobson [1987]), and informedness appears to influence whether or not a sample person agrees to be interviewed. Some models of vote choice do not rely so much on levels of information. For example, models based on the respondent's assessment of economic conditions (e.g., Kinder and Kiewiet [1981]) or on negative voting (e.g., Fiorina and Shepsle [1989]) seem to have slim connections to the respondent's decision to comply: what does one's assessment of the economy or feelings toward political figures have to do with any of the four relationships?

Other political scientists estimate models of *candidate evaluation* to explore such problems as how a candidate's issue positions or ideology influence citizens' feelings about the candidate. Some models explaining how people evaluate political figures are based on ideology (e.g., Powell 1989). However, being able to identify a candidate's ideology requires political information (Zaller 1985). Further, the respondent's level of information is related to his or her responsiveness to the survey, and so we might expect that this model would be affected by nonresponse.

A fourth collection of models aspires to explain what influences people's *policy positions*. Unless the survey happens to be about the particular policy in question, one would not expect that one's position on policy matters would influence whether or not one would agree to participate in a survey.[8] In this chapter, I evaluate how nonresponse affects attitudes toward abortion.

Finally, in an effort to examine models outside of political science (unfortunately constrained to political science data sets), this chapter evaluates how models of family income may be affected by nonresponse. This chapter looks at how education and social position influence family income.

In all of the tables of corrections to follow, I display only the Administrative Selection Model (table 6.1). The tables displaying all the corrections using the Behavioral Selection Model (1988 NES only) and the Demographic Selection Model (1986 and 1988 NES) appear in appendix I. What I want to draw the reader's attention to is the pattern of changes in the coefficients, and a display of all the corrections distracts from this pattern. As the reader might notice, there is some variability to the estimated coefficients in the appendix, but with only a couple of exceptions, the pattern of changes (or no changes, as the case may be) holds throughout all three methods of correcting. The Demographic Selection Model is most likely to deviate from the other two corrections. This is for two reasons. For one, the Demographic Selection Model is not that good a predictor of compliance. Demographics are just not a very useful way to understand why certain people choose or refuse to participate. The second reason is that the demographic measures cause some of the models to become underidentified. In many of the models to follow, the demographic measures in the selection model rightly belong in the model of interest as well. I make note where exceptions arise and the selection models differ on whether or not an important change is taking place after correction for nonresponse.

---

8. Response rates to polls about campaign issues during an election may well be affected by respondents' interest in the issue. Pearl and Fairley (1985) found that respondents' attitudes toward a bill to change the drinking age affected their reluctance to participate in a survey about this bill.

Models of Political and Social Participation

Models of political participation are a good test of how survey nonresponse undercuts multivariate analyses. As I argue at the conclusion to chapter 3, there are some strong similarities between survey participation and political participation. People who are more interested in politics are more likely to participate in politics. As chapters 3 and 4 note, people who are interested in the survey are more likely to agree to be interviewed. Also, people who are more informed about politics are more likely to participate in politics. And chapter 3 demonstrates that people who more readily agree to be interviewed are better informed about politics than people who resist being interviewed.

The dependent variable in models of political participation may be strongly related to why people agree to be interviewed. From the simulations in chapter 5, we know that researchers should be most wary of nonresponse bias when the cases are censored by the level of the dependent variable. While political participation differs from survey participation in some important ways, the similarities between the two forms of participation warrant examination for the effects of nonresponse. In this section, I look at two variants of models of political participation: a model of turnout in the general election as a function of class, and a model of turnout in the general election as a function of residency.

Turnout and Demographics

Wolfinger and Rosenstone (1980) model turnout in the general election as a function of education, income, race, and age. The fundamental question they want to understand with this model is how different demographic attributes affect turnout. Poor people vote at lower rates than wealthier people, but is the lower turnout due to income, education, race, or what? Wolfinger and Rosenstone find that education is far and away the most important determinant of turnout.

With the 1986 and 1988 NES, we can replicate their approach to the problem.[9] The dependent variable is *Turnout,* where voters are coded 1 and nonvoters coded 0.[10] *Education* is a scale ranging from 0 to 1,

---

9. Wolfinger and Rosenstone use the CPS data collections, with response rates nearing 95 percent and 50 times as many respondents as for the NES data. They also estimate probit models instead of the generalized least squares approach used here.
10. This is using the so-called validated vote measure, where in a separate follow-up study to the interview itself NES interviewers verified whether or not the respondent had voted via administrative records.

where the points on the scale refer to the highest degree received by the respondent. (Full coding of this and other measures for the models in this chapter appear in Appendix H. In all the models of this chapter, I use the original authors' codings of the variables.) *Age* is measured in years. *Black* and *Hispanic* are dummy variables denoting whether the respondent is black or of Hispanic origin. *Income* is the NES 22-point scale for the respondent's family income (or respondent's income, if the respondent lives alone). Table 6.4 displays the uncorrected and corrected estimates for this model.

The uncorrected estimates replicate Wolfinger and Rosenstone's findings. The respondent's level of education is far and away the most important determinant of whether or not the respondent votes in the general election. There are weak, positive relationships between age, income, and probability of turnout. Whether or not the respondent is black or Hispanic appears not to be a statistically significant cause of turnout. In 1988, education is the only statistically significant predictor of turnout.

Upon correcting for nonresponse, two features emerge. The effect of education on the likelihood of turnout increases after correction for nonresponse, and this effect holds for all three corrections in 1986 and 1988 (see table 6.4 in appendix I). While the magnitude of the change is relatively slight, the pattern of the change is consistent with a hypothesis

TABLE 6.4. Turnout in the General Election as a Function of Demographics, Uncorrected and Corrected Estimates, 1986 and 1988 NES

	1986 NES		1988 NES	
	Uncorr. (GLS)	Corr. (Nonlin.)	Uncorr. (GLS)	Corr. (Nonlin.)
Education	**.470**	**.500**	**.710**	**.820**
	(.06)	(.06)	(.09)	(.10)
Age	**.020**	**.020**	.010	.010
	(.001)	(.001)	(.001)	(.001)
Black	.010	−.010	−.070	−.070
	(.03)	(.04)	(.04)	(.04)
Hispanic	−.050	−.070	.020	.030
	(.04)	(.04)	(.11)	(.11)
Income	**.007**	**.008**	.001	.001
	(.002)	(.002)	(.001)	(.001)
(Constant)	**−.510**	**−.590**	**−.220**	**−.340**
	(.07)	(.07)	(.06)	(.08)
$\rho\sigma$		−.470		−.010
		(.26)		(.35)

Boldfaced entries are statistically significant at $p < .05$. The dependent variable is *Turnout*, where voters are coded 1, and nonvoters are coded 0. Standard errors are entered in parentheses below coefficients.

that survey nonresponse is, to some degree, censoring upon the dependent variable measuring participation. From Tobin's model, explicated in chapter 5, we would expect to see some attenuation of the regression coefficients, as we do here. Substantively, the meaning of these changes is that we underestimate the importance of education on participation because we oversample from more participative people.

The most significant change takes place in the constant term for both the 1986 and 1988 NES. The constant term becomes more negative in both cases, from $-.51$ to $-.59$ in 1986, and from $-.22$ to $-.34$ in 1988. This change means that we overestimate a respondent's likelihood of turnout if we do not correct for nonresponse. This is indirect evidence that these surveys with significant levels of nonresponse oversample voters *even after validating their voting*, and that survey nonresponse is a cause of the pervasive overestimates of turnout in survey research.[11]

A more direct way of gauging the extent to which these surveys overestimate turnout due to nonresponse is to compare predicted probabilities of participation in the uncorrected and corrected models. If we treat a predicted probability of turnout of 50 percent as a cutoff threshold for likely turnout, we may then compare the predicted turnout rates. Using the uncorrected model in 1986, we would estimate that 66.8 percent of the population would turn out in the election. Using the estimates for the field administration correction for 1986 (those printed in table 6.4 in the second column), we obtain a 48 percent turnout rate, a difference of nearly 18 percent. (We would obtain similar differences for the other corrections, and for 1988.) We have long known that surveys overestimate turnout, and these results demonstrate that survey nonresponse is one of the significant causes of those overestimates.

Lastly, one might be tempted to draw some provisional interpretations of the estimates for the coefficient on $\rho\sigma$ under the three different corrections for the two years (see tables I.1 and I.2 for the full estimates). One might first be struck by the considerable variability in the estimates for the magnitude of $\rho\sigma$ across the different corrections. Recall that this coefficient represents the estimate of the correlation between the error terms in the outcome and selection models. Since the regressors for the selection equations all differ, it should not startle the reader to note that the estimates of $\rho\sigma$ all differ. The reader might also note that the estimates of $\rho\sigma$ don't usually attain statistical significance. This is also not out of the ordinary for this family of corrections; indeed, the equivalent coefficients for the models evaluated by Heckman (1976, 1979) and

---

11. DeNardo (1989) makes a similar point with respect to the "surge and decline" hypothesis, that the National Election Studies oversamples core voters.

Achen (1986) don't attain conventional levels of statistical significance either. The key to evaluating the corrections lies in the substantive coefficients of the model.

Turnout and Residency

Whether or not one votes in the general election is surely a function of more than mere demographic traits. One's connection to the community, one's level of partisanship, one's interest in the election, and the registration requirements of one's community are examples of other plausible factors that influence turnout. Squire, Wolfinger, and Glass (1987) estimate a model of turnout in the general election as a function of residential mobility.

According to Squire, Wolfinger, and Glass, one-third of all adults move every two years. Every time that one moves, one must reregister. Turnout among people who have moved is as low as that of groups with traditionally low turnout (e.g., young people or people with low levels of education). Moving impedes voting.

We can replicate the model estimated by Squire, Wolfinger, and Glass with the 1986 and 1988 NES.[12] The dependent variable is *Turnout*, again using the validated voting measure, with voters coded 1 and nonvoters coded 0. *Closing Date* represents the number of days between election day and when a voter must be registered. *Age* is the respondent's age in years. *Income* is the 22-category NES scale. *Own Home?* is a dummy variable, where home owners are coded 1 and renters are coded 0. *Married?* is a dummy variable, where married respondents are coded 1, unmarried respondents coded 0. *Political Interest* is a scale measuring how much attention the respondent pays to politics, ranging from 1 (hardly at all) to 4 (most of the time). *Public Officials Care?* is a dummy variable, where respondents who believe public officials care what the respondents think are coded 1, others coded 0. Finally, *Years at Address* measures the number of years that the respondent has lived at the current address.

Table 6.5 shows the uncorrected and corrected estimates of the Squire, Wolfinger, and Glass model of turnout. The uncorrected estimates replicate the main point of the original model: mobility impedes turnout. The coefficient on the number of years the respondent has lived at that address is positive and statistically significant. Although

---

12. As with the Wolfinger and Rosenstone model, Squire, Wolfinger, and Glass estimate a probit model of turnout. There is little harm done to their model by estimating with generalized least squares.

the number itself may look small, the results from both 1986 and 1988 suggest that the respondent's chances of voting increase by 1 percent for every year the respondent stays at the same address.

One can tease some further interesting observations from this replication of the Squire, Wolfinger, and Glass model. Other demographic variables associated with an enduring residency in a community contribute positively toward turnout. The signs on the coefficients for age, income, owning a home, and being married are all positive and, in most cases, statistically distinguishable from zero. Political interest is substantively one of the strongest coefficients in the two models. A unit increase (on a scale of 4 points) in interest meant approximately a 10 percent increase in the respondent's probability of voting in the general election. The signs on the coefficient for the *Public Officials Care?* variable cross over the two years but, for the uncorrected estimates, are not statistically significant.

We might have expected to see changes to the corrected estimates

TABLE 6.5. Turnout in the General Election as a Function of Residency, Uncorrected and Corrected Estimates, 1986 and 1988 NES

	1986 NES		1988 NES	
	Uncorr. (GLS)	Corr. (Nonlin.)	Uncorr. (GLS)	Corr. (Nonlin.)
Closing Date	−.03	−.05	−.004	−.004
	(.02)	(.02)	(.001)	(.001)
Age	.04	.01	.003	.004
	(.02)	(.02)	(.0007)	(.004)
Income	.09	.01	.01	.01
	(.03)	(.03)	(.02)	(.02)
Own Home?	.001	.08	.08	.07
	(.001)	(.02)	(.03)	(.05)
Married?	.01	.03	.04	.03
	(.001)	(.01)	(.03)	(.09)
Public Officials Care?	−.03	−.05	.02	.04
	(.02)	(.02)	(.02)	(.02)
Political Interest	.11	.11	.09	.09
	(.01)	(.01)	(.008)	(.01)
Years at Address	.01	.01	.01	.01
	(.001)	(.001)	(.003)	(.007)
(Constant)	−.17	−.29	.03	−.05
	(.04)	(.05)	(.05)	(.05)
$\rho\sigma$		.17		−.13
		(.08)		(.32)

Boldfaced entries are statistically significant at $p < .05$. The dependent variable is *Turnout*, where voters are coded 1, and nonvoters are coded 0. Standard errors are entered in parentheses below coefficients.

that replicate table 6.4. The coefficient on *Income* in table 6.4 rose slightly after correction; here, that same coefficient either becomes smaller (as it does in 1986), or it holds steady. And if *Political Interest* is related to nonresponse, we should be surprised that the coefficient on political interest is unchanged after correction for nonresponse.

The most important change takes place, again, in the constant term. The constant term drops for both the 1986 and 1988 data after correcting for nonresponse. As I argued in the preceding text, this change is evidence that the NES oversamples voters as a consequence of nonresponse, which leads to an overestimate of the rate of turnout in the general population.

The effect of correction for nonresponse on these models of turnout is small, but substantively very significant. The consistent pattern is that nonresponse causes an overestimate of the constant term in models of turnout. This may seem to some readers as though the main effect of the correction comes in the least interesting coefficient. The change in that least interesting coefficient is meaningful but subtle—direct evidence of nonresponse as a cause of overestimates of turnout pervasive in survey research. Some of the models to follow display much more pronounced nonresponse bias.

Models of Voting

From November 1948 onward, one of the major objectives of the NES study was to "illuminate some of the perplexities of the presidential vote" (American National Election Studies 1948, i). It would be a monumental task to determine how much survey nonresponse affects the breadth of voting models, but it is possible to review the effects of nonresponse on some models that reflect some of the important work in the discipline. Specifically, in this section I examine how nonresponse affects regression estimates of voting models based on *economic circumstance, political information*, and *negative voting*.

Sociotropic Voting

Kinder and Kiewiet's 1981 article in the *British Journal of Political Science* contrasts pocketbook voting with sociotropic voting. They question whether people vote on the basis of their own economic situation (pocketbook voting), or on the basis of perceptions of the state of the national economy (sociotropic voting). They find that the national considerations overwhelm personal circumstances as a predictor of votes.

None of the variables in the sociotropic model need have anything to do with survey nonresponse. The dependent variable—who one votes for—seems wholly unrelated to compliance. The respondent's assessment of the national economy seems also unrelated. Perhaps it is possible that the respondent's sense of his or her own financial position would affect the respondent's attitude toward others or to self-image, but even this link seems dim. By the simulations in chapter 5, one would *not* expect that the regression estimates of the sociotropic model would change after correction for nonresponse.

We can replicate Kinder and Kiewiet's model with the 1986 and 1988 NES. The dependent variable is *Vote for Congress*, with those voting for the Republican coded 1, and those voting for the Democrat coded 0. There are two measures for the pocketbook aspects of voting: *Dissatisfaction with Income*, where respondents who are better off financially are coded 1 and respondents who are worse off coded −1; and *Unemployment Experiences*, a scale from +4 for those currently working and never unemployed over the past year to −5 for those currently unemployed and never working over the past year. There are four measures of sociotropic aspects of voting: *Business Conditions*, reflecting whether respondents felt that business conditions were better (+1) or worse (−1) over the past year; *Government Performance*, coded +1 if the respondent thought the federal government's policies improved the economy, −1 if the policies made things worse; *Unemployment as National Problem* and *Inflation as National Problem* coded 1 if the respondent mentioned unemployment or inflation as one of the nation's most important problems. There is also a variable controlling for *Party Identification* coded +1 for Republicans and −1 for Democrats.

Table 6.6 reproduces Kinder and Kiewiet's key findings for both 1986 and 1988: the coefficients on personal economic experience are miniscule, while the coefficients on national economic assessments are substantial. The measure for pocketbook voting (Dissatisfaction with Income and Unemployment Experiences) are substantively slight and indistinguishable from zero statistically. The coefficients for the measures of sociotropic voting (Unemployment and Inflation as National Problems) are substantively sizable, particularly for 1986. Respondents who viewed unemployment as the most important national problem were 31 percent less likely to vote for Republican house candidates than those who did not.

Upon correction for nonresponse, the point estimates of the coefficients don't change all that much. The constant term changes only slightly, even though that term is still susceptible to selection bias when selection is not related to the model of interest. And although the small changes to the coefficients on class in the turnout model exhibited a pattern, there isn't a clear pattern in the small changes here.

This is reassuring, and not just to Kinder and Kiewiet. At the outset, I conjectured that the corrections would not affect the sociotropic model since neither independent nor dependent variables in the model were related to nonresponse. While my predictions are not all successful in the models to follow, that this prediction stood bodes well for the approach of comparing corrected and uncorrected estimates.

Information and Voting

An alternate approach to understanding why people vote for particular candidates looks to the voter's level of information. Does what one knows about candidates influence one's vote? Most observers of elections know that incumbents hold an advantage over challengers in elections to the House of Representatives: few challengers succeed and most incumbents are re-elected. One of the recurring explanations for

TABLE 6.6. Vote for Congress as a Function of Personal and National Economic Assessments, Uncorrected and Corrected Estimates, 1986 and 1988 NES

	1986 NES		1988 NES	
	Uncorr. (GLS)	Corr. (Nonlin.)	Uncorr. (GLS)	Corr. (Nonlin.)
Dissatisfaction with Income	.03	.02	−.01	−.02
	(.03)	(.03)	(.02)	(.02)
Unemployment Experiences	.01	.01	.01	.01
	(.01)	(.01)	(.01)	(.01)
Business Conditions	.001	.02	−.01	−.01
	(.02)	(.02)	(.02)	(.02)
Government Performance	−.01	−.01	.01	.01
	(.02)	(.02)	(.01)	(.01)
Unemployment as National Problem	−.31	−.35	.02	.03
	(.05)	(.05)	(.05)	(.05)
Inflation as National Problem	.14	.12	−.08	−.11
	(.10)	(.10)	(.06)	(.09)
Party Identification	**.24**	**.24**	**.27**	**.28**
	(.02)	(.02)	(.02)	(.02)
(Constant)	**.40**	**.39**	**.39**	**.39**
	(.04)	(.04)	(.03)	(.03)
$\rho\sigma$		.33		−.65
		(.64)		(.53)

Boldfaced entries are statistically significant at $p < .05$. Dependent variable is *Vote for Congress*, where vote for the Democrat is coded 0, vote for the Republican is coded 1, nonvoters missing. Standard errors are entered in parentheses below coefficients.

the incumbent's advantage in successive elections is that the incumbent enjoys better name recognition and identification than the challenger. After all, the incumbent has been in the limelight (such as it is, for a member of the House) for the past two years, while a challenger must introduce his or her name to the public.

Information-based models of voting may very well suffer from nonresponse bias. As chapter 3 shows, respondents appear to be better informed about politics and more attentive to politics than nonrespondents. While the dependent variable—who one votes for—is probably not related to sample selection, information as an independent variable may very well be related to why some respondents comply and others refuse.[13]

Jacobson (1987) uses a series of models to illustrate how incumbency, information, and affect interact. In the first of several models, Jacobson simply looks at the vote for the House candidate as a function of party identification and incumbency. The dependent variable, *Vote for Congress,* is a dummy variable coded 1 if the respondent voted for the Democratic candidate, and coded 0 if the respondent voted for the Republican candidate. (Nonvoters are discarded from the analysis.) *Party Identification* is the NES scale coded from −1 for strong Republicans to +1 for strong Democrats, with independents coded 0. Jacobson also includes two dummy variables for incumbency: *Democratic Incumbent* and *Republican Incumbent* coded 1 if the incumbent is of the respective party, 0 otherwise. (The omitted category is the situation in which no incumbent is running.) The GLS results from this model, estimated for the 1986 and 1988 NES, along with the corrections, appear in table 6.7.

The uncorrected estimates duplicate Jacobson's findings. This simple model demonstrates that incumbency substantially affects election outcomes when one doesn't account for alternate explanations. Respondents voting in districts with Republican incumbents were 27 percent and 42 percent more likely to vote for the Republican candidate in 1986 and 1988, respectively. Respondents voting in districts with Democratic incumbents were 24 percent and 12 percent more likely to vote for the Democratic candidate in 1986 and 1988. In this simplest of Jacobson's models, incumbency appears to have a significant effect on voting for congressional candidates.

Note that the corrections for nonresponse don't do much to the models either. No coefficient changes by more than .01, and many are

---

13. However, we should recall from the residency-based model of turnout that changes to information-related variables are not definite. *Political Interest* in that model did not change appreciably in either 1986 or 1988.

identical. At this level, nonresponse doesn't appear to affect this voting model.

Jacobson pushes the analysis further, in order to demonstrate how incumbency reflects both name recognition, affect toward the candidate, and contacts with the candidates. In fact, Jacobson demonstrates his points with four further models. While I do not persist in examining effects of nonresponse for each of his successive models, I do want to show what happens with just a minor change to the first model. (Similar effects persist in models three through five.) If one adds a simple scale measuring the respondent's level of recall/recognition of the candidates, one has a very simple illustration of information and voting. The scales, *Familiarity with Democrat* and *Familiarity with Republican,* are coded 1 if the respondent recalled the name of the respective candidate, .5 if the respondent could recognize the name of the candidate from a list, and 0 if the respondent could not recognize the name of the candidate. Adding these two variables to the first model and re-estimating the uncorrected and corrected coefficients yields table 6.8.

Unlike the earlier model, there are important changes to the coefficients when one corrects for nonresponse. Specifically, the uncorrected models significantly *underestimate* the importance of political information. The coefficients on familiarity with the Democrat or Republican *double* on correction for nonresponse, in both the 1986 and 1988 NES. This makes sense, especially in the context of the difference in levels of

TABLE 6.7. Vote for Congress as a Function of Incumbency and Party Identification, Uncorrected and Corrected Estimates, 1986 and 1988 NES

	1986 NES		1988 NES	
	Uncorr. (GLS)	Corr. (Nonlin.)	Uncorr. (GLS)	Corr. (Nonlin.)
Party ID	**.14**	**.15**	**.16**	**.17**
	(.05)	(.05)	(.04)	(.04)
Rep. Incumbent	**−.27**	**−.27**	**−.42**	**−.42**
	(.06)	(.06)	(.06)	(.06)
Dem. Incumbent	**.24**	**.25**	**.12**	**.12**
	(.05)	(.07)	(.06)	(.06)
(Constant)	**.59**	**.58**	**.70**	**.69**
	(.07)	(.10)	(.07)	(.07)
$\rho\sigma$		.18		.10
		(.47)		(.66)

Boldfaced entries are statistically significant at $p < .05$. Dependent variable is *Vote for Congress,* where vote for the Democrat is coded 1, vote for the Republican is coded 0, nonvoters missing. Standard errors are entered in parentheses below coefficients.

information about the candidates displayed in table 3.11. Recall that the amenable respondents could recall the name of the incumbent representative at a rate many times that of the reluctant respondents. By including only the most informed respondents, the effect of nonresponse on models using political information is to underestimate the importance of information.

This second table demonstrates a pitfall of nonresponse bias. With one specification of the problem, nonresponse may not affect your results. The first model, including only the incumbency dummy variables and Party Identification, changed only slightly on correction for nonresponse. But when the specification changes, nonresponse may significantly alter your conclusions. Just the addition of the two information variables— variables closely related to the process of survey participation—brought nonresponse effects into these very simple models.

Negative Voting

One persistent piece of political folklore is that voters weigh negatives about candidates heavier than positives. Fiorina and Shepsle (1989)

TABLE 6.8. Vote for Congress as a Function of Incumbency, Party Identification, and Familiarity with the Candidates, Uncorrected and Corrected Estimates, 1986 and 1988 NES

	1986 NES		1988 NES	
	Uncorr. (GLS)	Corr. (Nonlin.)	Uncorr. (GLS)	Corr. (Nonlin.)
Party ID	.10	.14	.12	.16
	(.04)	(.04)	(.04)	(.04)
Rep. Incumbent	−.22	−.19	−.41	−.35
	(.06)	(.05)	(.05)	(.06)
Dem. Incumbent	.15	.14	.03	.04
	(.05)	(.07)	(.04)	(.06)
Familiar w/ Dem.	.15	.33	.09	.24
	(.03)	(.05)	(.03)	(.04)
Familiar w/ Rep.	−.13	−.24	−.13	−.26
	(.04)	(.05)	(.03)	(.05)
(Constant)	.61	.51	.77	.67
	(.07)	(.07)	(.05)	(.07)
$\rho\sigma$		.83		1.33
		(.43)		(.78)

Boldfaced entries are statistically significant at $p < .05$. Dependent variable is *Vote for Congress*, where vote for the Democrat is coded 1, vote for the Republican is coded 0, nonvoters missing. Standard errors are entered in parentheses below coefficients.

challenge this observation, claiming that negative voting is an artifact resulting from the disproportionate number of supporters that an incumbent must have in comparison to the challenger. They operationalize negative voting as those voters who disapprove of an incumbent's performance. Negative voting occurs among the incumbent's supporters (people who would have voted for the candidate otherwise), while positive voting occurs among the challenger's supporters.

Fiorina and Shepsle prove their points with the creative combination of a formal model delineating a principal-agent view of negative voting with a regression analysis of two election studies' data sets. The principal independent variables in the three variants of their models are dummy variables denoting whether the respondent is of the *same* party *identification* as the candidate, *different identification;* and whether the respondent *approves* or *disapproves* of the incumbent and of the president's performance. They alter the dependent variable in three ways: a vote for or against the incumbent House candidate, a vote for or against the Republican House candidate, and a vote for or against the Republican, restricting the analysis to Republican party identifiers. They demonstrate that what appears to be negative voting in the first model against the incumbent disappears when one takes into account the party of the candidate and the voter. I reproduce only the first of their three models to demonstrate that negative voting is exaggerated in the uncorrected models.

None of the variables in their analysis are implicated in the respondent's decision to participate in the survey. The vote for the candidates, party identification, and approval or disapproval are divorced from all of the four survey relationships. By the results in the simulation in chapter 5, we would not expect that the coefficients would change upon correction for nonresponse.

Table 6.9 displays the first of their three analyses exploring negative voting. The coefficient *Disapprove Incumbent* represents negative voting. In both 1986 and 1988, the effect of negative voting is substantial—a respondent who disapproved of the incumbent's performance would be 44 percent less likely to vote for the incumbent in 1986 and 28 percent less likely in 1988. Also, notice that the effect of negative voting is larger than the effect of positive voting (the coefficient on *Approve Incumbent*), although this difference is much more pronounced in 1986 than in 1988. There is a small change to the size of the negative voting effect after correction for nonresponse: in both 1986 and 1988, the effect of negative

TABLE 6.9. Vote for Incumbent House Candidate and Approval, Uncorrected and Corrected Estimates, 1986 and 1988 NES

	1986 NES		1988 NES	
	Uncorr. (GLS)	Corr. (Nonlin.)	Uncorr. (GLS)	Corr. (Nonlin.)
Same Party ID	**.10**	**.10**	**.11**	**.14**
	(.05)	(.04)	(.04)	(.04)
Different Party ID	**−.16**	**−.18**	**−.22**	**−.24**
	(.06)	(.05)	(.05)	(.04)
Approve Incumbent	**.17**	**.20**	**.18**	**.22**
	(.04)	(.03)	(.03)	(.04)
Disapprove Incumbent	**−.44**	**−.40**	**−.28**	**−.23**
	(.06)	(.04)	(.06)	(.03)
(Constant)	**.72**	**.71**	**.70**	**.64**
	(.06)	(.05)	(.05)	(.05)
$\rho\sigma$		.11		1.04
		(.39)		(.60)

Boldfaced entries are statistically significant at $p < .05$. Dependent variable is *Vote for Incumbent*, where vote for the incumbent is coded 1, vote for the challenger is coded 0, nonvoters missing. Standard errors are entered in parentheses below coefficients.

voting drops by 4–5 percent, suggesting that nonresponse causes surveys to overestimate the importance of negative voting.[14]

Despite my predictions that nonresponse bias would *not* affect the negative voting models, nonresponse bias caused an overestimate of the significance of negative voting (disapproval). This finding enhances Fiorina and Shepsle's conclusion that there is no generalized negative voting effect.

One plausible story behind this effect is that respondents who are incensed at the incumbent are more motivated to participate in surveys. Angry respondents are probably both more attentive and informed than most respondents. They not only know their representative but they also know something about that representative that they dislike. Perhaps these respondents jump at the opportunity to vent political spleen by participating in the survey.

The alternate story is that selection is indeed unrelated to the variables, but that the pattern here simply emerges from chance inconsistency. After all, the previous chapter does demonstrate that multivariate estimates are affected by nonresponse bias even if the variables in the equation of interest are unrelated to selection. But given that there is a

---

14. The alternate selection models suggest the effect is more extreme: approval is larger and disapproval is smaller than even the corrected estimates reported here.

consistent pattern here, something more systematic appears to be taking place.

As the familiarity and negative voting models demonstrate, nonresponse sometimes affects estimates of voting models. Given the importance of voting models in political science, these changes alone suggest that the NES is on the right track by collecting information about nonrespondents and applying sometimes extraordinary efforts to convert refusals.

Models of Candidate Evaluation

Political scientists frequently examine another class of models with survey data: models explaining how people evaluate political figures. What determines whether a respondent feels positively or negatively toward a candidate? What determines whether or not a respondent has any information about the candidate and his or her political positions? In this section, I examine two models of candidate evaluation, one based on the policy preferences of respondents and candidates, and another explaining the respondent's information about the incumbent candidate's votes in Congress.

Issue Position and Candidate Evaluation

Rabinowitz and MacDonald (1989) contrast two models of candidate evaluation based on the respondent's and the candidate's policy positions. One model is *spatial*—respondents prefer candidates who are "closest" to themselves in a hypothetical space charting policy positions. Downs (1957) popularized this model, and it has been extensively used over the years. The second model is *directional*—Rabinowitz and MacDonald argue that people see policy matters in a more diffuse sense than the spatial model assumes, and that people prefer candidates on the basis of a *direction* of policy-making.

Directional Distance inflates positions far from one's own. In the spatial model, the distance between the respondent and the candidate is the average distance over several issue scales. Spatial Distance is calculated as the mean over n issues:

$$\text{Spatial distance} = 1/n \sum_{i=1}^{n} \text{candidate's position}_i$$
$$-\text{respondent's position}_i \qquad (6.1)$$

In the directional model, the distance between the respondent and the candidate reflects how far both are from a neutral position. The directional distance is calculated as:

$$\text{Directional distance} = \sum_{i=1}^{n}(\text{candidate's position}_i$$
$$-\text{neutral position}_i)$$
$$\times\,(\text{respondent's position}_i$$
$$-\text{neutral position}_i) \tag{6.2}$$

For example, suppose that on defense policy, the respondent is very conservative (score of 1), the Republican is neutral (4), and the Democrat is very liberal (7). If defense policy were the only issue that mattered, then the spatial distances would be 3 (to the Republican) and 6 (to the Democrat), while the directional distances would be 2.75 (to the Republican) and 9 (to the Democrat). It matters more to the directional-evaluating respondent that the Democrat is very different than that the Republican is neutral.

The dependent variable in the two models is the respondent's "feeling thermometer" evaluation of Reagan. (A respondent who feels very positively toward Reagan would rate him at 100 degrees, while a respondent who feels neutral toward Reagan would rate him at 50 degrees.) There are three issues in the 1986 NES where the respondent placed both Reagan's position and his or her own position: defense spending, Central American policy, and government spending. In 1988, the issues included defense spending, government services, cooperation with the USSR, a guaranteed standard of living, improving the status of blacks, and improving the status of minorities. Using the preceding formulas (6.1, 6.2), we can calculate the spatial and directional distance between the respondent and Reagan. Rabinowitz and MacDonald add three controlling variables. *Party Identification* ranges from 0 for strong Democrats to 6 for strong Republicans. *Black* and *South* are dummy variables denoting whether or not the respondent is black or from the South.

Neither the dependent variable (affect toward Reagan) nor any of the independent variables seems to be related to why people participate in surveys. While it might be possible that respondents who feel more extremely about Reagan would more gladly welcome the opportunity to present their views, this seems even less plausible than the direct questions of disapproval in the previous section (Fiorina and Shepsle's

TABLE 6.10. Evaluation of Reagan as a Function of Issue Proximity, Spatial and Distance Calculations, Uncorrected and Corrected Estimates, 1986 and 1988 NES

	1986 NES		1988 NES	
	Uncorr. (GLS)	Corr. (Achen)	Uncorr. (GLS)	Corr. (Achen)
Spatial Model				
Proximity to Reagan	**.32**	**.32**	**.30**	**.30**
Party ID	**.36**	**.36**	**.49**	**−.47**
Black	**−.14**	**−.14**	−.05	−.05
South	.09	.08	.15	.15
(Constant)	0	0	0	0
$\rho\sigma$		−.005		.03
Directional Model				
Distance from Reagan	**−.35**	**−.35**	**−.30**	**−.30**
Party ID	**.22**	**.33**	**.44**	**.44**
Black	**−.13**	**−.11**	−.05	−.05
South	.06	.06	.15	.15
(Constant)	0	0	0	0
$\rho\sigma$		−.01		.03

Boldfaced entries are statistically significant at $p < .05$. Dependent variable is *the respondent's feeling thermometer score for Ronald Reagan*. Cell entries are the *standardized* regression coefficients.

model). Consequently, we should not expect to see significant change to any of the estimated coefficients after correction for nonresponse.

Table 6.10 presents a regression of affect toward Reagan on the issue distance and controlling variables, using both a spatial and directional issue distance calculation.[15] While Rabinowitz and MacDonald claim that the directional distance model is clearly superior to the spatial model, that is not so apparent. In 1986, to be sure, the effect of directional distance *is* larger than the effect of spatial distance (the standardized coefficients are larger), but in 1988, the coefficients are exactly the same.[16]

There is virtually no difference to any of the coefficients in either of Rabinowitz and MacDonald's models after correction for nonresponse.[17] As I anticipated at the outset, these models of candidate evaluation do not appear to be affected by survey nonresponse.

---

15. Rabinowitz and MacDonald use standardized regression coefficients, which are what I report in this table.

16. Rabinowitz and MacDonald employ the two different calculations on a wide range of candidates, and perhaps their findings would be replicated for 1988 for a choice of different candidates.

17. The correction based on the demographic selection mechanism for both 1986 and 1988 suggests that proximate and directional distances are underestimated.

Information about Ideology

Models of candidate evaluation implicitly assume that the respondent has some information about the candidate. After all, if one is to calculate the distance between oneself and Ronald Reagan, one needs to know where Reagan resides. However, the overwhelming evidence is that most respondents operate on the basis of very little political information. Powell (1989) explores who is likely to "guess" about a candidate's ideology or issue positions.

I operationalize the dependent variable in Powell's model as whether or not the respondent had to guess about the candidate's voting record. Respondents who admit not knowing the candidate's voting record are coded 1, 0 otherwise. The independent variables are a series of dummy variables for demographics. Education is measured as three dummies depending on the respondent's highest level of education: *Less Than High School, High School,* and *Some College* (respondents with a college degree are the omitted category). The respondent's age is categorized as *Less than 30* or *Greater Than or Equal to 65.* The respondent's residency is categorized as *Less than 5 years* or *6 to 10 years.* There is also a dummy variable for sex, with men coded 1, women coded 0.

The dependent variable in this model—knowledge about the representative's voting record—may very well be related to survey nonresponse. Knowledge about the representative's votes is a measure of political informedness, and chapter 3 suggests that better informed respondents are more likely to participate than less informed respondents. Consequently, we should expect to see some changes to the estimated coefficients after correction for nonresponse.

Table 6.11 displays the model estimated for 1986 and 1988. The uncorrected estimates for 1986 reproduces Powell's original findings (albeit with respect to admitting not knowing about the representative's votes, instead of admitting guessing on the liberalism-conservatism scale). Note the mildly curvilinear relationship with respect to the education dummies for 1986. Respondents who had less than a high school education and those with a high school diploma were roughly equal in their probability of not knowing their representative's votes (38–39 percent increase). The same curvilinear relationship does *not* occur in 1988. Upon correction for nonresponse, the relationship is no longer curvilinear: with increasing education, respondents are less likely to admit not knowing the representative's votes. This makes sense: why should respondents with better education be equally likely to be unfamiliar with their representative's record or (more telling) be willing to admit as much?

There is a second point about the changes in levels of education: nonresponse obscured functional form in the 1986 NES (but not in the 1988 NES). Before correction for nonresponse, respondents with high school degrees were as likely as respondents with less than a high school education to claim not to know about the representative. After correction, respondents with a high school education were significantly less likely (by 11 percent) to claim ignorance than the respondents without a high school education. What appears to be a flat relationship between education and political information in the 1986 NES appears monotonically positive after correction for nonresponse.

There are a few other differences between the pattern we see in table 6.11 and Powell's original results. Older respondents, in the uncorrected results, would be *more* likely to admit unfamiliarity with the representative's voting record than middle-aged respondents. For the

TABLE 6.11. Lack of Knowledge of Representative's Votes as a Function of Demographics, Uncorrected and Corrected Estimates, 1986 and 1988 NES

	1986 NES		1988 NES	
	Uncorr. (GLS)	Corr. (Nonlin.)	Uncorr. (GLS)	Corr. (Nonlin.)
< High School	**.38**	**.42**	**.15**	**.19**
	(.02)	(.03)	(.03)	(.04)
High School	**.39**	**.31**	**.12**	**.12**
	(.02)	(.02)	(.03)	(.03)
Some College	**.32**	**.24**	**.06**	**.05**
	(.02)	(.03)	(.03)	(.02)
Male	−.05	−.04	**−.12**	**−.14**
	(.02)	(.02)	(.02)	(.02)
Age < 30	**.17**	**.23**	**.08**	**.09**
	(.02)	(.02)	(.02)	(.03)
Age ≥ 65	.08	.03	−.06	−.07
	(.03)	(.03)	(.03)	(.03)
Resident < 5 Years	**.27**	**.31**	**.17**	**.19**
	(.02)	(.02)	(.03)	(.04)
Resident 6–10 Years	**.19**	**.17**	.06	.06
	(.02)	(.02)	(.04)	(.04)
(Constant)	**.09**	**.10**	**.04**	**.06**
	(.01)	(.01)	(.01)	(.01)
$\rho\sigma$		1.43		.42
		(.26)		(.24)

Boldfaced entries are statistically significant at $p < .05$. Dependent variable is *Don't Know about the Representative's Votes* where respondents who admit not knowing about their representative's votes are coded 1, others coded 0. Standard errors are entered in parentheses below coefficients.

elderly in her original results, Powell notes a sharp decrease in the likelihood of guessing about the representative's position. Upon correction for nonresponse, the coefficients for 1986 become indistinguishable from zero; while not confirming her original findings, the corrected results do not dispute them. Powell's original article does not find much of an effect of the respondent's residency on familiarity with the representative; here, both the uncorrected and corrected estimates for 1986 show modest effects.

Models of Policy Position

The fourth class of models I evaluate in this chapter for nonresponse bias are models explaining respondents' policy position. Although not as prolific as models of voting, models explaining the bases of policy position abound. Furthermore, considering the importance of polling in the identification of the political agenda, we should be especially concerned about the potential for nonresponse bias in models of policy position. In this section, I look at a model examining attitudes toward abortion.

Abortion

Abortion is probably the single most divisive issue of our time, and public opinion polls figure prominently in the debate. This issue tests whether or not nonresponse affects political debate. One of the curiosities of surveys on public opposition to abortion is that blacks disproportionately disapprove of abortion compared with whites, even after one controls for socioeconomic status and region.

Hall and Ferree (1986) examine Combs and Welch's earlier (1982) finding that blacks are more opposed to abortion than whites. They demonstrate that black respondents are more likely to oppose abortion even after one controls for socioeconomic status, religion, and attitudes toward sex. In their models, they use the GSS tests on whether or not abortion should be permitted in any of six different circumstances, treating the different circumstances as part of an additive scale. Since the data sets for which we have selection mechanisms are the 1986 and 1988 NES, and since the NES uses a different measure for attitudes toward abortion, we must vary the structure of their model (table 6.12).

The dependent variable in this variation on Hall and Ferree's model is whether the respondent believes that abortion should never be permitted (coded 1) or otherwise (coded 0). We can regress the dichotomy on a variety of measures of socioeconomic status, region, and religion.

Education is coded in years. The respondent's *Income* is the NES 22-point scale of income, ranging from 0 for respondents earning less than $3,000 per year to 22 for respondents earning more than $70,000 per year. *South at 16* is a dichotomous variable indicating whether or not the respondent is from the South, or lived in the South at age 16 (coded 1), or otherwise (coded 2). (The nonstandard coding of dichotomous variables reflects Hall and Ferree's original coding.) *Size of Place* represents the size of the respondent's community, coded 1 for rural areas, 2 for suburbs, and 3 for cities. *Size of Place at 16* represents the size of the respondent's community when the respondent was 16 years old, coded 1 for nonrural areas, 2 for rural areas. *Frequency Attend Church* is a scale denoting how often the respondent goes to church, ranging from 1 for every week to 5 for never. If religion is important to the respondent, *Religion Important* is coded 1, coded 5 otherwise. *Religion Provides Guidance* is coded 3 if religion provides a great deal of guidance to the respondent, 2 if religion provides quite a bit of guidance, and 1 if religion provides some guidance. There are also dummy variables denoting if the respondent is *Catholic* or *Fundamentalist.*

This is another model where I do not expect to see consistent changes after correction for nonresponse. The dependent variable—strong opposition to abortion—seems unrelated to why a respondent would agree to participate in the survey. Some of the independent variables (*Race, Income,* and *Education*) may be related to nonresponse, but in a tertiary way through the intervening relationships.

Despite my expectations that there would not be significant changes after correction, two important changes do take place. The coefficient on the dummy variable for race (*Black*) rises by 2 percentage points (or about 20 percent over the uncorrected coefficient) after correction. This suggests that a straight application of Hall and Ferree's model understates their main point: blacks more frequently oppose abortion on any grounds, even after one controls for demographics. In addition, the constant term rises substantially for both 1986 and 1988 (by 11 percent in 1986 and by 16 percent in 1988). This change implies that the NES *underestimates* the number of people who believe that abortion should never be permitted.[18]

A more direct demonstration of how the NES underestimates the proportion of people who are opposed to abortion under any circum-

---

18. The corrections based on the demographic selection mechanism run in the *opposite* direction, suggesting that we overestimate black opposition to abortion. On the other hand, the corrections based on the LISREL model suggest that the administrative selection mechanism corrections are too small.

stances is to compare the reluctant and amenable respondents. Seventeen percent of the reluctant respondents, compared with 12 percent of the amenable respondents, believe that abortion should never be permitted.

I failed once before in my predictions about absence of nonresponse bias, with the negative voting model. But in some ways, the bias evident in this model is more troublesome. Politicians, journalists, social scientists, even ordinary people, all use survey results to gauge public sentiment on policy matters. The assumption is that the surveys yield fair pictures of public feeling. The results from this model of attitudes

TABLE 6.12. Attitudes toward Abortion as a Function of Demographics, 1986 and 1988 NES

	1986 NES		1988 NES	
	Uncorr. (GLS)	Corr. (Nonlin.)	Uncorr. (GLS)	Corr. (Nonlin.)
Black	**.08**	**.10**	**.05**	**.07**
	(.03)	(.02)	(.02)	(.02)
Education	**−.02**	**−.02**	**−.003**	−.01
	(.003)	(.003)	(.001)	(.003)
Income	.000	−.001	−.0003	−.0003
	(.000)	(.02)	(.0002)	(.03)
South at 16	−.01	−.01	.02	.02
	(.013)	(.01)	(.01)	(.02)
Size of Place	−.005	.004	**−.02**	**−.03**
	(.008)	(.02)	(.008)	(.01)
Size of Place at 16	**.04**	.03	−.01	−.0005
	(.02)	(.02)	(.01)	(.02)
Frequency Attend Church	**−.04**	**−.05**	**−.03**	**−.04**
	(.005)	(.006)	(.005)	(.006)
Religion Important	**−.02**	−.005	**−.01**	**−.02**
	(.003)	(.006)	(.004)	(.006)
Religion Provides Guidance	**.05**	.004	.008	.01
	(.006)	(.007)	(.007)	(.007)
Catholic	.01	.03	**.04**	**.07**
	(.014)	(.02)	(.01)	(.02)
Fundamentalist	**.04**	**.05**	.007	−.0002
	(.02)	(.02)	(.02)	(.02)
(Constant)	**.40**	**.50**	**.29**	**.45**
	(.05)	(.07)	(.04)	(.05)
$\rho\sigma$		−.74		**−.67**
		(.46)		(.30)

Boldfaced entries are statistically significant at $p < .05$ Dependent variable is *Abortion Never Permitted*, where respondents who believe that abortion should never be permitted are coded 1, 0 otherwise. Standard errors are entered in parentheses below coefficients.

toward abortion imply that surveys may not produce such a fair picture after all.

Family Income

The three data sets at hand reflect the concerns of scholars of American politics and limit tests of models pertinent to other disciplines. There is at least one economic model that may be tested with the NES data: the relationship between the respondent's income and life situation.

One important question is how much the respondent's income varies as the respondent's education increases, or if the respondent marries, divorces, loses a job, grows old, or is black. Such a model can be tested in the 1986 and 1988 NES (table 6.13).

The dependent variable for the model is the respondent's family income (or the respondent's own income if the respondent is single). The measure of *Family Income* is the 22-category income scale, ranging from a value of 0 for respondents earning less than $3,000 per year to 22 for respondents who earn more than $70,000 per year. There are five independent, dummy variables in this analysis denoting whether the respondent is *Over 65, Married, Divorced, Working Now,* or *Black.* In addition, the respondents' level of education is measured on a scale that varies from 0 for those with less than a third grade education to 1 for those with an advanced degree.

Is the respondent's income related to the respondent's likelihood of participating in the survey? While income is related to the respondent's attitudes toward the interview (see chapters 3 and 4), the connection to compliance is indirect. There is the possibility, at any rate, that the dependent variable (*Family Income*) is related to the respondent's chances of entering the sample.

What is most striking about this model is that the coefficients are virtually identical across all four columns. This model is not only stable over 1986 to 1988, but it also appears to be unaffected by nonresponse. The respondent's education contributes enormously to the respondent's income. In comparison to the lowest end of the scale, respondents with an advanced degree earned 11 categories higher on the income scale (at least a difference of $15,000, perhaps as high as $60,000). Sensibly, the respondent's working and marital status also contribute to the family's income. Married respondents earned 4 NES income categories more (a difference of at least $8,000) than nonmarried respondents. Working respondents earned 3 NES income categories more (a difference of at least $5,000) than nonworking respondents. But perhaps the most interesting point is that black respondents are likely to earn less than nonblack respondents, even after one accounts for education, age, working status and marital status. Black respondents earned two income categories, which may be as little as $3,000 or as much as $25,000.

Although some models employing measures of class are affected by survey nonresponse, this model demonstrates that not all models may change after correction. One question remaining to be resolved is whether or not class itself is related to nonresponse directly or only via intervening relationships. The implication of the absence of nonresponse bias in this model of income is the latter.

Summary

What difference does nonresponse make for political science models? Many, perhaps most, of the models in this chapter escaped with only small changes to the coefficients. If all one were looking for were a rough guide to the relative importance of a set of variables in predicting political behavior, the corrections here for nonresponse don't alter such coarse conclusions. But there are times when nonresponse makes such a

TABLE 6.13. Family Income as a Function of Demographics, Uncorrected and Corrected Estimates, 1986 and 1988 NES

	1986 NES		1988 NES	
	Uncorr. (GLS)	Corr. (Achen)	Uncorr. (GLS)	Corr. (Achen)
Over 65	−.65	−.65	−.63	−.62
	(.36)	(.35)	(.36)	(.36)
Education	**11.22**	**11.21**	**11.22**	**11.19**
	(.57)	(.56)	(.58)	(.56)
Married	**4.02**	**4.03**	**4.01**	**4.00**
	(.26)	(.26)	(.26)	(.26)
Divorced	−.84	−.82	−.84	−.86
	(.35)	(.34)	(.35)	(.35)
Working Now	**3.12**	**3.13**	**3.11**	**3.05**
	(.27)	(.27)	(.28)	(.28)
Black	**−2.14**	**−2.15**	**−2.12**	**−2.14**
	(.34)	(.34)	(.34)	(.34)
(Constant)	**2.10**	1.87	**2.11**	**2.11**
	(.45)	(.67)	(.45)	(.45)
$\rho\sigma$		.61		**1.83**
		(1.89)		(.61)

Boldfaced entries are statistically significant at $p < .05$. Dependent variable is *Family Income*. Standard errors are entered in parentheses below coefficients.

substantive difference—doubling coefficients, for instance—that we need to attend to the potential for nonresponse bias. Is it possible to be more systematic about the sorts of models that are likely to be affected by nonresponse?

It seems straightforward to identify the instances when survey nonresponse is likely to make a difference. The most clear-cut nonresponse effects appear to be related to the respondent's level of information. In earlier chapters, I show that reluctant respondents were less informed and less interested in politics than amenable respondents. For example, reluctant respondents could recall the names of their legislators at about a quarter of the rate that amenable respondents could. Multivariate analyses also suffer. In the familiarity model, the coefficients for recall and recognition of the candidates *double* on correction for nonresponse. In the model testing the respondent's knowledge of how a legislator votes, nonresponse increased the proportion of less educated voters who admitted not knowing how their legislator votes. However, in the residency-based model of turnout, the coefficients on political interest were unchanged after correction for nonresponse.

Secondly, models of turnout in the general election overestimate the proportion of voters because of nonresponse. There are alternate explanations for overestimates of voters, but both of the turnout models tested here showed big changes in the constant term after correction. The measure of turnout controlled for one alternate explanation—fibbing about one's voting. And the 1986 NES was a post-test only, controlling for the remaining alternate explanation—turnout was stimulated by contacting respondents before the election.

Curiously, models relying on class may or may not be affected by nonresponse. The model of turnout and demographics displayed very slight attenuation—all the estimates of the importance of class were damped down before correction for nonresponse. But the direct test of nonresponse effects on class—the model of family income—was astoundingly stable, even across the two years.

It may not be straightforward to identify when one's models are safe. Models where the phenomena of interest are unrelated to survey participation would seem to be more safe than others, but there are no guarantees. As chapter 5 demonstrates, models where selection is related to variables outside the model of interest may also suffer from nonresponse bias for no other reason than because the error terms in our model of interest are related to selection. (In such a situation, we won't know or probably even be able to speculate about the direction of the bias.)

It is also possible that our models will be affected in unanticipated ways because we don't yet really know the set of variables related to nonresponse. I anticipated that two models would not change after correction when, in fact, the correction made quite a difference. In the models of negative voting, nonresponse caused underestimates of the effect of approval and overestimates of the effect of disapproval. In the model evaluating the attitudes of blacks toward abortion, nonresponse caused an underestimate of opposition to abortion among both blacks and the population as a whole. While it is conceivable that negative attitudes toward politicians may spur respondents to participate in surveys, it seems quite unlikely that opposition to abortion would cause respondents to refuse. If attitudes toward abortion are, in fact, related to responsiveness to surveys, they might be connected by virtue of some intermediary variables. It is plausible that attitudes toward self-image and attitudes toward abortion are related, for example.

Other models appeared to escape with virtually no difference after correction for nonresponse. The model of sociotropic voting, the models of candidate evaluation based on issue positions, and the model of family income displayed no consistent pattern after correction for nonresponse. But too much faith is inappropriate: as the models of voting based on recognition demonstrated, nonresponse bias may not be evident with one specification of the model, but apparent upon inclusion of only a few more variables.

Two points become clear. One, respondents are not the same as nonrespondents. Respondents differ from the nonrespondents not just in terms of demographic characteristics but also in terms of attitudes and political attributes. Two, if you do not account for nonresponse, you may make important mistakes. You will overestimate turnout or underestimate the importance of information. Fortunately, the method of correction is relatively simple to implement. The cost of this correction is that survey researchers have to continue to collect information about their nonrespondents.

CHAPTER 7

What If Nonresponse Worsens?

The nonresponse bias evident in the models of chapter 6 might be too small for some tastes. After all, if the analyst were merely looking for the sign of a coefficient, none of the models displayed a change of sign on statistically significant coefficients. The problem is that nonresponse bias in many surveys may well be much worse than the preceding analysis suggests. The models in chapter 6 employ academic surveys with quite respectable response rates, hovering around 70 percent. The response rates for commercial surveys and polls are often considerably lower. What would happen to the analysis if the NES were like the commercial polls? In this brief chapter, I simulate falling response rates and evaluate their effect on univariate and multivariate analyses.

Worsening Response Rates and Univariate Analysis

Recall the results of Crespi's (1988) survey of pre-election survey organizations. He found that one-third of these organizations would not conduct "callbacks" to attempt to reach individuals previously not contacted. Furthermore, nearly all of the organizations (82 percent) would not attempt to convert refusals. Of course, these organizations have appreciable reasons for waiving callbacks or refusal conversions—pre-election surveys are utterly dependent on timing. But one might well ask what would happen to analyses of academic or government surveys were those surveys to adopt the field practices of pre-election survey organizations.

In fact, it is possible to simulate falling response rates by adopting, post hoc, these practices. Begin by conducting the analysis on a full data set, and then selectively remove respondents. An artificial response rate may be produced for the 1988 NES Postelection Survey by first removing all refusal conversions. Then remove any respondent who was sent a persuasion letter. Then remove respondents who took more than six calls to reach, and so forth, down to one call. This yields a falling response rate displayed in table 7.1, along with some selected demographics.

With the exception of the very last call, the demographic measures and turnout change nearly monotonically with respect to the simulated response rate. As the simulated response rate falls, the respondents' age and the proportion of the respondents who are married increases. Both of these make sense: older respondents are more likely to be at home than younger respondents, and the mean age increases by five years as the response rate falls; married respondents are more likely to have someone at home to make appointments for the respondents, and the proportion of married respondents increases by about 3 percent (except for the very last step of the simulated decline).

As the simulated response rate falls, the proportion of respondents who are working outside the home, are men, or are black falls. The difference between the proportion of working respondents in the full sample and the lowest response rate is a staggering 23 percent. There is also an 8 percent decline in the proportion of the sample that is male.

Clearly, if the NES were to mimic the field practices of the organizations Crespi interviewed, the sample would change drastically. In some important ways, the samples would become less representative, too. Recall from chapter 2 that the NES overrepresents the proportion of the elderly and underrepresents the proportion of men. If the NES were to adopt these field practices, the NES samples would be even less representative in terms of the proportion of men and the elderly in the samples. One must wonder about the representativeness of the samples of those organizations that do not attempt to convert refusals or make only one trip to the household.

TABLE 7.1. Simulated Falling Response Rate and Selected Demographics, 1988 NES

	Simulated Response Rate	Percent Married	Percent Working	Percent Male	Percent Black	Mean Age
Full Sample	70	54.8	63.5	42.7	13.2	45.1
No Letters	65	54.3	63.5	42.8	13.1	44.8
No Conversions	64	54.5	63.5	42.6	13.0	44.8
< 7 Calls	58	55.8	61.2	41.6	12.9	45.7
< 6 Calls	56	55.8	59.9	41.5	12.9	46.0
< 5 Calls	52	55.7	58.4	41.0	13.0	46.6
< 4 Calls	48	56.6	55.6	40.0	13.0	47.1
< 3 Calls	41	57.0	50.5	39.0	12.8	48.3
< 2 Calls	28	53.5	38.4	34.1	15.1	50.0

Worsening Response Rates and Regression Analysis

We can use the same technique to examine what would happen to regression models were response rates to fall. We can begin by estimating a regression model with the full data set, and then withdrawing cases according to whether or not the NES administered a persuasion letter, a refusal conversion attempt, or successively fewer calls. By recording the estimates for coefficients at each stage, we have a simulation of the effect of declining response.

Moreover, we can use this simulation to see if the *corrections* can cope with falling response. Ideally, we would like to see that the corrected coefficients maintain a smoother, flatter line (i.e., one not sensitive to falling response rates). With this approach, we can see if the key results of the correction hold while response rates worsen. If we had an ideal selection model, we might well expect that the corrected estimates would be smoother, more insensitive to falling response.

There are two reasons why we might not be so confident. Note that we don't actually have the declining nonresponse, but that we have a kind of simulated nonresponse. In this case, the simulation of nonresponse is by excluding the more difficult to reach respondents, who are more reluctant to offer reasons for participating in the survey. We remain subject to the endogeneity problems I warn of in the introduction to chapter 6.

Second, we are limited in our choice of corrections. We can't simulate declining response with the field administration measures *and* use those same measures to correct for nonresponse. As appendix I shows, the LISREL Selection Model yields nearly identical results to the Field Adminstration selection model, and we can use this instead. As I point out throughout chapters 3 and 4, none of the three selection models is perfect—we lack key indicators for the posited relationships and must instead depend upon the dichotomous coding of open-ended questions. Further, as the introduction to chapter 6 comments, all three selection models must use measures that are endogenous to selection, to varying degrees. Consequently, perhaps we should not be too surprised to see variation in the corrected estimates as the simulated response rate worsens. Instead, the emphasis in this chapter is upon the qualitative differences between the uncorrected and corrected estimates. The pattern of qualitative differences holds throughout: where there was a substantively significant difference between the corrected and uncorrected coefficients in the model with current nonresponse levels, that substantive difference persists as the nonresponse rate worsens. For each of the corrections to follow, I use the Achen estimator for selection bias with dichotomous dependent variables.

It's hardly necessary for us to repeat the analysis of all the models in the previous chapter. Instead, I select three models to test based on their apparent sensitivity (or lack thereof) to nonresponse: the Wolfinger and Rosenstone turnout model (small changes after correction, except to the constant term), the Jacobson model of voting for Congress on the basis of familiarity (significant changes), and the Kinder and Kiewiet sociotropic voting model (no significant changes). I consider the effects to these models in turn.

Declining Response and Turnout Models

As the reader should recall, Wolfinger and Rosenstone model turnout as a function of demographic variables: education, income, age, race, and Hispanic origin. The corrections for nonresponse to this model produced one significant change (to the constant) and two smaller changes (to the coefficients on income and education). What happens to the uncorrected and corrected estimates as response rate falls?

Figures 7.1–7.6 display the changing uncorrected and corrected coefficients for each variable in the Wolfinger and Rosenstone turnout model. Three points are immediately apparent from these models. First, the estimates of the uncorrected coefficients may change dramatically as the response rate falls. Sometimes the declining response rate causes signs to change. In figure 7.1, the uncorrected coefficient for *Black* in the turnout model rises from −.06 to nearly +.12. In figure 7.2, the coefficient for *Hispanic Origin* starts off at +.05, dips below 0, then rises to +.18 as the response rate falls. The change in this coefficient means that being black in the full model implied *less* likelihood of turnout; in the model with the lowest response rate, being black implied *greater* likelihood of turnout. If coefficients change sign as response rate falls, we must be particularly worried about the consequences of nonresponse. As can be observed in the figures to follow in this chapter, when response rate falls below 30 percent (i.e., excluding all respondents who had been sent persuasion letters or refusal conversion attempts, or who were reached on more than two calls to the household), the estimates become very odd. And it is at this very low level of response that the estimates may change sign. This should, at minimum, warn us against adopting the kinds of shortcutting practices that Crespi found for pre-election polling firms.

Part of the effect that may account for such variability in the estimates is that the standard errors remain large and increase as the response rate falls (if only for the smaller sample size with fewer respondents).

Other coefficients merely bobble around a bit. The uncorrected coefficients on *Age* fluctuate by plus or minus .001 (fig. 7.3); the uncorrected coefficient on *Income* drops from about .006 to 0 (fig. 7.4); the uncorrected estimate of *Education* bobbles around .65, plus or minus .05 (fig. 7.5); and the constant term oscillates from −.2 to −.05 back to −.2 as the response rate falls (fig. 7.6). An immediate point to make is that as the response rate changes, additional noise enters into our estimates. Sometimes this noise works in a systematic way to change our conclusions (as they do when the sign changes).

The second major point is that the corrected estimates are no less sensitive to nonresponse than the uncorrected estimates. In fact, the corrected estimates tend to hew to the same up- and downswings as the uncorrected estimates as the response rate falls. If we had hoped that the Heckman and Achen corrections would miraculously restore the accuracy of our data from the perils of nonresponse, that hope is gone.

But the third point is that if the corrections make a substantive difference to our conclusions, the corrections continue to enforce the same difference as the response rate falls. The effect of correction on the *Black* and *Hispanic Origin* coefficients was tiny (for both 1986 and 1988, and with all the correction mechanisms). But there was one substantive change to the coefficients that was readily apparent: the corrected constant term is significantly less (more negative) than the uncorrected constant. And figure 7.6 shows that while the uncorrected constant bobbles around at about the same level, the corrected constant term becomes even more negative. Note also that the effect of correction on the *Age, Income,* and *Education* terms works in a consistent way: the corrected estimates are always greater than the uncorrected estimates. Furthermore, the desired "flat" path for the corrected coefficients is arguably present for these three coefficients, until the 30 percent response rate, when all estimates become strange.

While the corrections do not restore imperfect response rates to perfect response rates, the corrections continue to make sensible changes to the models. This simulation worked with a model where there were relatively subtle changes after correction for nonresponse. What happens to a more extreme case?

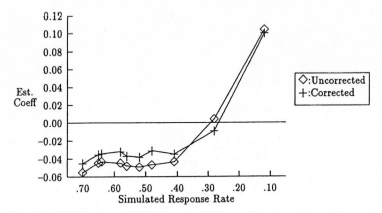

FIGURE 7.1. Simulated Response Rate and Race in Turnout Model, 1988 NES

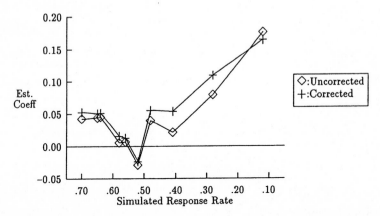

FIGURE 7.2. Simulated Response Rate and Hispanics in Turnout Model, 1988 NES

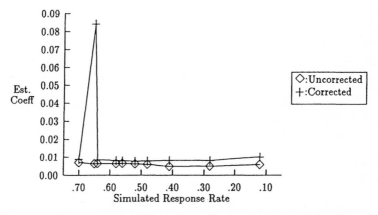

FIGURE 7.3. Simulated Response Rate and Age in Turnout Model, 1988 NES

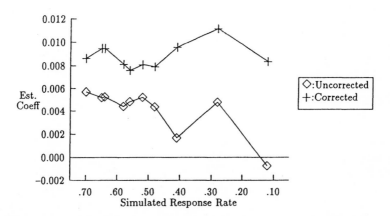

FIGURE 7.4. Simulated Response Rate and Income in Turnout Model, 1988 NES

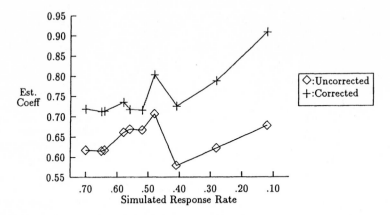

FIGURE 7.5. Simulated Response Rate and Education in Turnout Model, 1988 NES

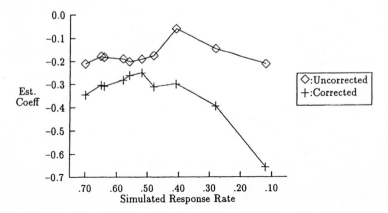

FIGURE 7.6. Simulated Response Rate and Constant in Turnout Model, 1988 NES

Declining Response and the Familiarity Model

Jacobson explores the sources of the incumbent candidate's advantage in congressional elections with his series of models. As the models progress, he demonstrates that what appeared to be a raw advantage for the incumbent (i.e., the coefficient on the dummy variable for incumbency dwarfed the others) disappears as one takes account of name recognition and contact. In chapter 6, I show that the effect of correction for nonresponse may not be apparent at one specification of a model, but when one adds new variables, the effect of correction may appear. In this case, there was a clear change to the coefficients on *Familiarity* with the candidates after correction for nonresponse.

I display what happens to the uncorrected and corrected coefficients in the familiarity model as the response rate falls in figures 7.7–7.12. The same three points that are apparent in the previous section are apparent here as well. There is significant instability in the coefficients, where some of the coefficients change dramatically in magnitude (although none change sign). The effect of incumbency, for both Democrats and Republicans, increases as the response rate falls. After the first drop in the simulated response (eliminating those who were sent a persuasion letter), the effect of familiarity with the Democrat and the Republican remains somewhat level, until the response rate drops below 30 percent. The corrected estimates are no more stable than the uncorrected estimates. The corrected estimates may be a bit more unstable than the uncorrected estimates for the effect of incumbency.

But the qualitative differences between the corrected and uncorrected estimates remain. At all levels of simulated nonresponse, the uncorrected estimates understate the importance of familiarity with the Democrat or the Republican. Where there is a clear effect of correction for nonresponse at current levels of nonresponse, that effect remains as the response rate worsens. In figures 7.9 and 7.10, the uncorrected estimates are always less in absolute value than the corrected estimates.

In both the turnout model and the familiarity model, there were some changes after correction in both 1986 and 1988, and with all of the selection mechanisms. Do we see the same three effects with a model that did *not* display differences due to nonresponse?

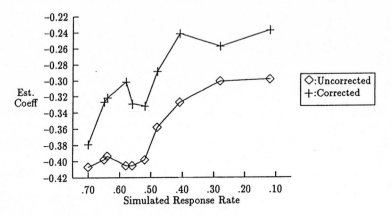

FIGURE 7.7. Simulated Response Rate and Democratic Incumbency in Familiarity Model, 1988 NES

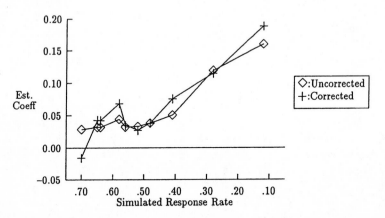

FIGURE 7.8. Simulated Response Rate and Republican Incumbency in Familiarity Model, 1988 NES

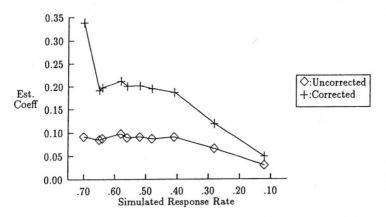

FIGURE 7.9. Simulated Response Rate and Familiarity with Democrat, Familiarity Model, 1988 NES

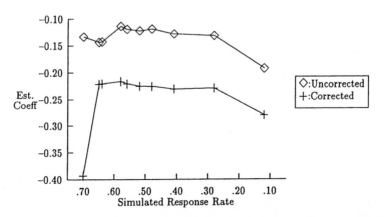

FIGURE 7.10. Simulated Response Rate and Familiarity with Republican in Familiarity Model, 1988 NES

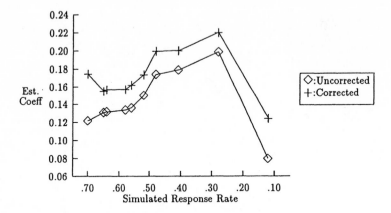

FIGURE 7.11. Simulated Response Rate and Party ID in Familiarity Model, 1988 NES

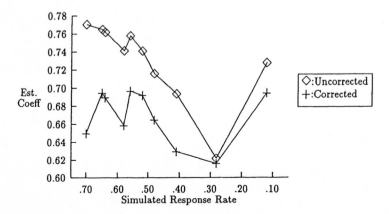

FIGURE 7.12. Simulated Response Rate and Constant in Familiarity Model

Declining Response and the Sociotropic Model

Kinder and Kiewiet developed a model contrasting voting on the basis of personal economic experience ("pocketbook voting") with voting on the basis of assessments of the national economy ("sociotropic voting"). That model showed miniscule changes after correction for nonresponse. I test the effect of declining response rates with this model that doesn't appear to suffer from nonresponse bias (see figs. 7.13–7.20).

In figures 7.13–7.20 I display the uncorrected and corrected estimates for the sociotropic model for 1988. Again, there is often considerable instability in these coefficients. In figures 7.13, 7.14, and 7.17, the coefficients for *Dissatisfaction with Income, Unemployment Experiences,* and *Unemployment as National Problem,* respectively, change sign *both* when uncorrected and corrected. If we had response rates below 50 percent, the implication of these graphs is that we would draw polar conclusions about the effect of personal economic experiences. If these simulations hold for true nonresponse below 50 percent, the immediate implication of these figures is that we should be especially wary. With this model, the corrected estimates are as unstable as the uncorrected estimates.

Are any of the corrected estimates consistently different from the uncorrected estimates? Two are close, except when the simulated response rate drops to 12 percent. In figure 7.18, the uncorrected coefficient for *Inflation as National Problem* is consistently smaller in absolute value (closer to zero) than the corrected estimates. Likewise, the uncorrected coefficient for *Government Performance* is consistently smaller than the corrected estimate, until the response rate reaches 12 percent. These two variables were among the most important in Kinder and Kiewiet's original finding that sociotropic assessments of the economy matter. The implication here is that we would underestimate those effects under extremely low response levels. Note, however, that the pocketbook assessments (figs. 7.13 and 7.14) waver on both sides of zero. The implication is that we underestimate the importance of this sociotropic assessment of the economy.

Even a model that is largely insensitive to current levels of nonresponse may become very sensitive to nonresponse should the rate worsen.

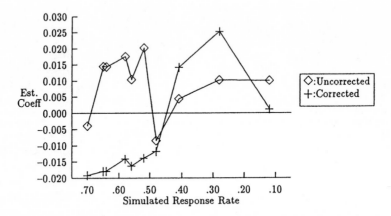

FIGURE 7.13. Simulated Response Rate and Dissatisfaction with Income in Sociotropic Model, 1988 NES

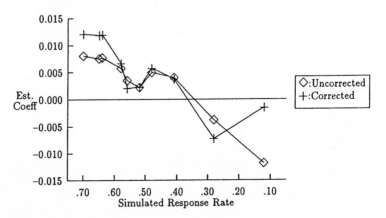

FIGURE 7.14. Simulated Response Rate and Unemployment Experience in Sociotropic Model, 1988 NES

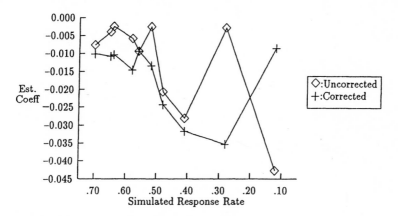

FIGURE 7.15. Simulated Response Rate and Business Conditions in Sociotropic Model, 1988 NES

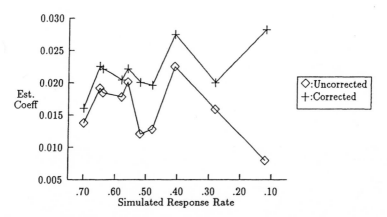

FIGURE 7.16. Simulated Response Rate and Government Performance in Sociotropic Model, 1988 NES

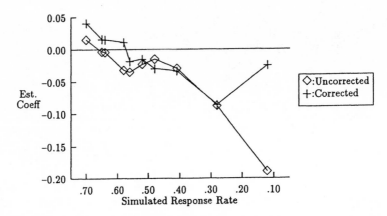

FIGURE 7.17. Simulated Response Rate and Unemployment as a National Problem in Sociotropic Model, 1988 NES

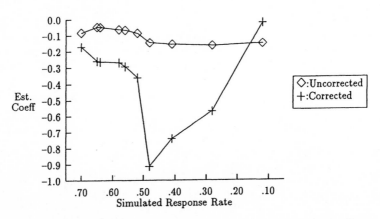

FIGURE 7.18. Simulated Response Rate and Inflation as a National Problem in Sociotropic Model, 1988 NES

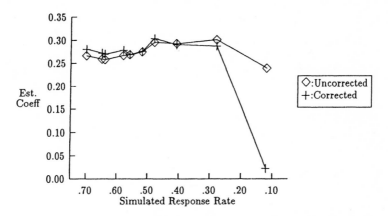

FIGURE 7.19. Simulated Response Rate and Party ID in Sociotropic Model, 1988 NES

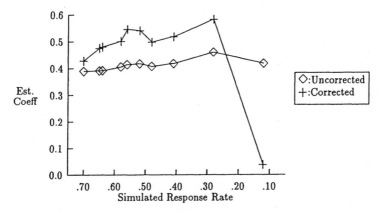

FIGURE 7.20. Simulated Response Rate and Constant in Sociotropic Model, 1988 NES

Conclusions

If chapter 6 gives us the naive sense of optimism that we can correct multivariate analyses for any level of nonresponse, by now we should realize that the Heckman and Achen corrections are not utter salvation. Emphatically, we will not get perfect estimates from imperfect data. Chapter 5 suggests that the errors in the Heckman and Achen corrections are themselves sensitive to nonresponse (specifically, to ρ, the correlation between the error terms in the selection and outcome equations). Furthermore, our knowledge of the sensitivity of those corrections comes from Monte Carlo simulations where we have a perfectly specified selection model. With our inherently imperfect selection equations, we introduce other sources of error into the correction. As nonresponse worsens, our estimates at the lower response rates become decreasingly comparable to our estimates at current response rates, and the corrections do not eliminate the problem.

This much said, the corrections do restore consistency to the estimates as long as they are based on the right selection model, as the simulations show in chapter 5. Further, the corrections under worsening nonresponse continue to be very useful even for these imperfect selection models, especially with regard to the substantive interpretations of our models of interest. Every time that the corrections for nonresponse made a difference to our models with current levels of nonresponse, the corrections made the same substantive difference at lower response rates. The turnout models continue to overestimate turnout and underestimate the importance of income and education. The familiarity models still underestimate the significance of the respondent's ability to recall or recognize the Republican and Democratic candidates. We might turn the problem around and ask what we have learned about the nonrespondents by these adjustments. Qualitatively, what is the difference to our substantive models once we take into account the increasing proportion of the public that refuses to take part in our studies?

Further, while the corrections are manifestly variable under the simulated nonresponse, we should reserve judgment about the ability of these corrections to generate stable estimates under alternate scenarios. For one, the standard errors of both the corrected and uncorrected estimates increase as the sample sizes diminish, which will appear as unstable estimates. For another, we know that the selection model used for the corrected estimates depends upon the dichotomous indicators and unorthodox structural modeling tricks discussed in chapter 4. The model is reasonable, but it is hardly a perfect selection equation, such as those tested by the Monte Carlo simulation in chapter 5.

Perhaps the most important observations we should draw about the simulations of declining response pertain to our methods of conducting survey research. We cannot let response rates slip further and still hope to compare estimates over time. It really is worthwhile for organizations like the Survey Research Center and the National Opinion Research Center to make multiple call backs, send persuasion letters, and try to convert refusals. These extra efforts to reduce nonresponse may be expensive, but they are also essential if we want data sets that fairly represent the public, not to mention are comparable over time. The results of this chapter argue for further attempts to model the process by which we elicit responses from the public. With better understanding of why people choose or refuse to participate in our surveys, we should gain more stable and accurate corrections for nonresponse.

Our estimates become least reliable when the response rate drops below 30 percent. In this simulation, that means when we exclude any respondent who refuses on the first contact and whom we cannot reach on two calls or less. If these patterns hold true for pre-election survey organizations, we may want to distrust the utility of these studies for regression-type analyses. Recall that 82 percent of the organizations surveyed by Crespi (1988) would not convert refusals, and that a third wouldn't call back the household. If the NES were to adopt these procedures, our response rate would fall well below 30 percent, and we would observe the wildly unstable results displayed in the figures of this chapter.

CHAPTER 8

Surveys and Misrepresentation

This book begins with a discussion of the meaning of representation in modern politics. Representation embodies not only people empowered to act on our behalf but also a description of who we are. When we refer to representatives as people entitled to act on our behalf, we refer to the "authorization" sense of representation. Representatives are political actors who create legislation, enforce laws, and express our opinions for us. A second sense of representation is "descriptive," a mirroring of the attributes and characteristics of the public. A "representative" legislature means, in part, one that fairly replicates the attitudes and characteristics of the public. Descriptive representation matters to us.

One way that we evaluate the representativeness of government is to see if every citizen has an equal opportunity to have his or her interests expressed. We become suspicious of the adequacy of representation when some votes count more than others (as in legislative apportionment) or when a legislature contains few minorities. These are worries about descriptive representation.

Polls and surveys are descriptive representation par excellence, conduits of information from citizens to decision makers. Polls and surveys represent us in the American political process. When we ask how representative polls and surveys are, think not only of the scientific sense of a representative sample, think also of the role of surveys in political representation.

Certainly, I have dwelt on the narrow, scientific sense of representation in surveys. But this narrow sense of representation is richer than one might have previously thought, and directly important to contemporary politics. When a survey researcher judges the representativeness of the sample, he or she may merely compare the proportion of people in different categories against the population. In a trivial sense, nonresponse is exactly the problem that we are missing people of some categories in the population. But here, we have tried to compare the motives of people who participate in surveys against those who don't, and to ask what difference nonresponse makes for our understandings of why people behave in certain ways.

I suggest that surveys, as one of the mechanisms for political representation, are not merely descriptive but "interpretive." The advantage that survey research provides to political decision-makers is not just a raw tabulation of categories but a sense of what those categories mean. What is the relationship between education and poverty? Do citizens become politically informed as a consequence of participating in politics, or is information a prerequisite for participation? Do voters choose between candidates because of pocketbook concerns, or a more general sense of the state of the economy? These questions matter to policy makers, not just to political scientists.

In this concluding chapter, I first recapitulate the key findings of the earlier chapters and then return to the problem of nonresponse in the context of political representation. These findings provide the basis for suggestions about what academics, survey researchers, the government, and the public could do about nonresponse.

Recapitulating Representation

There are some surprises among the major findings in this research, especially when placed in the context of representation. A sample may be representative at one level of analysis, but unrepresentative at another.

One surprise is that the academic surveys (GSS and NES) overrepresent minorities as a strict proportion of the sample. There are more blacks, poor people, less educated people, and elderly in the NES and GSS samples than in the population. Of course, these differences are not strictly due to nonresponse: errors due to the sampling frame and errors in the CPS could also account for differences between the NES, GSS, and CPS samples. And we might step back and wonder whether or not the CPS underrepresents the same groups. But if one stopped with chapter 2, one might conclude that surveys are a vehicle for enhanced representation of political and economic minorities.

A raw comparison of the academic samples and the CPS misses the story. Different groups fall out of different stages of the survey process. Interviewers have an easier time contacting the elderly, but the elderly are disproportionately likely to be incapable of being interviewed and less likely to comply. Interviewers are also more likely to contact people with greater incomes, but wealthier people are also the most likely to refuse on grounds of being too busy. Interviewers may have a more difficult time contacting Hispanics, and Hispanics are more likely than non-Hispanics to refuse on grounds of confidentiality. The information that some demographic groups fall out of different parts of the survey process and not others doesn't really inform us about *why* people are nonrespondents.

The more important observation of chapters 3 and 4 is that survey participation is a behavioral process. It makes more sense to think about the reactions that a potential respondent has toward strangers, the interviewer, or surveys in general than to ask whether or not particular classes refuse to participate. To be sure, there are some demographic patterns to the types of people who refuse to participate on different grounds, but these demographic patterns are of secondary importance to the reasons themselves.

Furthermore, survey participation is one of the most common instances of a very general situation, where one person asks another to comply with some request. When political scientists study the effectiveness of law enforcement, why people contribute to interest groups, or how voters respond to political advertising, they study "compliance." Just as it makes sense to think of compliance in these studies as a behavioral problem, we should think about survey participation in terms of *why* people participate, and not just *who* participates.

If we treat what respondents and refusals *say* as the reasons for their action as, in truth, the reasons for their actions, we learn something about why people choose or refuse to participate. We discover something about the refusals' relationship to strangers by whether or not they refused on the grounds of privacy or confidentiality. We learn about the respondents' relationship to the interviewer by the interviewers' record of the the respondents' attitude, or by whether or not respondents agreed to participate because they empathized with the interviewer. We know, above all, that respondents' interest in the survey, available time, prior experiences, and level of informedness are aspects of the respondents' relationship to the interview. The respondents' reasons help us learn why some people participate in surveys.

If we use these reasons as legitimate indicators of why the selected respondents choose or refuse to comply, we gain useful insights into what is likely to affect responsiveness. Instead of attempting to boost response rates solely by exhorting the interviewers to go out for one more week, with a model of survey participation we are in a better position to direct our resources. The models I evaluate in chapter 4 all suggest that the respondent's relationship to the interview far and away dominates among the four relationships. The implication is that we will be more successful in boosting response rates if we try to raise the respondent's interest in the interview, compensate the respondent for his or her time, and make interviews more enjoyable experiences than by consoling the respondent about the confidentiality of the study or lecturing interviewers on ways to improve rapport.

The other goal of this book is to make explicit how nonresponse undermines scientific research and, by implication, political uses of survey data. In principle, every statistical use of survey data is jeopardized by nonresponse—whether that use is a simple scatterplot, comparison of means, regression analysis, or crosstabulation. In the case of a simple comparison of means, nonresponse alters both the estimate of the mean *and* the estimate of variance. Because nonresponse contracts the estimated variance, anyone who uses unadjusted survey data will be more certain about findings, even if the finding itself is in error.

By comparing corrected estimates to uncorrected ones for several well-regarded models of politics, I found several instances where nonresponse affects how we understand politics. We know that nonresponse is a reason why surveys overestimate the number of people who vote in elections. Surveys oversample voters. We know that survey nonresponse causes us to underestimate the effect of some measures of political information, like name recognition and knowledge about a legislator's voting record. Survey nonresponse causes us to overestimate the importance of whether or not voters dislike candidates. These changes are important to a good deal of political science research. We depend on surveys to understand why people vote for particular candidates. If we underestimate information and overestimate negative voting, nonresponse muddles two factors that many political scientists hold central to voting.

To be sure, most of the coefficients in the models of chapter 6 changed only slightly, if at all. Devil's advocates, contrary to their usual position, might choose to be sanguine about the consequences of current levels of nonresponse. If the only aspect of a regression analysis we cared about was the signs of slope coefficients and whether or not they were statistically discernible from zero, we probably would not fear nonresponse at *current* levels. But we *do* pay attention to the relative magnitude of slope coefficients, and how they change over time. We want to know if blacks continue to be more likely to vote than whites (after accounting for income), if the role of class is declining in politics, or how opposition to abortion is shifting. For answers to questions like these, we attend to subtle changes in survey statistics, and we benefit from more accurate estimates.

More so, the effect of corrections here may be underestimated. We know that all three of the selection mechanisms I use in chapter 6 are misspecified. We would rather have more and better measures of the relationships but settle for proxies. One result of settling for misspecified selection models is that we may yet find more significant changes to regression coefficients after we correct for nonresponse, perhaps even among the models here that showed little difference. What this book shows is that there are instances when nonresponse clearly affects our understanding of politics *even when we use the misspecified selection models.* The potential remains for even greater effects.

A relaxed attitude toward the magnitude of nonresponse bias is especially unwarranted if nonresponse rates continue to worsen. In the penultimate chapter, I show that if nonresponse continues to worsen that our conclusions about politics will become less reliable. As the simulated response rates fall, virtually every coefficient changes, and some quite drastically. If response rates plummet, we won't know from survey research whether being black or Hispanic means a greater or lesser likelihood of voting. If the nonresponse problem becomes worse, we won't be able to tell if personal economic conditions are more important in determining whom a citizen votes for than national economic conditions. If nonresponse becomes worse, then we will no longer be able to trust our estimates or to compare them over time. The devil's advocate who won't worry about current levels of nonresponse must be concerned about what will happen should response rates continue to fall. Further, while the corrections developed in chapter 5 and applied in chapter 6 continue to produce the same qualitative differences as response rates continue to worsen, we can not expect that the two-stage corrections will salvage plainly miserable response rates. Nonresponse is a clear and present danger to political science.

Representation or Misrepresentation?

These findings have implications for the quality of representation that surveys provide. We might think of the problems nonresponse poses to political representation in terms of *who* is represented, and *what effect* nonresponse has on politics.

At one level, we know that surveys overrepresent people who are underrepresented elsewhere in politics. In chapter 2, I show that the NES and GSS samples included disproportionately high numbers of the elderly, blacks, and poor. But we also know something about why people participate in surveys, and this information affects the quality of representation for those very groups. We know that the respondent's race and ethnic origin interacts with the respondent's relationship to strangers and the interviewer. Hispanics appear to be more likely than non-Hispanics to refuse to participate on grounds of a fear of breach of confidentiality or a desire to preserve privacy. Respondents who are of a different race than the interviewer are more likely to be perceived as hostile, threatening, or rude than respondents of the same race as the interviewer. These findings mean something in the context of polls and surveys as a tool of political representation. These findings suggest that surveys represent Hispanics who *do not* fear a breach of confidentiality, which may well be a misrepresentation. Surveys may overrepresent people who are trusting and cooperative with people of another race. Race becomes a barrier to survey participation because of the relationships that race evokes. One might wonder if the federal authorities harassed Hispanics less frequently or if race were less divisive, whether or not these relationships would be less important.

Furthermore, because the behavioral aspects of survey participation dominate class correlates, there is an implication that surveys attract the least representative people of lower economic classes. If interest in politics and information about politics influence whether or not a respondent chooses to participate in a survey, then respondents are more interested and informed than most people in their class. If true, what this means is that the poor *respondent* is more like the wealthy respondent than the poor *refusal* in terms of interest and information, trust for others, and general participativeness. The net effect of nonresponse is to depress the differences between classes, to reduce the importance of class in understanding politics. We end up with respondents of all classes who are more like each other than members of their own class. This means that nonresponse undermines the importance of class in understanding politics. Given that we have seen considerable recent ink in both the political science journals and the press devoted to the declining importance of class in American politics, it is especially interesting if nonresponse depresses the observed effects of class. One has to wonder whether or not the declining role of class is an artifact of rising survey nonresponse.

There are very real, consequential effects of nonresponse on politics. One need only look as far as the decennial Census to locate concrete problems with nonresponse. The Census may be nominally a complete tabulation of the residents of the United States, but the Census undercounts people in certain groups. Notably, young, black males in urban areas may be undercounted by as much as 18 percent (Maurice and Nathan 1982). In 1980, the Census missed 5 percent of the total population. In 1990, the missing proportion may well be much larger: the initial nonresponse rates for the 1990 Census were 10 percent higher than expected. Of course, the Census is not a survey, but the undercount problem is a problem of nonresponse.

The Census determines congressional apportionment, as provided in the Constitution itself. In this sense *at minimum,* the nonresponse problem for the Census directly implicates political representation, altering whether or not a citizen in New York has as much political representation as a citizen in Kansas. The founders of the United States themselves argued for the fundamental importance of accurate Census counts.

> Every word of these provisions imports the intention of the Constitution that the *whole* People shall be represented. Every apportionment therefore which leaves a portion of the People totally *unrepresented* fails to carry into effect the prescription of the Constitution (Letter dated Feb. 28, 1832, quoted in testimony to the House Subcommittee on Census and Population, Jan. 30, 1990, 134)

The gross undercount in 1980 exceeded 8.5 million persons, greater than the populations of eleven states, counted individually. A Census that misses the equivalent of an Alaska, Wyoming, or Vermont, can not be held to be representative in the sense that the founders mandated.

By some estimates, New York lost one congressional seat as a result of the undercount in 1980 (*New York Times,* Feb. 18, 1990). But the problem with the undercount is that specific subpopulations of the United States count less than others. There is an unpleasant similarity between the Census undercount and the original three-fifths rule for counting black Americans in terms of representation. Joseph Kadane, in testimony before the House Subcommittee on Census and Population, eloquently identified the similarity:

> When the constitution was written, a black person, then almost certainly a slave, counted for 60% of a white person. By 1980, a black person would count for about 94% of a white person. The 1990 census might be the first in which every American, black or white, counts the same, if a reasonable adjustment is done. This is a civil rights issue. (House Subcommittee on Census and Population, Jan. 30, 1990, 108)

We did not achieve parity between whites and blacks in the 1990 Census, and it is far from evident that a reasonable adjustment could be done.

The Census undercount is not simply a problem of a missing legislator in a few of the largest cities. Recall the *billions* of dollars that are allocated on the basis of Census figures. Some estimate that New York City lost as much as $670 million due to the undercount (*New York Times,* Feb. 18, 1990). But the Census is only a decennial event, whereas surveys happen in this country every day. The Census nonresponse is but the tip of the iceberg.

We depend upon the CPS's monthly estimates of income in many ways. These estimates contribute to the development of the Consumer Price Index, our primary means to assess inflation. And the stock market might fluctuate by millions of dollars in a single day, depending on the release of these CPS income estimates. The irony embedded in our increasing reliance on these numbers is that the number of respondents who refuse to divulge their income to the CPS interviewers has *quintupled* in the last 40 years (Joint Economic Committee, Mar. 1 and 29, 1990). As of 1987, 28 percent of the CPS sample refused to respond to the income questions. The effect of the item nonresponse to this question remains unknown, but potentially ripples throughout our economy.

One of the best modes of reconnaissance in the war on drugs is survey research on drug use. While the Drug Enforcement Administration proudly displays every large seizure of illegal drugs, without knowing what is happening to consumption, the signal is decidedly equivocal: does a large arrest signify that fewer drugs will then enter the market or that demand is sufficiently great to cause a large circulation of drugs into the United States, of which the seizure is but a small portion? We have to know whether consumption of drugs is rising or falling in order to gauge the success of the war on drugs. Yet there is a gap between the results of the National Institutes on Drug Abuse surveys and evident epidemic drug problems in many communities. As several members of the House Appropriations Subcommittee questioned the administrators of the Alcohol, Drug Abuse and Mental Health Administration, the very population that is most at risk—high school dropouts—fell out of the High School Seniors Survey (House Subcommittee on Appropriations, Apr. 22, 1991, 564–69). Likewise, our National Household Surveys can not track drug abuse among the homeless, many of whom may have addictive disorders.

Nonresponse affects not just *who* is represented, it also affects how this representation carries into politics. Political scientists use survey data to answer questions about human behavior. Why do people vote? Does personal economic situation outweigh one's sense of the national economy when one chooses between candidates? Why was Reagan such a popular president? What is the relationship between religion, socio-economic status, and attitudes toward abortion?

While I frame these questions in a way only a social scientist could love, a different formulation of these questions permeates political life.

Candidates for all manner of national political offices regularly rely on survey data. These candidates need to know which people are likely to vote at all, and if they do vote, who they would choose. One implication of chapter 6 is that survey nonresponse leads to overestimates of the number of people who turn out for elections. From chapters 6 and 7, we also know that survey nonresponse causes us to underestimate the importance of income. Combined, the two findings suggest that nonresponse causes us to overestimate turnout by the wealthy. By implication, nonresponse causes political candidates' polls to overestimate turnout among wealthier groups. If these polls contribute to the direction of candidates' strategy—and there is ample evidence that they do (Salmore and Salmore 1985; Sabato 1981; Jacobson 1987; Bogart 1972; Aldrich 1980)—survey nonresponse may cause an underrepresentation of poorer economic groups' concerns in the discourse surrounding campaigns.

There are other implications of the effects of nonresponse on our understanding of why people vote for different candidates. Nonresponse causes us to overestimate the importance of negative voting, and to underestimate the importance of approval voting. A rather salient and distasteful feature of recent major campaigns has been the profusion of negative advertising, much of it developed and tested with campaign polls. Nonresponse in campaign polling adds to the incentives for negative advertising by overestimating the importance of negative voting.

Public opinion surveys are a means for decision-makers to learn about the needs and the desires of the public. On a mechanical level, surveys tally the characteristics of the public, providing a tool to understand the relationship between problems and characteristics. The Public Health Service is one of the most active agencies of the government in survey research. Surveys are a means to identify the causes of substance abuse, how disease spreads, and the correlates of mental health. In chapter 3, we learn that Hispanics are more likely to be suspicious of the interviewer and that respondents of a different race than the interviewer are more likely to have an acrimonious rapport. Do these class effects on the survey process percolate to the findings of federal agencies about health, economics, or welfare?

Nonresponse is a problem of political misrepresentation. What could have been an opportunity to redress barriers to political participation by reducing the costs of participation and balancing against intensely held opinions is a lost opportunity. Nonresponse undercuts the work of social scientists, journalists, and government researchers. Do we leave it at that?

What Is to Be Done?

Surveys matter to a wide range of people—academics depend on surveys to explore human behavior, federal agencies rely on surveys to obtain accurate counts of the public, campaigners use surveys to design strategy, newspapers incorporate polls as standard news, even the general public seems to have a fascination with survey results. Nonresponse affects all of these people. What could academics, survey researchers, the government, and the public do about nonresponse?

To Academic Researchers

If there is any audience to whom this work and its findings should matter the most, it is academics who use survey research. Academics must become aware that survey nonresponse will undermine their work.

Recall the magnitude of the effects of correction for nonresponse in chapter 6 to the range of models. To be sure, some of the changes were small, a matter of a few percent. For example, the changes to the slope coefficients in the turnout models were all changes of at most a few percentage points. But some of the other changes were substantial. The changes to the coefficients on recall and recognition of the candidates in the familiarity model doubled on correction. And even some of the subtle changes meant something. The constant term in the turnout models— arguably the least interesting coefficient in any model—decreased by several percent, providing direct proof that nonresponse causes surveys to overestimate turnout. Political scientists will continue to overestimate the number of people who participate in politics until they account for nonresponse. We will overestimate the effect of negative voting, and underestimate the importance of information and class, until we correct for nonresponse.

It may be no accident that the direction of change to the coefficients after correction was to *increase* the importance of key variables. Tobin (1958) proved over three decades ago that if a sample is selected on the dependent variable, all of the coefficients will be underestimated. And while nonresponse is a more complicated process of selection, the general finding of attenuation bears up in every model in chapter 6 that evinced some change after correction.

If there is a threat by nonresponse to academic research that appears here, it is that nonresponse undermines social scientific work and prevents us from confirming theories or hypotheses when they should be confirmed. Attenuation means that the coefficients will be smaller relative to their standard errors than they should be.

The process of correction for nonresponse is relatively simple. Chapter 6 demonstrates that one may develop corrections for nonresponse based solely on information that most survey organizations collect as a matter of course. In order for a survey organization to gauge how well it is doing in the field, that organization needs to know how many contacts an interviewer must make and whether respondents need special persuasion to participate. These measures are the very basis of the nonresponse corrections used throughout chapter 6.

We can improve on the reliability of the corrections by approaching the problem from other directions, by examining the respondents' reasons for refusal or response as well as their demographic characteristics. And certainly, we have every incentive to improve the selection models. Improvement in these models aids the corrections, helps us understand compliance better, and provides further guidance to ways to improve response rates. But a minimally satisfactory correction for nonresponse requires inexpensively gathered information. Moreover, the techniques to apply these corrections may be implemented in any statistical package that conducts regression analysis, even in many microcomputer spreadsheets.

Survey organizations not only need to collect this information but they ought to routinely disseminate information about the nonrespondents. This information provides the basis for sensible use of survey data. It's not sufficient for survey organizations to gather data strictly for internal use. Secondary analysts need the data on nonrespondents in order to develop and apply corrections for nonresponse. An organization could conceivably release simply an estimate of the extra term for corrections (the residual of the selection model for the Achen corrections, or the Inverse Mill's Ratio of the predicted values of the selection model in the Heckman corrections). Just as we should doubt the validity of data weighted by unknown weighting classes, we should also doubt the validity of models adjusted without knowing what goes into the adjustment. The far better solution is to release the information about the nonrespondents so that we may make adjustments appropriate to our models.

There remain problems in the study of how nonresponse affects scientific research, and academics of various disciplines are best suited to approaching these problems. Chapter 5 presents how nonresponse may undermine simple, one-equation regression models. But most social science disciplines have progressed far beyond such simple analyses. While one can see by analogy how nonresponse may also affect more complicated analyses, considerable work remains. How does nonresponse affect multiple equation models? How does error due to nonresponse compare with measurement error in models that assume imperfect indicators of latent variables (i.e., LISREL or confirmatory factor analysis models)? Most recently, methodologists in political science and economics have moved far beyond regression analyses to modeling the systematic component of stochastic processes with Maximum Likelihood techniques. How does nonresponse affect our work if we model the error itself?

Nonresponse explicitly affects time series analyses of political data. Indeed, I presented the problem of nonresponse as one worsening over time: refusal rates, for instance, have more than trebled over the last three decades in the NES. The problem is not simply one of assuming that the data collected in the 1950s are less prone to nonresponse error than current data. As I discuss in chapter 5, nonresponse *error* is the product of *both* nonresponse rates and the difference between respondents and nonrespondents. It may well be that the data collected over 30 years ago with refusal rates below 10 percent are just as prone to nonresponse error as the data collected today. Moreover, the underlying process may have changed over time. Perhaps concerns about confidentiality and privacy were more important in the Vietnam-Watergate era than either today or in the 1950s. Perhaps suspiciousness of strangers has risen over time. At the same time that we really need to know if nonresponse undercuts time series analyses of political and social data, we face a much more difficult (and perhaps more interesting) problem in assessing the error due to nonresponse. Plenty of work remains to be done on the causes and consequences of nonresponse.

To Survey Researchers

Nonresponse is an explicit threat to the business of survey research. Nonresponse threatens generalizability, increases the cost of gathering an acceptable sample size, may make interviewing a less attractive career. Extensive levels of nonresponse threaten the very legitimacy of surveys: how many people now believe that surveys are a waste of time or an intrusion into private affairs? To the survey researchers, I offer two suggestions.

First, survey researchers should publicize response rates. In the 1970s, the American Association of Public Opinion Researchers codified a set of guidelines for appropriate display of survey results. Survey organizations should identify who sponsored the survey and who conducted it, the exact question wording, size of the samples, and precision of the findings, and they should indicate the sample selection procedure. Included among the recomendations, but rarely a fixture of reported survey results, is the suggestion that survey organizations publicize the completion rates for the survey. Instead, what one sees in the newspapers is an obfuscating claim that a survey with so many respondents has a margin of error of X percent. What is never made clear is that X percent incorporates only one aspect of survey error. While nonresponse *rates* are only a part of nonresponse *error,* these rates are a vital test of the fairness of the surveys.

Second, survey researchers should identify the characteristics of the people who refuse to participate in your surveys. Most of the attention by the survey industry to nonresponse has been ameliorative—what can we do to reduce nonresponse rates? This approach is only half of the problem. No matter what we do, some people will refuse to participate. What do we do about the nonresponse that remains? We have techniques that produce unbiased and consistent estimates of the population, even with nonresponse. We can impute for missing data, apply two-stage corrections for nonresponse in multivariate analyses, or model the likelihood of response. With all these approaches, there is a common requirement: we need to know which people participate in surveys and why.

Survey researchers will probably remain most interested in what can be done to reduce nonresponse rates. The model developed in chapters 3 and 4 has implications for what might be done. If the respondent's relationship to the interview is the dominant of the four relationships, then attempts to boost response rates should focus on this. In these two chapters, I point to interest, experience, informedness, and time as aspects of the respondent's relationship to the interview. Can we make interviews seem less like tests to respondents and more enjoyable? Can we make the surveys more interesting and less time-consuming?

Survey researchers, then, are left with two very good reasons to devote efforts toward gathering information about nonrespondents and correcting for nonresponse rather than making excessive efforts to reduce nonresponse. One, we will always have some nonresponse and will always be in a position of assessing how nonresponse affects our analysis. Two, continued attempts to convert refusal rates raise ethical concerns. At some point, efforts to boost response rates become prohibitively expensive. We know some people will continue to refuse or continue to elude contact with the interviewer. Even after all conceivable attempts to cut nonresponse rates, we will still confront some amount of nonresponse. Furthermore, there is an ethical reason not to devote all our resources toward reducing nonresponse. We must respect the wishes of refusals who absolutely do not want to participate in our studies. Continuing to badger these refusals to comply with the interview abuses the refusals' right to privacy and is tantamount to harassment.

To Policymakers

While survey researchers and academics depend on surveys for their livelihoods, we all depend on the government's use of surveys. The extent to which surveys permeate political life touches every phase of the policy process. I have two suggestions about what government agencies might do in response to nonresponse.

First and foremost, policymakers should remember that the people who respond to surveys may be an increasingly biased sample of the public. If the net effect of screening out the least informed people is to reduce the apparent effect of information in our analysis, we need to keep this in mind when viewing any survey where information is an aspect of the analysis.

When survey researchers adjust data, those researchers should make the adjustments explicit enough to enable researchers to repair the fixes if needed. There is something to be said for leaving the data unaltered. A census is a count—perhaps a biased one—and there's something appealing about its simplicity. If it turns out to be necessary to adjust the decennial Census, then it is imperative that we know how the data are adjusted. Fortunately, the track record of the government surveys is one of openness with regard to the methods of adjustment. But the same suggestion goes for commercial polls and academic surveys, and with those studies, it is often unclear when or how or if the data are adjusted—for "likely voters," for proportions of demographic categories, to compensate for nonresponse, or whatever.

To the Public

While academics, survey researchers, and the government depend on surveys, we all ultimately depend on the public responding to the surveys. We have already seen a number of books and articles advising the public on how to be intelligent consumers of poll data (e.g., Wheeler 1976; Ginsberg 1986; Bradburn and Sudman 1988; Asher 1988). To that chorus, I make three suggestions.

First, the public should be aware that surveys contain more error than the newspapers typically admit. There is something deceptively precise about survey results, especially as the media use these results. There are several reasons why survey results are not as exact as they seem. Other books warn about surveys laden with measurement error and sampling error. What I suggest is that nonresponse error is a hitherto largely ignored component of error in all published survey results. When newspapers list survey results and the X percent sampling error, we should remember that X percent is based on the claim that the respondents to the surveys are a random sample of the population. We know that respondents differ from nonrespondents in important ways, especially in terms of overall participativeness or interest in politics. The newspapers' claim of X percent sampling error ignores the many other, nonsampling, sources of error.

Second, if we are asked to participate in a survey, we should demand to know who is conducting the survey and why. Fraudulent uses of surveys abound, and the responsible parties should be reprimanded. A local water treatment company attempts to lure customers with the opening line, "We're conducting a survey of water quality," and then proceeds to try to sell water filters. A local newspaper tries the same by claiming to be running a survey of newspaper readership, as a ruse to sell subscriptions. These may seem innocuous, but they threaten real survey work by causing people to be wary of sales pitches whenever a stranger comes to the door or calls on the phone. For a newspaper that often uses survey results, conducts their own (real) surveys, and presumably depends on the accuracy of survey results, to masquerade as a survey in order to huckster sales is egregious.

But third, if the survey is legitimate, we should take the time to respond. Surveys can be pleasant, a chance to express our views, perhaps even a way to think about problems we haven't given much thought to before. Surveys are a means for government to identify what we want. We were selected for the survey not because we're the same as everyone else, but because we represent a part of American diversity. When the interviewer comes to our doors or calls on the phone, the interviewer is asking us to represent ourselves in an increasingly vital part of the American political process.

Appendixes

APPENDIX A

Tables of Demographics

TABLE A.1. Age of Respondents, Bracketed, 1978–1988 CPS, NES, GSS and NES Telephone

	1978	1980	1982	1984	1986	1988
				CPS		
18–29	27	29	30	29	30	27
30–49	38	36	34	34	34	39
50–64	19	19	20	21	22	18
65+	16	16	16	16	15	16
Mean	44	43	43	43	43	44
				NES		
18–29	27	25	22	23	23	21
30–49	35	33	35	38	39	40
50–64	21	21	21	18	18	18
65+	18	21	22	21	20	20
Mean	45	46	47	46	45	46
				GSS		
18–29	25	23	27	25	20	22
30–49	35	35	31	37	38	39
50–64	20	20	21	18	18	16
65+	20	23	21	21	24	23
Mean	46	47	47	46	47	47
			NES Telephone			
18–29			23	31		24
30–49			38	39		46
50–64			19	20		16
65+			21	10		14
Mean			45	41		40

Cell entries are percentage of each age group for each year. CPS data are weighted by standard person weight (the CPS adjustment for probability of selection and nonresponse). NES and GSS data are weighted by the probability of selection (the inverse of number of eligible adults in household).

TABLE A.2. Race of Respondents, 1978–1988 CPS, NES and GSS

	1978	1980	1982	1984	1986	1988
			CPS			
White	89	88	88	86	87	86
Black	10	11	11	11	11	11
Other	1	1	2	3	2	3
			NES			
White	87	87	87	86	82	82
Black	11	13	12	12	16	14
Other	1	1	1	2	2	4
			GSS			
White	88	90	87	84	84	83
Black	11	10	11	13	13	13
Other	1	1	2	3	2	4
			NES Telephone			
White			92	89		90
Black			5	9		5
Other			2	2		5

Cell entries are percentage of each race group for each year. CPS data are weighted by standard person weight (the CPS adjustment for probability of selection and nonresponse). NES and GSS data are weighted by the probability of selection (the inverse of number of eligible adults in household).

TABLE A.3. Gender of Respondents, 1978–1988 CPS, NES and GSS

	1978	1980	1982	1984	1986	1988
			CPS			
Male	47	47	47	47	47	48
Female	53	53	53	53	53	52
			NES			
Male	42	41	43	42	41	40
Female	58	59	58	58	59	60
			GSS			
Male	40	42	39	39	40	41
Female	60	58	61	61	60	60
			NES Telephone			
Male			39	46		45
Female			62	54		55

Cell entries are percentage of each gender for each year. CPS data are weighted by standard person weight (the CPS adjustment for probability of selection and nonresponse). NES and GSS data are weighted by the probability of selection (the inverse of number of eligible adults in household).

TABLE A.4. Education of Respondents, 1978–1988 CPS, NES and GSS

	1978	1980	1982	1984	1986	1988
				CPS		
Less than HS	27	26	24	23	21	21
High School	37	38	38	38	38	38
College	35	36	38	39	41	41
				NES		
Less than HS	30	27	24	26	22	22
High School	36	36	33	34	35	35
College	34	37	44	41	43	43
				GSS		
Less than HS	33	33	32	29	31	27
High School	34	32	33	32	32	30
College	33	35	35	39	38	43
			NES Telephone			
Less than HS			19	12		12
High School			60	65		65
College			21	23		24

Cell entries are percentage of each education group for each year. CPS data are weighted by standard person weight (the CPS adjustment for probability of selection and nonresponse). NES and GSS data are weighted by the probability of selection (the inverse of number of eligible adults in household).

TABLE A.5. Income of Respondents, 1978–1988 CPS, NES and GSS

	1978	1980	1982	1984	1986	1988
			CPS			
< $5,000	14	11	9	8	7	9
$5,000–$9,999	19	17	15	13	12	13
$10,000–$19,999	36	32	28	26	24	22
$20,000–$24,999	13	15	12	11	11	9
$25,000–$49,999	15	22	29	32	34	40
$50,000+	3	4	14	18	23	16
			NES			
< $5,000	7	14	14	12	10	11
$5,000–$9,999	15	19	16	16	15	13
$10,000–$19,999	38	29	28	25	23	24
$20,000–$24,999	16	14	13	11	11	10
$25,000–$49,999	22	21	24	28	31	29
$50,000+	3	4	6	8	11	12
			GSS			
$5,000–$9,999	21	17	15	13	12	13
$10,000–$19,999	35	31	17	27	23	21
$20,000–$24,999	14	14	27	14	11	10
$25,000+	15	24	28	19	44	48

Cell entries are percentage of each income group for each year. CPS data are weighted by standard person weight (the CPS adjustment for probability of selection and nonresponse). NES and GSS data are weighted by the probability of selection (the inverse of number of eligible adults in household).

TABLE A.6. Respondent's Place of Residence, 1978–1988 CPS, NES and GSS

	1978	1980	1982	1984	1986	1988
			CPS			
Central Cities	26.2	25.6	25.7	25.6	24.4	26.9
Balance of SMSA	36.1	36.8	36.7	37.7	36.1	35.4
Non-SMSA	29.5	29.2	29.1	28.2	23.2	21.8
Not Identified	8.2	8.4	8.6	8.5	16.3	15.9
			NES			
Central Cities	29.4	30.0	29.8	25	28.1	26.3
Balance of SMSA	38.1	32.7	35.1	40.4	40.3	40.6
Non-SMSA	25.7	25.0	21.8	24.9	24.9	24.9
Not Identified	6.8	7.6	13.2	9.7	6.7	8.3
Mean Population						
(1,000s)	235	284	366	302	375	387
			GSS			
Central Cities	23.4	25.6	24.6	25	22.3	21.4
Balance of SMSA	23.0	19.0	15.7	29.4	31.3	31.7
Non-SMSA	34.8	38.3	41.7	33.1	31.8	36.3
Not Identified	18.8	17.1	17.8	12.6	14.5	10.6
Mean Population						
(1,000s)	273	463	466	372	339	371

Cell entries are percentage of each residency group for each year. CPS data are weighted by standard person weight (the CPS adjustment for probability of selection and nonresponse). NES and GSS data are weighted by the probability of selection (the inverse of number of eligible adults in household).

Coding of Open-ended Reasons for Refusal

1986 NES

Very Ill: Long-term illness; short-term illness; illness of unspecified length; R senile, feebleminded, "too old," language difficulty, disability, illiterate.

Family Stress: Illness in R's family; R under severe stress: death in family, divorce, etc.

Too Busy: R genuinely too busy: holds several jobs, study conflicted with other family events; too busy, not further specified (NFS).

Not Interested: R doesn't vote; not interested in politics.

Bad Experience: "It is a waste of time, no good will come out of it"; other surveys mentioned (tired of answering surveys, bad experience with other surveys).

Confidentiality: Right to privacy mentioned; "I don't do surveys/don't discuss politics or religion"; general evasiveness, suspicious, not coming to the door, talking through closed door; religious beliefs mentioned as reasons for not granting interview.

1988 NES

Very Ill: R is senile, mentally retarded, or otherwise incompetent; R speaks neither English nor Spanish; R is deaf; R is very ill.

Family Stress: Death, severe illness of someone not R; jail, divorce, loss of job; a family member is adamantly opposed to R doing the interview.

Too Busy: Respondent asks for payment for time; survey is too long/an hour is too long; "we're just too busy" (NFS); "we're just too busy, moving"; "we're just too busy"—family business, seasonal, imminent wedding, etc.; R is too busy (NFS); R is almost never home—working two jobs, traveling, seasonal crunch at work, etc.

Not Interested: "We're not interested, don't vote"; R is not interested, doesn't vote; R is not registered and does not vote; R doesn't know enough; "we don't want to be bothered."

Bad Experience: "Surveys are a waste of time"; previous bad experience—general household reference.

Confidentiality: Confidentiality box checked; too personal—"we don't talk to anyone about politics, etc."; against (our) religion.

1989 DAS Refusals

Very Ill: Senile or incompetent; very ill; deaf.

Family Stress: Stressful family situation; other family member opposes R's participating in survey.

Too Busy: Asks for payment; survey is too long; moving; R almost never home; too busy (NFS); R is away; "I don't have time"; work schedule.

Not Interested: "We (R) are not interested in current affairs"; "we (R) do not vote, are not registered"; "we are not interested (NFS)"; "I just don't want to do it"; "I don't know about these things"; "we don't want to be bothered."

Bad Experience: "Surveys are waste of time"; previous bad experience with surveys; general objections to surveys; objects to persistent requests by interviewer.

Confidentiality: Suspicious of survey; confidentiality; against religion; too personal.

1989 DAS Respondents

Good Experience: Enjoys surveys; thought it would be fun; R might learn something; R views survey as personally useful; wasn't going to hurt R; didn't cost R anything; doesn't mind questions; no reason not to answer survey; believes surveys help solve community problems; wants to do something about a specific problem; gives a picture of the community; lets government know what people want; interested in community affairs/problems; general belief in importance of surveys.

Openness: Enjoys expressing opinions; R has "nothing to hide."

Interest: Curious about the survey; interested in surveys; never been interviewed before; it's different; survey is a diversion.

Empathy: Support for University of Michigan; general mention for University of Michigan; empathy/sympathy for interviewer; knows how difficult surveys can be; R acted as interviewer previously; sympathetic to college students; happy to help students; wants to help interviewer with school; positive feelings toward interviewer; interviewer appeared trustworthy/likable/friendly/nice; not afraid of interviewer; no negative feelings toward interviewer.

Helper: Wants to help out; "I'm a nice person"; "I like to help people"; R doesn't like to say no; felt obligated; somebody has to do it.

Not Busy: Not too busy; nothing to do; had the time; didn't know how long survey was.

APPENDIX C

Cookbook Corrections for Nonresponse

Heckman's Method is suitable where the outcome equation is a linear model and the dependent variable is continuous.

1. Code a dummy variable for response to the survey, $Y1$, where respondents are coded 1, and nonrespondents are coded 0.

2. Identify a set of independent variables, $Z1, Z2, \ldots$, to predict whether or not the sample person responds to the survey. The Zi's must include at least one variable which does *not* appear in the equation of interest.

3. Estimate a probit model of $Y1$ as a function of the Zi, and save the predicted values:

$$\hat{\delta}_1 Z_1 + \hat{\delta}_2 Z_2 + \ldots + \hat{\delta}_k Z_k$$

4. Compute the Inverse Mill's Ratio of the predicted values from the previous step $(\hat{\delta}_1 Z_1 + \ldots + \hat{\delta}_k Z_k)$:

$$\text{IMR}(\hat{\delta}_1 Z_1 + \ldots + \hat{\delta}_k Z_k) = \frac{\phi(\hat{\delta}_1 Z_1 + \ldots + \hat{\delta}_k Z_k)}{\Phi(\hat{\delta}_1 Z_1 + \ldots + \hat{\delta}_k Z_k)}$$

5. Estimate the outcome equation of a continuous dependent variable, $Y2$, as a function of independent Xi and the $\text{IMR}(\hat{\delta}_1 Z_1 + \ldots + \hat{\delta}_k Z_k)$ generated in the previous step.

Achen's Method I is suitable when the dependent variable is continuous.

1. Repeat steps one and two from the Heckman Method.

209

2. Estimate a linear probability model with ordinary least squares regressing $Y1$ on the k $Z_1, Z_2, \ldots, Z_k$. Save the *residuals* in $\hat{u}_i$.

3. Estimate the outcome equation of a continuous dependent variable, $Y2$, as a function of the m independent $X_1, X_2, \ldots, X_m$ and the residual term, $\hat{u}_i$, with ordinary least squares.

Achen's Method II is suitable when the dependent variable is dichotomous (e.g., yes or no).

1. Repeat steps one through three from the Achen Method to obtain an estimate of the residual, $\hat{u}_i$.

2. Estimate a linear probability model regressing $Y2$ on the m X_1, X_2, $\ldots, X_m$ with ordinary least squares (this is the *outcome equation*). Save the *estimated coefficients*.

3. Estimate the following function with nonlinear least squares, using the estimated coefficients from the previous step as starting values:

$$
\begin{aligned}
Y1_i \;=\; & \beta_0 + \beta_1 X_1 + \ldots \beta_m X_m \\
& + \rho\hat{u}(\beta_0 + \beta_1 X_1 + \ldots \beta_m X_m) \\
& \times [1 - (\beta_0 + \beta_1 X_1 + \ldots \beta_m X_m)]
\end{aligned}
$$

APPENDIX D

Calculation of Standard Errors, Achen Continuous Model

Achen (1986) develops these calculations for the standard errors of the regression coefficients in his linear two-stage correction for censored samples. Following the format for the equations laid out previously, the model of interest is

$$Y_i = \beta' X_i + \epsilon_i \tag{D.1}$$

and the selection mechanism is

$$Y_i \text{ is observed if and only if } \delta' Z_i + u_i > 0 \tag{D.2}$$

Then, let p be the predicted values from the selection mechanism (D.2), and let q be 1 minus p

$$
\begin{aligned}
p &= Z\hat{\delta} \\
q &= 1 - p
\end{aligned}
$$

Let P be the diagonal matrix of the predicted values from the selection mechanism (D.2):

$$P = diag(p_i)$$

Let $\hat{\Sigma}$ be the diagonal matrix:

$$\hat{\Sigma} = diag(p_i q_i)$$

In order to perform the correction for censored samples, first estimate the selection equation (D.2) and save the estimated residuals, $\hat{u}_i$. Include the estimated residuals ($\hat{u}_i$) as an additional regressor in the outcome equation (D.1):

$$Y = \beta' X_i + \rho \hat{u}_i + \epsilon_i$$

Let $\hat{\sigma}^2$ be the estimate of the variance in the error term (ϵ_i):

$$\hat{\sigma}^2 = var(Y_i - \hat{\beta}' X_i)$$

Define the following matrices for shorthand:

$$
\begin{aligned}
Z_2 &= [X \quad q] \\
\hat{G} &= Z_2' Z_2 \\
\hat{A} &= Z_2' Z (Z' \hat{\Sigma}^{-1} Z)^{-1} Z' Z_2 \\
\hat{B} &= \frac{Z_2(I - P^2)Z_2}{3}
\end{aligned}
$$

Then the variance on the coefficients in the corrected equation (D.3) is:

$$var[\beta \quad \rho] = \hat{\sigma}^2 \hat{G}^{-1} + \hat{\rho}^2 \hat{G}^{-1}(\hat{A} - \hat{B})\hat{G}^{-1}$$

APPENDIX E

Calculation of Standard Errors, Achen Dichotomous Model

Achen (1986) develops the following calculations for standard error in his nonlinear correction for selection bias in a dichotomous outcome model. Following the format for the equations laid out above, the model of interest is

$$Y_i = \beta'X_i + \epsilon_i \qquad (E.1)$$

and the selection mechanism is

$$Y_i \text{ is observed if and only if } \delta'Z_i + u_i > 0 \qquad (E.2)$$

Then, let p_1 be the predicted values from the selection mechanism (E.2), and let q_1 be 1 minus p_1

$$p_1 = Z\hat{\delta}$$
$$q_1 = 1 - p_1$$

And let p_2 be the predicted values from the outcome equation (E.1), and q_2 be 1 minus p_2

$$p_2 = X\hat{\beta}$$
$$q_2 = 1 - p_2$$

Let ρ be the nonlinear least squares estimate on the nonlinear interaction term $[\hat{u}(\beta'x_i)(1 - \beta'x_i)]$. Let Σ be

$$\hat{\Sigma} = diag(p_1 q_1) = \begin{bmatrix} p_{11}q_{11} & 0 & 0 \\ 0 & \ddots & 0 \\ 0 & 0 & p_{1n}q_{1n} \end{bmatrix} \qquad (E.3)$$

213

Let Z_{2i} be the concatenated matrix

$$Z_{2i} = \left[(1 + \rho q_{1i} - 2\rho p_{2i} q_{1i}) X_i \quad p_{2i} q_{2i} q_{1i} \right]$$

Let r and s be

$$r_i = X_i \beta + \rho p_{2i} q_{1i} q_{2i}$$
$$s_i = 1 - r_i$$

Let Λ be the diagonal matrix

$$\hat{\Lambda} = diag(s_1 r_1) = \begin{bmatrix} s_{11} r_{11} & 0 & 0 \\ 0 & \ddots & 0 \\ 0 & 0 & s_{1n} r_{1n} \end{bmatrix}$$

For shorthand, define three matrices, A, C, and G

$$A = X' Z_{2i} \left(X' \Sigma^{-1} X' \right)^{-1} X' Z_{2i}$$
$$C = Z'_{2i} \Lambda Z'_{2i}$$
$$G = Z'_{2i} Z_{2i}$$

Then the variance of the coefficients of the nonlinear correction is

$$var \begin{bmatrix} \beta & \rho \end{bmatrix} = G^{-1} (\rho^2 A + C) G^{-1}$$

Sample SHAZAM Run for Achen Dichotomous Model

SHAZAM (White 1978) is a general purpose econometrics computer program offering many features conducive to the corrections proposed by Heckman and Achen. Not the least of these features is a full matrix algebra facility.[1] The following is a full SHAZAM setup to estimate a model of turnout in the general election as a function of demographic measures, akin to one estimated by Wolfinger and Rosenstone (1980). Chapter 6 discusses this model in more detail, but the model is a suitable one to demonstrate (1) the nonlinear correction for dichotomous dependent variables (here, turnout in the general election), and (2) the calculation of the standard errors.

```
format (11f10.3)
read (11) valturn black hisp age agesq income educ
 comply pletter refconv logcalls / format
set nowarnskip
* drop nonsample cases
skipif(comply.eq.9)
ols comply pletter refconv logcalls / resid=uhat predict=p1
* truncate the residual uhat to 0 to 1 bounds
if (uhat.gt.0.999) uhat=0.999
if (uhat.lt.0.001) uhat=0.001
* skip missing data
skipif(black.eq.9)
skipif(hisp.eq.9)
skipif(educ.eq.9)
skipif(valturn.eq.9)
skipif(age.eq.99)
skipif(income.eq.9)
```

---

1. There are, of course, other statistics packages with matrix algebra facilities (e.g., SAS, SST). I choose SHAZAM for the inexpense of running the program on an enormous range of platforms and for the transparent nature of the matrix algebra.

```
* first ols estimate of the turnout model
ols valturn black hisp age income educ / predict=yhat
if (yhat.lt.0.001) yhat=.001
if (yhat.gt.0.999) yhat=.999
* Note that SHAZAM applies the sqrt of the weight
genr wt=1/(yhat*(1-yhat))
* gls estimate of the turnout model,
* using weight generated above
ols valturn black hisp age income educ / weight=wt coef=glsb
* save the starting betas as the gls coefficients,
* reordering for nl
matrix stb=lag(glsb,1)                              .
matrix stb(1,1)=glsb(6,1)
matrix stb=(stb')|1
* set the starting value for rho to be 1
matrix stb(1,7)=1
* nonlinear least squares, saving predicted values,
* using starting values from gls
nl 1 / ncoef=7 predict=p2 coef=nlb start=stb
eq valturn = a+b*black+c*hisp+d*age+e*income+f*educ+ &
 o*uhat*(a+b*black+c*hisp+d*age+e*income+f*educ)* &
 (1-(a+b*black+c*hisp+d*age+e*income+f*educ))
end
genr one=1
* x1 is the matrix of the independent vars for
* the selection eqn
matrix x1=one|logcalls|refconv|pletter
* x2 is the matrix of the independent vars
* for the outcome eqn
matrix x2=one|black|hisp|age|income|educ
matrix q1=1-p1
* oddity of SHAZAM: to multiply item-by-item two vectors,
* multiply one by the inverse of the inverse of the other
matrix sigma=p1/(1/q1)
* in the odd event that sigma is zero,
* set to a very small number
if (sigma.eq.0) sigma=.000001
genr siginv=1/sigma
matrix q2=1-p2
gen1 rho=nlb(7,1)
matrix con=1+rho*q1-2*rho*p2/(1/q1)
```

```
matrix z2=con*x2|(p2/(1/q2)/(1/q1))
matrix r=p2+rho*p2/(1/q2)/(1/q1)
matrix s=1-r
matrix lambda=r/(1/s)
matrix g=z2'z2
matrix a=z2'x1*inv((siginv*x1)'x1)*x1'z2
matrix c=(lambda*z2)'z2
matrix delta=inv(g)*(rho*rho*a+c)*inv(g)
matrix vcv=sqrt(diag(delta))
```

APPENDIX G

Efficiency and Sensitivity of Corrections

We can compare the consistency and increasing inefficiency of the estimates with a simple Maximum Likelihood model. An extension of the linear regression model aptly describes the process. A log-likelihood function for an OLS model with one independent variable, where the variance (σ_i^2) is different for each observation i is:

$$\ln L = -\frac{n}{2}\ln(2\pi) - \frac{1}{2}\sum_{i=1}^{n}\ln(\sigma_i^2) - \frac{1}{2}\sum_{i=1}^{n}\frac{e_i - \alpha - \beta\rho_i}{\sigma_i}^2 \qquad (G.1)$$

Of course, this model cannot be estimated: there is a separate σ^2 for each observation plus α and β, or $(n+2)$ parameters to estimate from n observations. A simplifying assumption is necessary. One plausible assumption is that the spread of the error increases with the ρ:

$$\sigma_i^2 = e^{s+k\rho_i}$$

(The exponentiation is necessary because σ_i^2 must be positive.) With this assumption, the new log-likelihood becomes:

$$\ln L = -\frac{n}{2}\ln(2\pi) - \frac{1}{2}\sum_{i=1}^{n}s + k\rho_i - \frac{1}{2}\sum_{i=1}^{n}\frac{(e_i - \alpha - \beta\rho_i)^2}{e^{s+k\rho_i}}$$

If the corrections are consistent, we expect that both α and β will be zero. If the estimates are highly efficient, then the base variance (with $\rho = 0$, or s) will be small (or negative). The relative inefficiency as ρ in-

TABLE G.1. Maximum Likelihood Estimates of Consistency and Efficiency of Heckman and Achen Corrections for Selection Bias

	Heckman				Achen			
	a	b	s	k	a	b	s	k
Selection on Y								
Error(β_0)	0.00	0.00	−4.92	5.41	.02	.01	−2.87	8.68
Error(β_1)	0.00	0.00	−5.55	4.07	−.01	−.02	−5.16	8.42
Error(β_2)	0.00	0.00	−4.37	4.47	−.02	.01	−2.56	8.00
Selection on X								
Error(β_0)	.13	−.10	.56	1.73	.72	−.21	−1.71	.59
Error(β_1)	−.07	.13	−.53	1.87	−.51	.15	−1.79	.15
Error(β_2)	0.00	.01	−5.98	2.54	0.00	0.00	−6.02	2.61
Selection on Z								
Error(β_0)	−.01	.06	5.04	3.08	−.01	.07	4.98	3.02
Error(β_1)	0.00	0.00	−6.08	2.75	.02	−.03	−6.08	2.75
Error(β_2)	0.00	0.00	6.14	2.74	0.00	0.00	−6.14	2.75

Error is the true value−estimated value. The coefficients (a, b, s, k) are parameters in the log-likelihood

$$\ln L = -\frac{n}{2}\ln(2\pi) - \frac{1}{2}\sum_{i=1}^{n} s + k\rho_i - \frac{1}{2}\sum_{i=1}^{n} \frac{(e_i - \alpha - \beta\rho_i)^2}{e^{s+k\rho_i}}$$

creases should appear as a positive estimate of k.[1] Maximum-Likelihood estimates of this function relating the bias (α and β) and the relative efficiency (k) for both Heckman and Achen models for all three selection scenarios appear in Table G.1.

The two methods yield estimates which are relatively close to each other. In the case of selection on the dependent variable (Y), the Heckman estimates are more efficient (the coefficient for s is always less than the corresponding coefficient in the Achen estimates). The Heckman

---

1. The gradients for the log-likelihood function are:

$$\frac{\partial}{\partial \alpha}\ln L = \sum_{i=1}^{n} \frac{e_i - \alpha - \beta\rho_i}{k\rho_i}$$

$$\frac{\partial}{\partial \beta}\ln L = \sum_{i=1}^{n} \frac{(e_i - \alpha - \beta\rho_i)^2}{k^2\rho_i}$$

$$\frac{\partial}{\partial k}\ln L = -\frac{1}{2}\sum_{i=1}^{n}\frac{1}{k} + \frac{1}{2}\sum_{i=1}^{n} \frac{(e_i - \alpha - \beta\rho_i)^2}{k^2\rho_i}$$

estimates when the data are censored on Y are also less sensitive to increasing correlation between the error terms of the selection and outcome models. But these differences are small.

In the case of selection on the independent variable (X), the Heckman estimates are more efficient initially (s is always less than the equivalent estimate for the Achen models). However, the Heckman estimates are more sensitive to increasing ρ: the coefficient on the increase in variance (k) is always larger for Heckman's method.

In the case of selection on an unrelated variable (Z), the two methods are equally sensitive to the size of ρ, and equally efficient at the situation when $\rho = 0$.

Most important, the coefficients on the bias (α and β) are tiny for both the Heckman and Achen approaches. The impressive aspect of both corrections is that they yield consistent and efficient estimates, when failing to correct for nonresponse clearly introduces bias.

Coding of Variables

Turnout and Class

- *Dependent Variable—Turnout:* Respondents who voted in the general election are coded 1; respondents who did not vote are coded 0. This uses the "validated voting" measure.

- *Education:* Respondents with less than four years of education are coded 0; respondents with five to seven years of education are coded .14; respondents who had eight grades of education are coded .29; respondents with some high school, but no diploma, are coded .43; respondents with a high school diploma are coded .57; respondents with some college education are coded .71; respondents with a college degree are coded .86; and respondents with an advanced degree are coded 1.

- *Age:* This variable denotes the respondent's age in years.

- *Black:* Respondents who are black are coded 1, 0 otherwise.

- *Hispanic Origin:* Respondents who are of Hispanic origin are coded 1, 0 otherwise.

- *Income:* This variable reports the respondent's family income (or own income, if the respondent lives by himself or herself) using the 22 NES categories, ranging from 0 for respondents who earn less than $3,000 a year to 22 for respondents who earn $75,000 or more a year.

Turnout and Residency

- *Dependent Variable—Turnout:* Respondents who voted in the general election are coded 1; respondents who did not vote in the general election are coded 0. This uses the "validated voting" measure.

- *Closing Date:* This variable codes the number of days between election day and the final date of registration.

- *Income:* This variable reports the respondent's family income (or own income, if the respondent lives by himself or herself) using the 22 NES categories, ranging from 0 for respondents who earn less than $3,000 a year to 22 for respondents who earn $75,000 or more a year.

- *Own Home?:* Respondents who own their home are coded 1, 0 otherwise.

- *Education Squared:* This variable is the respondent's number of years of education, squared.

- *Married?:* Married respondents are coded 1, 0 otherwise.

- *Political Interest:* This variable is the NES scale measuring how much attention the respondent pays to politics, ranging from 1 (hardly at all) to 4 (most of the time).

- *Public Officials Care?:* Respondents who believe that public officials care what the respondents think are coded 1, others coded 0.

- *Years at Address:* This variable codes the number of years that the respondent has lived at the current address.

Sociotropic Voting

- *Dependent Variable—Vote for Congress:* Respondents who voted for the incumbent party (Republicans) are coded 1, respondents who voted for the opposition party (Democrats) are coded 0, and nonvoters are missing data.

- *Dissatisfaction with Income:* Respondents who claimed to be better off financially than during the past year are coded +1, respondents who claimed to be about the same financially are coded 0, and respondents who claimed to be worse off financially are coded −1.

- *Unemployment Experiences:* Respondents working at present who were never out of work in the past year are coded +4; respondents working at present but who were out of work sometime in the past year are coded −1; respondents who are temporarily laid off at present but had not been out of work in the past year are coded −3; respondents unemployed at present but who had worked sometime in the past year are coded −4; respondents who are unemployed at present and had not worked anytime in the past year are coded −5.

- *Business Conditions:* Respondents who said that business conditions are better at the present time than a year ago are coded +1; respondents who said business conditions are worse are coded −1.

- *Government Performance:* Respondents who said that the economic policies of the federal government had made things better are coded +1; respondents who said that federal economic policies had made things worse are coded −1.

- *Inflation as National Problem, Unemployment as National Problem:* Respondents who identified inflation or unemployment as a national problem are coded +1, coded 0 otherwise.

- *Party Identification:* Respondents who are Republican (strong identifier, weak identifier, or an independent leaning to Republican) are coded +1; respondents who are independent are coded 0; respondents who are Democrats are coded −1.

Recall and Recognition of Candidates and Voting

- *Dependent variable—Vote for Congress:* Respondents who voted for the Democrat for Congress are coded 1; those who voted for the Republican candidate are coded 0; nonvoters are missing data.

- *Party Identification:* Democratic party identifiers (strong identifiers, weak identifiers, those leaning towards the Democrats) are coded +1; Republican party identifiers are coded −1; independents are coded 0.

- *Democratic Incumbent, Republican Incumbent:* These variables are coded 1 if the incumbent is of the respective party (and running), coded 0 otherwise.

- *Recall/Recognize Democrat, Recall/Recognize Republican:* These variables are coded 1 if the respondent can recall the candidate's name, .5 if the respondent recognizes the name from a list, and 0 otherwise.

Negative Voting

- *Dependent Variable, Model I—Vote for Incumbent:* Respondents who voted for the incumbent house candidate are coded 1; respondents who voted for the challenger are coded 0; nonvoters are missing data.

- *Dependent Variable, Models II and III—Vote for Republican:* Respondents who voted for the Republican candidate are coded 1; respondents who voted for the Democratic candidate are coded 0; nonvoters are missing data.

- *Same Party ID:* Respondents of the same party identification as the incumbent are coded 1, others coded 0.

- *Different Party ID:* Respondents of the opposite party identification of the incumbent are coded 1, others coded 0.

- *Independent:* Respondents who identified themselves as independents are coded 1, others coded 0.

- *Approve Incumbent:* Respondents who expressed approval of the incumbent are coded 1, others 0.

- *Disapprove Incumbent:* Respondents who disapproved of the performance of the incumbent are coded 1, others 0.

Distance and Proximity Models

- •*Dependent Variable—Reagan Feeling Thermometer:* Respondents expressed their warmth toward Reagan on a scale ranging from 0 (for those who feel very cold toward Reagan) to 100 (for those who feel very warm toward Reagan), with 50 representing neutrality toward Reagan.

- •*Spatial Distance:* The respondents' spatial distance toward Reagan is computed as the arithmetic mean of the respondents' placement of Reagan on an issue less the respondents' self-placement. In 1986, the issues included defense spending, Central American policy, and government spending. In 1988, the issues included defense spending, government services, cooperation with the USSR, a guaranteed standard of living, improving the status of blacks, and improving the status of minorities.

- •*Directional Distance:* Using the same set of issues for the spatial distance scale, directional distance is the sum over the issues of the product of the distance of the respondent's placement of the candidate from a neutral position and the distance of the respondent's self-placement from a neutral position.

- •*Party Identification:* The respondent's party identification ranges from 0 for strong Democrats to 6 for strong Republicans, with independents coded at 3.

- •*Black:* If the respondent is black, this variable is coded 1, 0 otherwise.

- •*South:* If the respondent lives in the Census region "South," this variable is coded 1, 0 otherwise.

Information about Voting Record

- •*Dependent Variable—Don't Know about the Representative's Votes:* Respondents were asked if they generally agreed or disagreed with their representative's votes. Respondents who professed not knowing how their representative votes are coded 1. Respondents who agreed or disagreed with their representative's votes are coded 0.

Respondents in districts with no incumbent representative running are missing data.

- *Education:* The respondent's education is bracketed into three categories. *Less Than High School* is coded 1 for respondents without a high school diploma, 0 otherwise. *High School* is coded 1 for respondents who have a high school diploma, but no further education, 0 otherwise. *Some College* is coded 1 for respondents with some amount of college education (but no degree), 0 otherwise. The omitted category is respondents with a college degree.

- *Age:* The respondent's age is categorized in two ways. *Age Less Than 30* is coded 1 for respondents who are less than 30 years old, 0 otherwise. *Age Greater Than or Equal to 65* is coded 1 for respondents who are 65 or more years old, 0 otherwise. The omitted category is respondents between 30 and 65 years old.

- *Male:* This variable is coded 1 for men, 0 for women.

- *Residency:* The number of years that the respondent has lived at the current address is categorized in two ways. *Resident Less Than 5 Years* is coded 1 for respondents who have lived at their current address for less than 5 years, 0 otherwise. *Resident 6 to 10 years* is coded 1 for respondents who have lived at their current address between 6 and 10 years, 0 otherwise. The omitted category includes respondents who have lived at the same address for more than 10 years.

Attitudes toward Abortion

- *Dependent Variable—Abortion Never Permitted:* This variable is coded 1 for respondents who believe that abortion should never be permitted, 0 for respondents who believe that abortion should be allowed under some other circumstance or always as a matter of personal choice. Respondents who refused to answer this question are missing data.

- *Education:* The respondent's education is coded in years.

- *Income:* This variable reports the respondent's family income (or own income, if the respondent lives by himself or herself) using the

22 NES categories, ranging from 0 for respondents who earn less than $3,000 a year to 22 for respondents who earn $75,000 or more a year.

- *South at 16:* This variable is coded 1 for respondents who currently live in the South or lived in the South at age 16, 2 otherwise. (The nonstandard coding of dichotomous variables reflects Hall and Ferree's original coding.)

- *Size of Place:* This variable denotes the size of the respondent's community, coded 1 for rural areas, 2 for suburbs, and 3 for cities.

- *Size of Place at 16:* This variable represents the size of the respondent's community when the respondent was 16 years old, coded 1 for nonrural areas, 2 for rural areas.

- *Frequency Attend Church:* This variable is a scale denoting how often the respondent goes to church, ranging from 1 for every week to 5 for never.

- *Religion Important:* This variable is coded 1 if religion is important to the respondent, 5 otherwise.

- *Religion Provides Guidance:* This variable is coded 3 if religion provides a great deal of guidance to the respondent, 2 if it provides quite a bit of guidance, and 1 if it provides some guidance.

- *Catholic:* This variable is coded 1 if the respondent is Catholic, 0 otherwise.

- *Fundamentalist:* This variable is coded 1 if the respondent is a Fundamentalist, 0 otherwise.

Family Income

- *Dependent Variable—Family Income:* This variable reports the respondent's family income (or own income, if the respondent lives by himself or herself) using the 22 NES categories, ranging from 0 for respondents who earn less than $3,000 a year to 22 for respondents who earn $75,000 or more a year.

- *Over 65:* This variable is coded 1 if the respondent is over 65 years old, 0 otherwise.

- *Education:* This variable codes the respondent's level of education in years.

- *Married:* Respondents who are currently married are coded 1, 0 otherwise.

- *Divorced:* Respondents who are currently divorced (and not married to another spouse) are coded 1, 0 otherwise.

- *Working Now:* Respondents who are currently employed at least 20 hours a week are coded 1, 0 otherwise.

- *Black:* Respondents who are black are coded 1, 0 otherwise.

APPENDIX I

Complete Tables for Models

TABLE I.1. Turnout in the General Election as a Function of Demographics, Uncorrected and Corrected Estimates (All Forms), 1986 NES

| | 1986 NES | | |
	Uncorr.	FAdm.	Demo.
Education	.470	.497	.584
	(.060)	(.060)	(.108)
Age	.017	.019	.010
	(.003)	(.003)	(.001)
Black	.013	−.013	.028
	(.027)	(.041)	(.037)
Hisp	−.051	−.074	.154
	(.037)	(.039)	(.099)
Income	.007	.008	.007
	(.002)	(.002)	(.003)
(Constant)	−.511	−.592	−.545
	(.065)	(.067)	(.081)
$\rho\sigma$		−.474	1.095
		(.261)	(1.156)

The dependent variable is *Turnout*, where voters are coded 1, and nonvoters are coded 0. Standard errors are entered in parentheses below coefficients. *FAdm.* is the Field Administration Selection Model; *Demo.* is the Demographic Selection Model.

TABLE I.2. Turnout in the General Election as a Function of Demographics, Uncorrected and Corrected Estimates (All forms), 1988 NES

	1988 NES			
	Uncorr.	FAdm.	Demo.	Behav.
Education	.713	.825	.722	.719
	(.086)	(.102)	(.104)	(.106)
Age	.007	.009	.008	.009
	(.001)	(.001)	(.001)	(.008)
Black	−.070	−.067	.024	−.045
	(.040)	(.040)	(.041)	(.039)
Hisp	.024	.033	.162	.053
	(.115)	(.110)	(.065)	(.110)
Income	.002	.001	.014	.009
	(.000)	(.001)	(.003)	(.002)
(Constant)	−.223	−.336	−.428	−.345
	.063	(.081)	(.112)	(.096)
$\rho\sigma$		−.010	−12.677	−.459
		(.342)	(31.653)	(.560)

The dependent variable is *Turnout*, where voters are coded 1, and nonvoters are coded 0. Standard errors are entered in parentheses below coefficients. *FAdm.* is the Field Administration Selection Model; *Demo.* is the Demographic Selection Model; *Behav.* is the Behavioral Selection Model.

TABLE I.3. Turnout in the General Election as a Function of Residency, Uncorrected and Corrected Estimates (All Forms), 1986 NES

	1986 NES		
	Uncorr.	FAdm.	Demo.
Closing Date	−.004	−.004	−.003
	(.001)	(.019)	(.002)
Age	.039	.006	.005
	(.019)	(.006)	(.001)
Income	.091	.009	.007
	(.027)	(.017)	(.002)
Own Home?	.005	.076	.054
	(.001)	(.018)	(.028)
Married?	.009	.025	.015
	(.002)	(.010)	(.027)
Public Officials Care?	−.029	−.046	−.067
	(.018)	(.021)	(.027)
Political Interest	.107	.107	.099
	(.007)	(.008)	(.014)
Years at Address	.006	.011	.011
	(.002)	(.000)	(.004)
(Constant)	−.170	−.287	−.240
	(.039)	(.047)	(.068)
$\rho\sigma$		.175	2.124
		(.082)	(.805)

The dependent variable is *Turnout*, where voters are coded 1, and nonvoters are coded 0. Standard errors are entered in parentheses below coefficients. *FAdm.* is the Field Administration Selection Model; *Demo.* is the Demographic Selection Model.

TABLE I.4. Turnout in the General Election as a Function of Residency, Uncorrected and Corrected Estimates (All Forms), 1988 NES

	1988 NES			
	Uncorr.	FAdm.	Demo.	Behav.
Closing Date	−.004	−.004	−.004	−.004
	(.030)	(.001)	(.001)	(.001)
Age	.003	.004	.004	.004
	(.020)	(.001)	(.001)	(.001)
Income	.010	.010	.009	.012
	(.003)	(.002)	(.002)	(.002)
Own Home?	.080	.070	.083	.070
	(.008)	(.030)	(.031)	(.030)
Married?	.040	.030	.069	.037
	(.001)	(.027)	(.026)	(.026)
Public Officials Care?	.020	.040	.046	.036
	(.001)	(.002)	(.023)	(.023)
Political Interest	.090	.090	.098	.094
	(.030)	(.008)	(.083)	(.009)
Years at Address	.010	.010	.005	.008
	(.020)	(.004)	(.005)	(.004)
(Constant)	.030	−.050	−.106	−.049
	(.050)	(.020)	(.052)	(.069)
$\rho\sigma$		−.130	1.371	−.058
		(.321)	(.446)	(.054)

The dependent variable is *Turnout*, where voters are coded 1, and nonvoters are coded 0. Standard errors are entered in parentheses below coefficients. *FAdm.* is the Field Administration Selection Model; *Demo.* is the Demographic Selection Model; *Behav.* is the Behavioral Selection Model.

TABLE I.5. Vote for Congress as a Function of Personal and National Economic Assessments, Uncorrected and Corrected Estimates (All Forms), 1986 NES

	1986 NES		
	Uncorr.	FAdm.	Demo.
Dissatisfaction w/ Income	.025	.020	.057
	(.026)	(.025)	(.048)
Unemployment Experience	.007	.008	.049
	(.009)	(.001)	(.027)
Business Conditions	.000	−.001	−.105
	(.025)	(.024)	(.027)
Gov't Performance	−.014	−.013	.001
	(.020)	(.019)	(.027)
Unemp. National Prob.	−.306	−.352	−.153
	(.046)	(.046)	(.101)
Inflation National Prob.	.138	.121	.167
	(.104)	(.101)	(.108)
Party ID	.244	.243	.210
	(.022)	(.022)	(.162)
(Constant)	.404	.394	.366
	(.039)	(.041)	(.054)
$\rho\sigma$		.327	−4.143
		(.640)	(1.808)

Dependent variable is *Vote for Congress*, where vote for the Democrat is coded 0, vote for the Republican is coded 1, non-voters missing. Standard errors are entered in parentheses below coefficients. *FAdm.* is the Field Administration Selection Model; *Demo.* is the Demographic Selection Model.

TABLE I.6. Vote for Congress as a Function of Personal and National Economic Assessments, Uncorrected and Corrected Estimates (All Forms), 1988 NES

| | 1988 NES | | | |
	Uncorr.	FAdm.	Demo.	Behav.
Dissatisfaction w/ Income	−.007	−.016	.011	−.002
	(.025)	(.021)	(.038)	(.030)
Unemployment Experience	.008	.011	.003	.002
	(.007)	(.007)	(.016)	(.011)
Business Conditions	−.008	−.009	−.092	−.040
	(.021)	(.022)	(.061)	(.030)
Gov't Performance	.012	.013	.026	.010
	(.014)	(.014)	(.024)	(.018)
Unemp. National Prob.	.018	.035	.002	−.013
	(.048)	(.049)	(.083)	(.065)
Inflation National Prob.	−.085	−.113	−.685	−.232
	(.058)	(.089)	(.938)	(.119)
Party ID	.269	.278	.270	.287
	(.019)	(.020)	(.135)	(.025)
(Constant)	.389	.395	.562	.412
	(.028)	(.033)	(.233)	(.045)
$\rho\sigma$		−.649	−7.000	.955
		(.530)	(11.200)	(1.167)

Dependent variable is *Vote for Congress*, where vote for the Democrat is coded 0, vote for the Republican is coded 1, nonvoters missing. Standard errors are entered in parentheses below coefficients. *FAdm.* is the Field Administration Selection Model; *Demo.* is the Demographic Selection Model; *Behav.* is the Behavioral Selection Model.

TABLE I.7. Vote for Congress as a Function of Incumbency, Party Identification, and Familiarity with the Candidates, Uncorrected and Corrected Estimates (All Forms), 1986 NES

| | 1986 NES | | |
	Uncorr.	FAdm.	Demo.
Party ID	.136	.146	.167
	(.048)	(.050)	(.001)
Republican Incumbent	−.265	−.268	−.417
	(.060)	(.057)	(.007)
Democrat Incumbent	.241	.245	.120
	(.053)	(.074)	(.005)
(Constant)	.591	.578	.691
	(.067)	(.103)	(.015)
$\rho\sigma$		.181	.102
		(.472)	(1.221)
Party ID	.100	.136	.143
	(.041)	(.044)	(.044)
Republican Incumbent	−.221	−.186	−.122
	(.057)	(.053)	(.053)
Democrat Incumbent	.154	.136	.229
	(.053)	(.066)	(.066)
Familiar w/ Dem	.154	.331	.400
	(.031)	(.047)	(.049)
Familiar w/ Rep	−.135	−.235	−.313
	(.035)	(.049)	(.054)
(Constant)	.606	.515	.367
	(.067)	(.072)	(.071)
$\rho\sigma$		.832	3.253
		(.429)	(.052)

Dependent variable is *Vote for Congress,* where vote for the Democrat is coded 1, vote for the Republican is coded 0, nonvoters missing. Standard errors are entered in parentheses below coefficients. *FAdm.* is the Field Administration Selection Model; *Demo.* is the Demographics Selection Model.

TABLE I.8. Vote for Congress as a Function of Incumbency, Party Identification, and Familiarity with the Candidates, Uncorrected and Corrected Estimates (All Forms), 1988 NES

	1988 NES			
	Uncorr.	FAdm.	Demo.	Behav.
Party ID	.162	.167	.168	.190
	(.041)	(.040)	(.057)	(.043)
Republican Incumbent	−.415	−.417	−.384	−.423
	(.064)	(.063)	(.084)	(.065)
Democrat Incumbent	.119	.120	.118	.156
	(.056)	(.061)	(.062)	(.069)
(Constant)	.696	.691	.696	.623
	(.066)	(.072)	(.103)	(.086)
$\rho\sigma$		.102	−.794	1.335
		(.655)	(1.734)	(.977)
Party ID	.122	.159	.206	.175
	(.038)	(.040)	(.039)	(.039)
Republican Incumbent	−.406	−.350	−.423	−.379
	(.050)	(.062)	(.109)	(.065)
Democrat Incumbent	.028	.039	−.053	−.015
	(.035)	(.060)	(.118)	(.071)
Familiar w/ Dem.	.093	.239	.344	.339
	(.026)	(.044)	(.046)	(.041)
Familiar w/ Rep.	−.134	−.258	−.456	−.393
	(.033)	(.047)	(.052)	(.044)
(Constant)	.769	.669	.674	.650
	(.055)	(.072)	(.117)	(.076)
$\rho\sigma$		1.327	3.263	3.725
		(.775)	(.556)	(.446)

Dependent variable is *Vote for Congress,* where vote for the Democrat is coded 1, vote for the Republican is coded 0, nonvoters missing. Standard errors are entered in parentheses below coefficients. *FAdm.* is the Field Administration Selection Model; *Demo.* is the Demographics Selection Model; *Behav.* is the Behavioral Selection Model.

TABLE I.9. Vote for Incumbent House Candidate and Approval, Uncorrected and Corrected Estimates (All Forms), 1986 NES

	1986 NES		
	Uncorr.	FAdm.	Demo.
Same Party ID	.098	.098	.130
	(.051)	(.043)	(.067)
Different Party ID	−.162	−.184	−.270
	(.058)	(.046)	(.066)
Approve Incumbent	.166	.199	.307
	(.040)	(.032)	(.034)
Disapprove Incumbent	−.437	−.396	−.276
	(.061)	(.043)	(.039)
(Constant)	.719	.709	.577
	(.062)	(.051)	(.066)
$\rho\sigma$		.107	2.060
		(.391)	(.321)

Dependent variable is *Vote for Incumbent*, where a vote for the incumbent is coded 1, vote for the challenger is coded 0, nonvoters and voters in nonincumbent races missing. *FAdm.* is the Field Administration Selection Model; *Demo.* is the Demographic Selection Model. Standard errors are entered in parentheses below coefficients.

TABLE I.10. Vote for Incumbent House Candidate and Approval, Uncorrected and Corrected Estimates (All Forms), 1988 NES

	1988 NES			
	Uncorr.	FAdm.	Demo.	Behav.
Same Party ID	.107	.142	.205	.230
	(.043)	(.043)	(.055)	(.051)
Different Party ID	−.217	−.235	−.240	−.239
	(.048)	(.044)	(.047)	(.044)
Approve Incumbent	.182	.224	.265	.283
	(.034)	(.044)	(.033)	(.030)
Disapprove Incumbent	−.280	−.233	−.194	−.172
	(.061)	(.031)	(.045)	(.042)
(Constant)	.702	.644	.547	.507
	(.052)	(.048)	(.061)	(.056)
$\rho\sigma$		1.044	1.692	2.963
		(.601)	(.388)	(.538)

Dependent variable is *Vote for Incumbent,* where a vote for the incumbent is coded 1, vote for the challenger is coded 0, nonvoters and voters in nonincumbent races missing. *FAdm.* is the Field Administration Selection Model; *Demo.* is the Demographic Selection Model; *Behav.* is the Behavioral Selection Model. Standard errors are entered in parentheses below coefficients.

TABLE I.11. Evaluation of Reagan as a Function of Issue Proximity, Spatial and Distance Calculations, Uncorrected and Corrected Estimates (All Forms), 1986 NES

	Uncorr.	FAdm.		Demo.	
	OLS	Uhat	IMR	Uhat	IMR
Spatial					
Proximity	.296	.295	.296	.311	.311
Party ID	.349	.349	.349	.382	.382
Black	−.127	−.127	−.127	−.003	−.003
South	.071	.071	.711	.045	.044
(Constant)	.000	.000	.000	.000	.000
$\rho\sigma$		−.005	.012	.026	.021
Directional					
Distance	−.344	−.343	−.343	−.359	−.359
Party ID	.329	.328	.329	.355	.355
Black	−.112	−.112	−.112	−.002	−.002
South	.062	.061	.062	.036	.035
(Constant)	.000	.000	.000	.000	.000
$\rho\sigma$		−.009	.011	.032	.028

Dependent variable is *the respondent's feeling thermometer score for Ronald Reagan.* Cell entries are the *standardized* regression coefficients. *FAdm.* is the Field Administration Selection Model; *Demo.* is the Demographic Selection Model. *Uhat* uses the Achen correction; *IMR* uses the Heckman correction.

TABLE I.12. Evaluation of Reagan as a Function of Issue Proximity, Spatial and Distance Calculations, Uncorrected and Corrected Estimates (All Forms), 1988 NES

| | 1988 NES | | | | | | |
| | Uncorr. | FAdm. | | Demo. | | Behav. | |
	OLS	Uhat	IMR	Uhat	IMR	Uhat	IMR
Spatial							
Proximity	.269	.267	.268	.276	.277	.269	.269
Party ID	.467	.467	.467	.493	.492	.468	.468
Black	−.054	−.054	−.055	.210	.105	−.054	−.054
South	.146	.147	.147	.150	.152	.145	.145
(Constant)	.000	.000	.000	.000	.000	.000	.000
$\rho\sigma$		.027	.029	−.143	−.404	.028	.029
Directional							
Distance	−.297	.296	−.296	−.312	−.313	−.299	−.299
Party ID	.441	.441	.441	.456	.455	.442	.442
Black	−.459	−.468	−.047	.214	.109	−.046	−.046
South	.145	.147	.147	.152	.154	.145	.145
(Cons.)	.000	.000	.000	.000	.000	.000	.000
$\rho\sigma$		.028	.029	−.143	−.040	.038	.039

Dependent variable is *the respondent's feeling thermometer score for Ronald Reagan*. Cell entries are the *standardized* regression coefficients. *FAdm.* is the Field Administration Selection Model; *Demo.* is the Demographic Selection Model; *Behav.* is the Behavioral Selection Model. *Uhat* uses the Achen correction; *IMR* uses the Heckman correction.

TABLE I.13. Knowledge of Representative's Votes as a Function of Demographics, Uncorrected and Corrected Estimates (All Forms), 1986 NES

| | 1986 NES | | |
	Uncorr.	FAdm.	Demo.
< High School	.379	.420	.355
	(.024)	(.026)	(.027)
High School	.390	.311	.235
	(.021)	(.022)	(.022)
Some College	.320	.239	.173
	(.024)	(.026)	(.024)
Male	−.050	−.037	−.052
	(.016)	(.017)	(.013)
Age < 30	.168	.226	.228
	(.021)	(.024)	(.023)
Age ≥ 65	.075	.031	.016
	(.027)	(.027)	(.021)
Resident < 5 yrs	.272	.312	.270
	(.022)	(.024)	(.024)
Resident 6–10 yrs	.189	.169	.129
	(.021)	(.023)	(.020)
(Constant)	.090	.097	.103
	(.011)	(.010)	(.012)
$\rho\sigma$		1.431	2.247
		(.257)	(.281)

Dependent variable is *Don't Know about Representative's Votes*, where respondents who admit not knowing about their Representative's votes are coded 1, others coded 0. Standard errors are entered in parentheses below coefficients. *FAdm.* is the Field Administration Selection Model; *Demo.* is the Demographic Selection Model.

TABLE I.14. Knowledge of Representative's Votes as a Function of Demographics, Uncorrected and Corrected Estimates (All Forms), 1988 NES

	1988 NES			
	Uncorr.	FAdm.	Demo.	Behav.
< High School	.147	.185	.216	.201
	(.030)	(.021)	(.019)	(.038)
High School	.120	.124	.135	.126
	(.029)	(.017)	(.015)	(.032)
Some College	.060	.053	.060	.057
	(.033)	(.020)	(.017)	(.035)
Male	−.122	−.144	−.127	−.153
	(.021)	(.014)	(.033)	(.025)
Age < 30	.079	.094	.152	.110
	(.021)	(.016)	(.013)	(.034)
Age ≥ 65	−.061	−.072	−.085	−.078
	(.033)	(.021)	(.018)	(.034)
Resident < 5 yrs	.166	.186	.212	.204
	(.034)	(.018)	(.015)	(.037)
Resident 6–10 yrs	.058	.065	.065	.068
	(.035)	(.018)	(.015)	(.035)
(Constant)	.620	.592	.501	.535
	(.041)	(.021)	(.063)	(.048)
$\rho\sigma$		.672	1.411	1.576
		(.391)	(.782)	(.440)

Dependent variable is *Don't Know about Representative's Votes*, where respondents who admit not knowing about their Representative's votes are coded 1, others coded 0. Standard errors are entered in parentheses below coefficients. *FAdm.* is the Field Administration Selection Model; *Demo.* is the Demographic Selection Model; *Behav.* is the Behavioral Selection Model.

TABLE I.15. Attitudes toward Abortion as a Function of Demographics, Uncorrected and Corrected Estimates (All Forms), 1986 NES

| | 1986 NES | | |
	Uncorr.	FAdm.	Demo.
Black	.078	.097	.022
	(.025)	(.023)	(.035)
Education	−.016	−.020	−.020
	(.003)	(.003)	(.004)
Income	.000	−.001	.000
	(.000)	(.017)	(.003)
South at 16	−.012	−.011	−.019
	(.013)	(.011)	(.024)
Size of Place	−.005	−.004	−.004
	(.008)	(.017)	(.013)
Size of Place at 16	.037	.028	−.028
	(.015)	(.017)	(.018)
Frequency Attend Church	−.038	−.047	−.063
	(.005)	(.006)	(.006)
Religion Important	−.022	−.005	−.017
	(.003)	(.006)	(.014)
Religion Provides Guidance	.049	.004	.008
	(.006)	(.007)	(.007)
Catholic	.012	.028	.047
	(.014)	(.021)	(.026)
Fundamentalist	.035	.053	.082
	(.019)	(.022)	(.022)
(Constant)	.394	.501	.785
	(.050)	(.066)	(.059)
$\rho\sigma$		−.739	−3.392
		(.457)	(.713)

Dependent variable is *Abortion Never Permitted*, where respondents who believe that abortion should never be permitted are coded 1, 0 otherwise. Standard errors are entered in parentheses below coefficients. *FAdm.* is the Field Administration Selection Model; *Demo.* is the Demographic Selection Model.

TABLE I.16. Attitudes toward Abortion as a Function of Demographics, Uncorrected and Corrected Estimates (All Forms), 1988 NES

| | 1988 NES | | | |
	Uncorr.	FAdm.	Demo.	Behav.
Black	.053	.074	.030	.129
	(.022)	(.023)	(.031)	(.033)
Education	−.003	−.013	−.013	−.021
	(.011)	(.026)	(.004)	(.004)
Income	.000	.000	−.002	−.001
	(.000)	(.031)	(.002)	(.002)
South at 16	.024	.022	.015	.017
	(.013)	(.016)	(.020)	(.020)
Size of Place	−.020	−.027	−.011	−.039
	(.079)	(.011)	(.013)	(.013)
Size of Place at 16	−.011	−.001	.005	.011
	(.013)	(.016)	(.022)	(.022)
Frequency Attend Church	−.032	−.041	−.033	−.060
	(.005)	(.006)	(.007)	(.069)
Religion Important	−.010	−.017	−.009	−.051
	(.004)	(.006)	(.016)	(.016)
Religion Provides Guidance	.008	.010	.011	.024
	(.007)	(.007)	(.010)	(.010)
Catholic	.042	.070	.039	.103
	(.015)	(.017)	(.026)	(.026)
Fundamentalist	.007	.000	.005	.022
	(.017)	(.020)	(.021)	(.021)
(Constant)	.294	.452	.381	.728
	(.038)	(.054)	(.069)	(.070)
$\rho\sigma$		−.674	1.128	−2.777
		(.302)	(.412)	(.413)

Dependent variable is *Abortion Never Permitted*, where respondents who believe that abortion should never be permitted are coded 1, 0 otherwise. Standard errors are entered in parentheses below coefficients. *FAdm.* is the Field Administration Selection Model; *Demo.* is the Demographic Selection Model; *Behav.* is the Behavioral Selection Model.

TABLE I.17. Family Income as a Function of Demographics, Uncorrected and Corrected Estimates (All Forms), 1986 NES

		1986 NES			
	Unc.	FAdm.		Demo.	
	OLS	Uhat	IMR	Uhat	IMR
Over 65?	−.65	−.69	−.70	−.62	−.65
	(.35)	(.35)	(.35)	(.35)	(.36)
Education	11.20	10.90	10.90	11.30	11.20
	(.57)	(.57)	(.57)	(.56)	(.58)
Married?	4.00	4.40	4.40	3.80	4.00
	(.26)	(.26)	(.26)	(.26)	(.26)
Divorced?	−.83	.81	.81	−.81	−.82
	(.34)	(.35)	(.35)	(.34)	(.35)
Working Now?	3.10	2.10	2.10	2.80	3.10
	(.27)	(.26)	(.26)	(.27)	(.28)
Black	−2.10	−2.10	−2.10	−1.40	−2.10
	(.33)	(.31)	(.31)	(.34)	(.33)
(Constant)	2.10	2.20	1.00	2.30	1.90
	(.44)	(.45)	(.33)	(.67)	(.50)
$\rho\sigma$		.58	6.40	−16.10	.61
		(.58)	(.45)	(1.8)	(.61)

Dependent variable is *Family Income*. Standard errors are entered in parentheses below coefficients. *FAdm.* is the Field Administration Selection Model; *Demo.* is the Demographic Selection Model. *Uhat* uses the Achen correction; *IMR* uses the Heckman correction.

TABLE I.18. Family Income as a Function of Demographics, Uncorrected and Corrected Estimates (All Forms), 1988 NES

| | | 1988 NES | | | | | |
| | Unc. | FAdm. | | Demo. | | Behav. | |
	OLS	Uhat	IMR	Uhat	IMR	Uhat	IMR
Over 65?	−.63	−.62	−.62	.25	−.64	−.70	−.69
	(.36)	(.36)	(.36)	(.24)	(.35)	(.36)	(.36)
Education	11.20	11.20	11.20	6.60	10.90	11.20	11.20
	(.58)	(.58)	(.58)	(.40)	(.56)	(.58)	(.58)
Married?	4.00	4.00	4.00	2.00	4.40	4.00	4.00
	(.26)	(.26)	(.26)	(.20)	(.25)	(.26)	(.26)
Divorced?	−.85	−.85	−.85	.22	.36	−.85	−.85
	(.35)	(.35)	(.35)	(.24)	(.35)	(.35)	(.35)
Working Now?	3.10	3.00	3.11	1.10	2.20	3.10	3.10
	(.28)	(.28)	(.28)	(.18)	(.26)	(.28)	(.27)
Black	−2.10	−2.10	−2.10	−8.00	−2.00	−2.10	−2.10
	(.33)	(.33)	(.33)	(.25)	(.31)	(.33)	(.34)
(Constant)	2.10	2.10	1.80	2.10	2.30	2.40	2.40
	(.44)	(.45)	(.45)	(.53)	(.44)	(.50)	(.50)
$\rho\sigma$		−.28	25.00	−71.20	−.53	−1.40	−.83
		(.31)	(.60)	(1.5)	(.20)	(.82)	(.49)

Dependent variable is *Family Income*. Standard errors are entered in parentheses below coefficients. *FAdm.* is the Field Administration Selection Model; *Demo.* is the Demographic Selection Model; *Behav.* is the Behavioral Selection Model. *Uhat* uses the Achen correction; *IMR* uses the Heckman correction.

References

Achen, Christopher H. 1986. *The Statistical Analysis of Quasi-Experiments*. Berkeley: University of California Press.

Aldrich, John H. 1980. *Before the Convention*. Chicago and London: University of Chicago Press.

Amemiya, Takeshi. 1985. *Advanced Econometrics*. Cambridge: Harvard University Press.

American National Election Studies. 1948. *American National Election Study, 1948*. Ann Arbor: Inter-University Consortium for Political and Social Research.

Anderson, Barbara A.; Silver, Brian D.; and Abramson, Paul R. 1988. "Interviewer race and attitudes of blacks." *Public Opinion Quarterly* 52:289–324.

Asher, Herbert. 1988. *Polling and the Public: What Every Citizen Should Know*. Washington, D.C.: CQ Press.

Atkin, Charles K., and Gaudino, James. 1984. "The impact of polling on the mass media." *Annals of the American Academy* 472:119–28.

Baker v. Carr 369 U.S. 186, 7 L. ed. 2d 663, 82 S Ct 691.

Batson, C. Daniel, and Coke, Jay S. 1981. "Empathy: A source of altruistic motivation for helping?" In *Altruism and Helping Behavior*, ed. J. Philippe Rushton and R. M. Sorrentins. Hillsdale, N.J.: Lawrence Erlbaum.

Beal, Richard S., and Hinckley, Ronald H. 1984. "Presidential decision making and opinion polls." *Annals of the American Academy* 472:72–84.

Benson, Sherwood; Booman, Wesley P.; and Clark, Kenneth E. 1951. "A study of interview refusals." *Journal of Applied Psychology* 35:116–19.

Benus, Jacob. 1971. "The problem of nonresponse in sample surveys.' In *Working Papers on Survey Research in Poverty Areas,* ed. John B. Lansing, Stephen B. Withey, and Arthur C. Wolfe. Ann Arbor: Institute for Social Research.

Berelson, B. R.; Lazarsfeld, P. F.; and McPhee, W. N. 1954. *Voting: A Study of Opinion Formation in a Presidential Campaign.* Chicago: University of Chicago Press.

Bogart, Leo. 1972. *Polls and the Awareness of Public Opinion.* New Brunswick, N.J.: Transaction Books.

Bradburn, Norman M., and Sudman, Seymour. 1988. *Polls and Surveys: Understanding What They Tell Us.* San Francisco: Jossey Bass Publishers.

Brehm, John J., and Mullin, William J. 1989. *Introduction to the Structure of Matter: A Course in Modern Physics.* New York: Wiley.

Bureau of the Census, U.S. Department of Commerce. 1990. *Federal Legislative Uses of Decennial Census Data.* 1990 CDR 14. Washington, D.C.

Byrne, D. 1971. *The Attraction Paradigm.* New York: Academic Press.

Campbell, Angus; Converse, Philip E.; Miller, Warren E.; and Stokes, Donald E. 1960. *The American Voter.* Chicago and London: The University of Chicago Press.

Campbell, Angus; Gurin, Gerald; and Miller, Warren E. 1954. *The Voter Decides.* Evanston, Ill.: Row, Peterson.

Cannell, Charles F.; Groves, Robert M.; Miller, Peter V.; and Thornberry, Owen T. 1987. *An Experimental Comparison of Telephone and Personal Health Interview Surveys.* Hyattsville, Md.: National Center for Health Statistics.

Cialdini, Robert. 1984. *Influence: The New Psychology of Modern Persuasion.* New York: Quill Books.

Cobb, Sidney; King, Stanley; and Chen, Edith. 1957. "Differences between respondents and nonrespondents in a morbidity survey involving clinical examination." *Journal of Chronic Diseases* 6:2, 95–108.

Combs, Michael, and Welch, Susan. 1982. "Blacks, whites and attitudes toward abortion." *Public Opinion Quarterly* 46:510–20.

Crespi, Irving. 1988. *Pre-Election Polling: Sources of Accuracy and Error.* New York: Russell Sage Foundation.

Crigler, Ann N. 1990. "Setting the congressional agenda: The public didn't do it." Paper presented at the annual meeting of the American Association for Public Opinion Research.

DeMaio, Teresa J. 1980. "Refusals: Who, where, and why?" *Public Opinion Quarterly* 44:223–33.

DeNardo, James. 1988. "The Strange Case of Surge and Decline: Sceptical Reflections on What We Know and Don't Know About the Architecture of Partisan Electorates." Paper presented at the annual meeting of the American Political Science Association.

Dohrenwend, Barbara S.; Colombotos, John; and Dohrenwend, Bruce P. 1968. "Social distance and interviewer effects." *Public Opinion Quarterly* 32:410–22.

Dohrenwend, Barbara S., and Dohrenwend, Bruce P. 1968. "Sources of refusals in surveys." *Public Opinion Quarterly* 32:74–83.

Downs, Anthony. 1957. *An Economic Theory of Democracy.* New York: Harper.

Eckert, William A., and Vinkenes, Mark S. 1990. "Public policy surveys for the Congress." Paper presented at the annual meeting of the American Association for Public Opinion Research.

Ellis, R. A.; Endo, C. M.; and Armer, J. M. 1970. "The use of potential respondents for studying nonresponse bias." *Pacific Sociological Review* 13:103–9.

Elving, Ronald D. 1989. "Proliferation of opinion data sparks debate over use." *Congressional Quarterly* Aug. 19, 2187–92.

Erikson, Robert S. 1981. "Why do people vote: Because they are registered." *American Politics Quarterly* 9:262.

Executive Office of the President. Office of Management and Budget. 1989. *1989 Catalog of Federal Domestic Assistance.* Washington, D.C.: Government Printing Office.

Farkas, Steve; Shapiro, Robert Y.; and Page, Benjamin I. 1990. "The dynamics of public opinion and policy." Paper presented at the annual meeting of the American Association for Public Opinion Research.

Fillion, F. L. 1976. "Exploring and correcting for nonresponse bias using follow-ups of nonrespondents." *Pacific Sociological Review* 19:401–8.

Fiorina, Morris P., and Shepsle, Kenneth A. 1989. "Is negative voting an artifact?" *American Journal of Political Science* 33:423–39.

Freedman, J. L., and Fraser, S. C. 1966. "Compliance without pressure: The Foot-in-the-Door Technique." *Journal of Personality and Social Psychology* 4:195–203.

Gaffney v. Cummings, 412 U.S. 736 (1973), 492.

Gallup, George, and Rae, Saul. 1940. *The Pulse of Democracy.* New York: Simon and Schuster.

Geer, John G. 1988. "Partisan realignments and the public opinion poll." Paper presented at the annual meeting of the American Political Science Association.

Germond, Jack W. 1980. "The impact of polling on journalism." In *Polling on the Issues,* ed. Albert H. Cantril. Cabin John, M.D.: Seven Locks Press.

Ginsberg, Benjamin. 1986. *The Captive Public: How Mass Opinion Promotes State Power.* New York: Basic Books.

Goldberger, Arthur S. 1981. "Linear regression after selection." *Journal of Econometrics* 15:357–66.

Goudy, William J. 1976. "Nonresponse effects on relationships between variables." *Public Opinion Quarterly* 40:360–9.

Goyder, John. 1986. "Surveys on surveys: Limitations and potentialities." *Public Opinion Quarterly* 50:27–41.

Greenberg, Daniel S. 1980. "The plague of polling." *Washington Post,* Sept. 16, A–17.

Gronke, Paul. 1990. "Assessing the sample quality of the 1988 Senate Election Study: A response to Wright." Technical report submitted to the National Election Studies Board of Overseers. Ann Arbor: Institute for Social Research.

Groves, Robert M. 1989. *Survey Errors and Survey Costs.* New York: Wiley.

Groves, Robert M., and Lyberg, Lars E. 1988. "An overview of nonresponse issues in telephone surveys," In *Telephone Survey Methodology,* ed. Robert M. Groves, Paul P. Biemer, Lars E. Lyberg, James T. Massey, William L. Nicholls II, and Joseph Waksberg. New York: Wiley.

Hall, Elaine J., and Ferree, Myra Marx. 1986. "Race differences in abortion attitudes." *Public Opinion Quarterly* 50:193–207.

Hansen, M. H., and Hurwitz, W. N. 1946. "The problem of nonresponse in sample surveys." *Journal of the American Statistical Association* 41:517–29.

Hawkins, Darnell F. 1975. "Estimation of nonresponse bias." *Sociological Methods and Research* 3:461–88.

Heckman, James J. 1976. "The common structure of statistical models of truncation, sample selection, and limited dependent variables and a simple estimator for such models." *Annals of Economic and Social Measurement* 5/4:475–92.

Heckman, James J. 1979. "Sample selection bias as a specification error." *Econometrica* 47:153–61.

Herrnson, Paul S. 1988. *Party Campaigning in the 1980s.* Cambridge: Harvard University Press.

Hornstein, H. A.; Fisch, E.; and Holmes, M. 1968. "Influence of a model's feeling about his behavior and his relevance as a comparison other on observers' helping behavior." *Journal of Personality and Social Psychology* 10:222–26.

House, James, and Wolf, Sharon. 1978. "Effects of urban residence and interpersonal trust and helping behavior." *Journal of Personality and Social Psychology* 36:9, 1029–43.

House Subcommittee on Appropriations. Subcommittee on the Departments of Labor, Health and Human Services, Education, and Related Agencies. 1991. "Departments of Labor, Health and Human Services, Education, and Related Agencies, appropriates for 1992." 102d Congress, Apr. 22.

House Subcommittee on Census and Population. 1990. "Proposed guidelines for statistical adjustment of the 1990 census." 101st Congress, Jan. 30, Serial 101-43.

Hyman, Herbert; Cobb, William J.; Feldman, Jacob F.; Hart, Clyde W.; and Stember, Charles Herbert. 1942. *Interviewing in Social Research*. Chicago: University of Chicago Press.

Jackson, John E. 1983. "Election night reporting and voter turnout." *American Journal of Political Science* 27:615–35.

Jacobson, Gary C. 1987. *The Politics of Congressional Elections*. 2d Edition. Boston: Little, Brown and Company.

Jacobson, Gary C., and Kernell, Samuel. 1981. *Strategy and Choice in Congressional Elections*. New Haven: Yale University Press.

Joint Economic Committee. 1990. "The Quality of Federal Statistics." 101st Congress, Mar. 1 and 29.

Kalton, Graham. 1983. *Compensating for Missing Survey Data*. Ann Arbor: Survey Research Center, Institute for Social Research, University of Michigan.

Kinder, Donald R., and Kiewiet, D. Roderick. 1981. "Sociotropic politics: The American case." *British Journal of Political Science* 11:129–61.

King, Gary. 1989. *Unifying Political Methodology: The Likelihood Theory of Statistical Inference*. Cambridge: Cambridge University Press.

Kingdon, John W. 1984. *Agendas, Alternatives, and Public Policies*. Boston: Little, Brown and Company.

Levy, Mark R. 1984. "Polling and the presidential election." *Annals of the American Academy* 472:85–96.

Lewis, I. A. 1987. "Muted voices—problems in polling Latinos." In *Ignored Voices: Public Opinion Polls and the Latino Community*, ed. Rodolfo O. de la Garza. Austin: University of Texas Press.

Lippmann, Walter. 1927. *The Phantom Public*. New York: MacMillan.

Little, Roderick J. A., and Rubin, Donald B. 1987. *Statistical Analysis with Missing Data*. New York: Wiley.

Maddala, G. S. 1983. *Limited-Dependent and Qualitative Variables in Econometrics.* Cambridge: Cambridge University Press.

Mansbridge, Jane J. 1980. *Beyond Adversary Democracy.* Chicago and London: University of Chicago Press.

Markus, Hazel, and Zajonc, Robert B. 1985. "The cognitive perspective in social psychology," In *Handbook of Social Psychology,* eds. G. Lindzey and E. Aronson. New York: Random House.

Maurice, Arthur J., and Nathan, Richard P. 1981. "The Census Undercount: Effects on Federal Aid to Cities," *Urban Affairs Quarterly* 17:251–84.

Milbrath, Lester W., and Goel, M.L. 1977. *Political Participation: How and Why Do People Get Involved in Politics?* Chicago: Rand McNally.

Mislevy, R. 1986. "Recent developments in the factor analysis of categorical variables." *Journal of Educational Statistics* 11:359–81.

Mitriani, I. 1982. *Simulation Techniques for Discrete Event Systems.* Cambridge: Cambridge University Press.

Muthén, Bengt. 1978. "Contributions to factor analysis of dichotomous variables." *Psychometrika* 43:551–60.

Nathan, Richard P. 1988. "The politics of printouts: The use of official numbers to allocate federal grants-in-aid." In *The Politics of Numbers,* eds. William Alonso and Paul Starr. Washington, D.C.: Russell Sage Foundation.

National Research Council. 1979. *Privacy and Confidentiality as Factors in Survey Response.* Washington, D.C.: National Academy of Sciences.

Nimmo, Dan. 1970. *The Political Persuaders.* Englewood Cliffs, N.J.: Prentice-Hall.

Nisbett, Richard E., and Wilson, Timothy D. 1977. "Telling more than we can know: Verbal reports on mental processes." *Psychological Review* 84(3):231–59.

O'Neil, Michael J. 1979. "Estimating the nonresponse bias due to refusals in telephone surveys." *Public Opinion Quarterly* 43:218–32.

Ostrom, Charles W., Jr, and Simon, Dennis M. 1985. "Promise and performance: A dynamic model of presidential popularity." *American Political Science Review* 79:334–58.

Paletz, David L.; Short, Jonathan Y.; Baker, Helen; Campbell, Barbara Cookman; Cooper, Richard J.; and Oeslander, Rochelle M. 1980. "Polls in the media: Content, credibility, and consequences." *Public Opinion Quarterly* 44:495–513.

Pateman, Carole. 1970. *Participation and Democratic Theory.* Cambridge: Cambridge University Press.

Patterson, Thomas E. 1980. *The Mass Media Election: How Americans Choose Their President.* New York: Praeger Scientific.

Pearl, Dennis K., and Fairley, Daniel. 1985. "Testing for the potential for nonresponse bias in sample surveys." *Public Opinion Quarterly* 49:553–60.

Petty, Richard E., and Cacioppo, John T. 1986. *Communication and Persuasion: Central and Peripheral Routes to Attitude Change.* New York: Springer-Verlag.

Pitkin, Hanna F. 1967. *The Concept of Representation.* Berkeley: University of California Press.

Platek, R. 1977. "Some factors affecting nonresponse." *Survey Methodology,* 3:191–214.

Platek, R. 1980. "Causes of incomplete data, adjustments and effects." *Survey Methodology* 6:93–132.

Powell, Lynda W. 1989. "Analyzing misinformation: Perceptions of congressional candidates' ideologies." *American Journal of Political Science* 33:272–93.

Presser, Stanley. 1984. "The use of survey data in basic research in the social sciences." In *Surveying Subjective Phenomena,* ed. Charles F. Turner and Elizabeth Martin. New York: Russell Sage Foundation.

Rabinowitz, George, and MacDonald, Stuart Elaine. 1989. "A directional theory of issue voting." *American Political Science Review* 83:82–121.

Ratzan, Scott C. 1989. "The real agenda setters: Pollsters in the 1988 presidential campaign." *American Behavioral Scientist* 32:451–63.

Reinhold, Robert. 1975. "Polling encounters public resistance: Decision making process threatened." *New York Times,* Oct. 22, 1.

Reynolds v. Sims 377 U.S. 533.

Rivers, Douglas, and Rose, Nancy L. 1985. "Passing the president's program: Public opinion and presidential influence in Congress." *American Journal of Political Science* 29:183–96.

Robins, Lee N. 1963. "The reluctant respondent." *Public Opinion Quarterly* 27:276–86.

Rochon, Thomas R., and Kabashima, I. 1988. "Electoral mobilization and political knowledge among blacks, 1952–1984." Paper presented at the Midwest Political Science Association meetings.

Roper, Burns. 1986. "Evaluating polls with poll data." *Public Opinion Quarterly* 50:10–16.

Rosenstone, Steven J. 1983. *Forecasting Presidential Elections.* New Haven and London: Yale University Press.

Rosentraub, Mark S., and Thompson, Lyke. 1981. "The use of surveys of satisfaction for evaluation." *Policy Studies Journal* 9:990–1000.

Rubin, Donald B. 1987. *Multiple Imputation for Nonresponse in Surveys.* New York: Wiley.

Runkel, David R., editor. 1989. *Campaign for President: The Managers Look at '88.* Dover, Mass.: Auburn House Publishing Company.

Sabato, Larry J. 1981. *The Rise of Political Consultants.* New York: Basic Books.

Salmore, Stephen A., and Salmore, Barbara G. 1985. *Candidates, Parties, and Campaigns.* Washington, D.C.: CQ Press.

Schleifer, Stephen. 1986. "Trends in attitudes toward and participation in survey research." *Public Opinion Quarterly* 50:17–26.

Schuman, Howard, and Converse, Jean M. 1971. "The effects of black and white interviewers on black responses." *Public Opinion Quarterly*, 35:44–68.

Schumpeter, Joseph A. 1942. *Capitalism, Socialism, and Democracy.* New York: Harper and Row.

Sharp, L. M. 1984. "Researchers and respondents in the 1980s." *Public Opinion Quarterly* 48:680–85.

Smith, Tom W. 1979. "Sex and the GSS: Nonresponse differences." *GSS Technical Report*, No. 17.

Smith, Tom W. 1983. "The hidden 25%: An analysis of nonresponse on the 1980 General Social Survey." *Public Opinion Quarterly* 47:386–404.

Squire, Peverill; Wolfinger, Raymond E.; and Glass, David P. 1987. "Residential mobility and voter turnout." *American Political Science Review* 81:45–65.

Steeh, Charlotte. 1981. "Trends in nonresponse rates." *Public Opinion Quarterly* 45:40–57.

Stimson, James A. 1989. "Political eras and representation: Measuring public mood." Paper presented at the annual meetings of the political methodology section of the American Political Science Association.

Sudman, Seymour. 1982. "The presidents and the polls." *Public Opinion Quarterly.* 46:301–10.

Swabey, Marie C. 1937. *Theory of the Democratic State.* Cambridge: Harvard University Press.

Taylor, Shelley E., and Fiske, Susan T. 1978. "Salience, attention, and attribution: Top of the head phenomena." *Advances in Experimental Social Psychology* 11:249–88.

Tobin, James. 1958. "Estimation of relationships for limited dependent variables." *Econometrica* 26:24–36.

United Jewish Organizations of Williamsburgh v. Carey, 430 U.S. 144 (1977).

Verba, Sidney, and Nie, Norman H. 1972. *Participation in America: Political Democracy and Social Equality.* New York: Harper and Row.

Weaver, Charles N.; Holmes, Sandra L.; and Glenn, Norval D. 1971. "Some Characteristics of Inaccessible Respondents in a Telephone Survey." *Journal of Applied Psychology* 60:2, 260–62.

Webster v. Reproduction Health Services, 57 L.W. 5024, 88-605 (1989).

Wheeler, Michael. 1976. *Lies, Damn Lies, and Statistics.* New York: Dell Publishing.

White, Kenneth J. 1978. "A general computer program for econometric methods—SHAZAM." *Econometrica* 46:239–40.

Wolfinger, Raymond E., and Rosenstone, Steven J. 1980. *Who Votes?* New Haven: Yale University Press.

Zaller, John. 1985. "Analysis of information items in the 1985 NES pilot study," Memo to the National Election Studies Board of Overseers.

Index

abortion, 7, 135, 154, 155

Abramson, Paul R., 57

academic surveys, 161

accessibility, 26–28, 30, 31, 35–40, 43–48, 66, 128–31, 161, 162. *See also* no contacts

Achen, Christopher H., 122–25, 127, 129, 133, 138, 178, 193

adjustment, 187. *See also* Census; corrections

administrative selection model, 128, 133, 135

age, 26, 28, 43, 46, 50, 60, 64, 66, 67, 136, 137, 140, 157, 158, 162. *See also* elderly

Ailes, Roger, 13

Aldrich, John H., 190

Amemiya, Takeshi, 123

amenable respondents, 43, 44, 61, 62

Anderson, Barbara A., 57

apportionment, 1, 2, 10–12, 186–88

approval ratings, 6

Armer, J. M., 43

Asher, Herbert, 193

Atkin, Charles K., 5

attitudes, 41, 43, 44, 51–68, 74, 76–92

Atwater, Lee, 13

Babbitt, Bruce, 14

bad experience, 74, 78, 80, 85, 87

Baker v. Carr, 1

bandwagon effects, 14

barriers, 40, 44. *See also* accessibility

Batson, C. Daniel, 56, 59

Beal, Richard S., 7, 13

behavioral selection model, 128, 131–33, 135, 163

benchmarks, 25–38

Benson, Sherwood, 31

Benus, Jacob, 28, 35

Berelson, B. R., 70

bias, 16, 17, 19, 93–117; to sample means, 94–97; to sample variance, 97–100; to regressions, 100–107. *See also* selection bias; weighting; imputation; corrections

blacks, 65, 117, 132, 137, 150, 154, 155, 157, 158, 164, 165, 182, 184–87. *See also* race

Bogart, Leo, 190

Booman, Wesley P., 31

Bradburn, Norman, 193

Brehm, John J., 19

Bureau of Labor Statistics, 11

Bush, George, 5, 13, 23, 29, 43

Byrne, D., 56

Cacioppo, John T., 69, 83

Caddell, Pat, 7, 13